Organization Theory and the Public Sector

Public-sector organizations are fundamentally different from their private-sector counterparts. They are multifunctional, follow a political leadership, and the majority do not operate in an external market. In an era of rapid reform, reorganization and modernization of the public sector, this book offers a timely and illuminating introduction to the public-sector organization that recognizes its unique values, interests, knowledge and power base.

Drawing on both instrumental and institutional perspectives within organization theory, as well as democratic theory and empirical studies of decision-making, the book addresses five central aspects of the public-sector organization:

- goals and values
- leadership and steering
- reform and change
- effects and implications
- understanding and design

The book challenges conventional economic analysis of the public sector, arguing instead for a political-democratic approach and a new prescriptive organization theory. A rich resource of both theory and practice, *Organization Theory and the Public Sector: Instrument, culture and myth* is essential reading for anybody studying the public sector.

Organization Theory and the Public Sector

Instrument, culture and myth

Tom Christensen,
Per Lægreid, Paul G. Roness
and Kjell Arne Røvik

LONDON AND NEW YORK

First published 2007
by Routledge
2 Park Square, Milton Park, Abingdon, Oxon OX14 4RN

Simultaneously published in the USA and Canada
by Routledge
270 Madison Ave, New York, NY 10016

Routledge is an imprint of the Taylor & Francis Group, an informa business

Typeset in Perpetua and Bell Gothic by
Florence Production Ltd, Stoodleigh, Devon
Printed and bound in Great Britain by
TJ International Ltd, Padstow, Cornwall

British Library Cataloguing in Publication Data
A catalogue record for this book is available from the British Library

Library of Congress Cataloging in Publication Data
Organization theory and the public sector/Tom Christensen . . . [et al.].
    p. cm.
    Includes bibliographical references and index.
  1. Public administration.   2. Organizational sociology
  I. Christensen, Tom.
  JF1351.O74 2007
  302.3'5 – dc22   2007015385

ISBN10: 0–415–43380–0 (hbk)
ISBN10: 0–415–43381–9 (pbk)
ISBN10: 0–203–92921–7 (ebk)

ISBN13: 978–0–415–43380–8 (hbk)
ISBN13: 978–0–415–43381–5 (pbk)
ISBN13: 978–0–203–92921–6 (ebk)

Contents

CONTENTS

Tables

About the authors

Tom Christensen is Professor of Public Administration and Organization Theory at the Department of Political Science, University of Oslo, Norway. His main research interests include national, central and comparative public administration and reform.

Per Lægreid is Professor at the Department of Administration and Organization Theory, University of Bergen, Norway. He has published numerous books and articles on public administration, administrative policy, organizational reform and institutional change.

Paul G. Roness is Professor at the Department of Administration and Organization Theory, University of Bergen, Norway. His main fields of interest are organization theory, administrative reforms in central government and state employees' unions.

Kjell Arne Røvik is Professor of Organization Theory at the Department of Political Science, University of Tromsø, Norway. His main research interest is the production, diffusion and adoption of popular management ideas among formal organizations.

Preface

This is a textbook in organization theory that focuses specifically on the public sector. An organization-theory approach to the public sector presupposes that one cannot understand the content of public policy and decision-making in public organizations without analysing the organization and operational modes of the public administration. The need for a textbook in organization theory that provides empirical examples from the public sector and draws on academic research in political science is obvious. Moreover, this need is particularly great in a period when public sectors are facing comprehensive reorganization and modernization processes. The book is anchored in an academic tradition that combines organization theory, political science and empirical studies of decision-making in formal public organizations.

We focus on three perspectives, one instrumental and two institutional. A key distinction between these perspectives is that an instrumental perspective looks at public organizations as tools for leaders, whereas institutional perspectives are open to the idea that organizations have their own culture, values and norms that exert an independent influence on decision-making. Hence organizations do not, in any simple and unproblematic way, adapt to shifting signals from leaders.

Within an instrumental perspective we distinguish between a *hierarchical variant*, where a leader's control and rational calculation are key factors, and a *negotiation-based variant*, which allows for articulation of interests, compromises and negotiation between actors with partly conflicting goals. As for institutional perspectives, we distinguish between a *cultural perspective* – where the main notion is of institutionalized organizations with a unique internal organizational culture and traditions – and a *myth perspective* – which embraces the idea of institutionalized environments, where the focus is on the significance of values and norms found in an organization's environment.

In spite of a significant grey area between public and private organizations, our point of departure is that public organizations are different from private organizations in fundamental ways. What distinguishes public organizations from private ones is that they have a citizen-elected leadership, are multifunctional and have to cope with partially conflicting considerations. Moreover, most public organizations do not operate within a free and competitive economic market. With this book, we aim to challenge the one-sided economic analysis of policy and society by drawing upon more central aspects of democratic theory and organization theory. From the vantage point of an organization theory approach anchored in political science, it is insufficient to focus attention just on economy and efficiency. The public sector's operational mode must be described, analysed and evaluated using a democratic–political approach that focuses on the sector's values, interests, knowledge and power base.

First, the main features of an *instrumental perspective*, a *cultural perspective* and a *myth perspective* are presented in individual chapters. Thereafter we outline four central aspects of public organizations: goals and values, leadership and steering, reform and change, and effects and implications. For each theme, we discuss how it is treated in light of the three perspectives. The book's concluding chapter deals with understanding and design. It discusses the relationship between the three perspectives and outlines how one might arrive at a *transformative approach* and a prescriptive organization theory.

We have tried to simplify and popularize insights culled through many research projects and years of teaching. Emphasis is placed on providing examples from empirical studies of the operational mode of representative public organizations and actual administrative reforms. We have chosen not to add references in the text, but for each chapter we have included a list of literature that covers the themes discussed. The selection could have been much larger, and we have therefore been unable to acknowledge adequately all the colleagues whose work we have drawn upon in writing this book. We have specified learning objectives at the beginning of each chapter, and a chapter summary and discussion questions appear at the end.

Acknowledgements

This book has materialized as a result of close collaboration between the authors and a professional network developed over the last twenty five years. It is based on a Norwegian textbook published in 2004 by Universitetsforlaget and we thank our Norwegian publisher for helping and encouraging us on this project. We wish to thank our colleagues in Norwegian public administration research who have aided us in writing the book. We have also taken recourse in the work of other colleagues in Scandinavia, in other parts of Europe and in Asia, Australia, New Zealand and the United States, and to these we extend our thanks.

We would also like to express our gratitude to the Department of Political Science at the University of Oslo, the Department of Political Science at the University of Tromsø, the Rokkan Centre and the Department of Administration and Organization Theory at the University of Bergen and the Research Council of Norway for funding the English translation. We are grateful to our publisher, Routledge, for believing in this project. Our final thanks go to Arlyne Moi who translated the text and to Melanie Newton for language assistance.

We have had the privilege of benefiting from Johan P. Olsen's guidance, enthusiasm and friendship for several decades. He has been an exemplary mentor and colleague. We gratefully dedicate this book to him.

Tom Christensen
Per Lægreid
Paul G. Roness
Kjell Arne Røvik
Oslo/Bergen/Tromsø, 2007

Abbreviations

Activity-based Costing	ABC
Activity-based Management	ABM
Business Process Re-engineering	BPR
Economic Value Added	EVA
European Union	EU
International Monetary Fund	IMF
Management by Objectives	MBO
Management by Objectives and Result	MBOR
Masters of Business Administration	MBA
New Public Management	NPM
Organisation for Economic Cooperation and Development	OECD
Scandinavian Airlines System	SAS
Total Quality Leadership	TQL
Total Quality Management	TQM
United Nations	UN
Value Process Management	VPM
World Trade Organisation	WTO

Chapter 1

Organization theory for the public sector

LEARNING OBJECTIVES

By the end of this chapter you should:

- have a clear understanding of the differences between organizations in the public and private sectors;
- be able to identify the main characteristics of the instrumental and institutional perspectives in organization theory;
- have some basic ideas about what the main dependent variables in the book are.

AN ORGANIZATION THEORY APPROACH TO THE PUBLIC SECTOR

This is a textbook on organization theory for the public sector with a particular focus on the way the public sector is organized in representative democracies. A central issue is the links between public organizations and the content of public policy. The people who shape public policy normally act on behalf of formal organizations. A key assumption is that these participants' organizational affiliations and the organizational setting in which they act will influence their way of thinking and their behaviour, and hence the content of public policy. An organization theory approach to the public sector assumes that it is impossible to understand the content of public policy and public decision-making without analysing the way political-administrative systems are organized and their modes of operation.

The relations between individuals and organizations, as well as between organizations themselves, will be central to our approach. It is the interplay between individual factors and organizational conditions that must be analysed, for we are faced with *organizations consisting of people* and with *people in an organizational context*. The internal features of an individual public organization will influence how it identifies problems and how it solves them, which consequences it emphasizes and what evaluation criteria it uses. At the same time, a public organization's mode of operation will be influenced by other formal organizations in the public and private sectors, in civil society and abroad.

Why do we need a book of this kind? First of all, organization theory has traditionally focused on private organizations in general and on private companies in particular. Second, organization theory has only to a limited extent been rooted in political science, drawing its academic substance more from sociology, management theory and psychology. Internationally, there has been little contact between political science and organization theory and not much interest either. Indeed, organization theory is more frequently found in business schools than in departments of political science. As a result, organizational research has been criticized for being too preoccupied with general theories about formal organizations and for having neglected the important political-administrative organizations and the connection between organizational design and the content of public policy. Third, the empirical focus has, to a large extent, been on the United States and has only occasionally been representative of other Western democratic systems.

By virtue of the fact that organizational studies increasingly are rooted in business schools, the attention and focus of organization theory has become distorted, leading to an exaggerated focus on the private sector and reduced attention to the public sector. Second, it has meant that ideas from economics tend to prevail at the expense of elements from political science. Third, organization theory is dominated by a focus on efficiency and output that emphasizes practical relevance at the expense of other organizational phenomena and considerations, basic research and the general development of knowledge. Fourth, we are seeing an increasing orientation towards the problems and possibilities of individual organizations (enterprises) and organizational strategies, and a shift of attention away from populations and groups of organizations and societal strategies. Fifth, there is a stronger focus on the technical environment, with an emphasis on economic, technological and market-related conditions, than on the institutional environment with its values, norms, ideologies and doctrines. One of the aims of this book is to counteract some of the distortions caused by these developments.

Today's organizational research and its theoretical basis constitute an interdisciplinary field. While it is difficult to identify one uniform nucleus, it is possible to filter out a number of traditions and perspectives that are built on partly complementary, partly competing theoretical rudiments and observations. In this book we will account for some directions rooted in a research tradition that can be traced back to the Carnegie Tech school of organization theory. This programme integrated Herbert Simon's notion of bounded rationality with empirical studies of the public administration's actual mode of operation. Key to the development of this direction is also Johan P. Olsen's longstanding cooperation with James G. March in which they combined organization theory, democratic theory and the study of decision-making behaviour in formal organizations. Their particular contribution in recent decades has been to introduce institutional perspectives into analyses of the organization and the mode of operation of political-administrative systems.

In recent years we have witnessed an increasing pluralism in theoretical perspectives and frames of reference in the study of public organizations and institutions. In this book we will concentrate our attention on a *structural-instrumental approach* and an *institutional approach*. A major distinction between instrumental and institutional perspectives is that instrumental perspectives view organizations as tools in the hands of leaders. Rationality is implicit in formal organizational structure; it imposes limitations on an individual's choice of action and creates a capacity to realize particular goals and values. Institutional perspectives, on the other hand, allow organizations to have their own institutional rules, values and norms, which in turn exert an independent influence on decision-making behaviour. Therefore, organizations do not, in any simple or unproblematic way, adjust to shifting managerial signals from leaders. This means that all institutions are organizations, but not all organizations are institutions. In practice, however, most organizations will have some institutional traits.

These two main approaches differ in three fundamental ways: first, in their understanding of what logic of action constitutes the basis for the behaviour of the organization's members; second, in their view of what politics is all about; and third, in their view of organizational change. The underlying logic of action in an instrumental perspective is a *logic of consequence*. This is based on a means–end rationality, where one tries to predict the future effects of an executed action. The two institutional perspectives we will present – one cultural- and one myth-oriented – are based on a *logic of appropriateness*. This means that a person acts in accordance with his or her experience of what has worked well in the past, or upon what feels fair, reasonable and acceptable in the environment the person works within.

Goals, from an instrumental perspective, are defined *exogenously*. They are formulated by leaders, and policy-making largely consists of finding suitable means to achieve the goals. Institutional perspectives allow for goals to gradually develop internally; thus, policy is also about forming opinions and discovering goals. Change, from an instrumental perspective, will occur as a rational adjustment to new goals and managerial signals, or to shifting external demands. Seen from institutional perspectives, particularly the cultural variety, organizations will be more robust and change will occur slowly through gradual adjustment, or through long stable periods interrupted by radical breaks.

3

Within instrumental perspectives we distinguish between a *hierarchically oriented variant*, where leaders' control and analytical–rational calculations are central, and a *negotiation-based variant*, which allows for the articulation of interests and for compromise and negotiation between organizations and actors whose goals and interests are partially conflicting. As for institutional approaches, we will distinguish between a *cultural perspective*, that is, the idea of institutionalized organizations, and a *myth perspective*, which entails the idea of an institutionalized environment, focusing on the values and norms present in an organization.

DIFFERENCES BETWEEN PUBLIC AND PRIVATE ORGANIZATIONS

About twenty-five years ago, the American political scientist Graham Allison wrote a seminal article where he posed the question: are public and private organizations fundamentally alike in all unimportant respects? With this question, Allison sided with the direction in organization theory that underscores the differences between organizations in the public and private sectors. In this book, we proceed from this basic assumption. The central elements of the argument supporting the conception that *public and private organizations are fundamentally different in key respects* are, first of all, that public interests differ from private interests, since the public sector must consider a broader set of norms and values. Many considerations must be weighed against each other, and democratic considerations, constitutional values and public welfare are given much more weight in public organizations than in private organizations. Second, the leaders of public organizations are accountable to citizens and voters rather than to special groups. Third, public organizations require a greater emphasis on openness, transparency, equal treatment, impartiality and predictability.

Opposed to this direction is a tradition within organization theory that rejects the conception of public organizations differing from private organizations in any fundamental respect, and we will pay some attention to this tradition. The ambition of this type of organization theory is to construct models and develop insights that are universal and valid for all types of organizations. Differences between public and private organizations are dismissed as stereotypes. The universalist direction advocates the need to underscore similarities and develop knowledge that is valid across organizations, in order to avoid the division between the public and the private, or between business-oriented and public-utility organizations. It stresses that variables such as size, tasks and technology can influence organizations more than their private or public status does.

The 'generic' approach, which reflects the last twenty years of reform programmes within the public sector, is labelled *New Public Management (NPM)*. This reform movement plays down the differences between the public and private sectors and stresses that organizational models and managerial methods from private organizations can be transferred to public organizations with great benefits. The doctrine claiming that public organizations are unique, and therefore subject to special laws, rules, procedures and forms of organization, is challenged by this competing doctrine, for it claims that public and private organizations have important common features and can therefore be subject to a common set of rules and organized according to the same principles.

Some scholars warn against constructing an overly simplified distinction between the public and private sectors, but they are also wary of equating the two all too readily. In a well-known book, the American scholar Barry Bozeman stresses that 'all organizations are public'. His aim is to build a bridge between public and private organization theories. He argues that more or less all organizations are subject to political authority and influence and to external governmental control. Therefore, it is important to warn against creating stereotypes in the discussion about public and private organizations. What marks the development of organizations today is that the clear-cut lines between the public and private sectors have dissolved in certain areas, and an increasing number of organizations operate in the grey area between public and private business. This implies hybrids in the border region between public and private organizations. Public–private partnership is not a new phenomenon, but it is now considered to be a particularly useful organizational form in many fields, for instance in development assistance and foreign aid. An organization may well be public in some respects but private in others – there may, for instance, be different arrangements for organization/personnel, financing and production equipment, as illustrated in Table 1.1.

Other relevant dimensions for determining what can be privatized are, first, to what extent the organization is subject to public regulation, and second, to what extent ownership is under the auspices of the public or the private sector. This implies that the division between the public and private sectors is, in many respects, more of a continuum than a dichotomy, a point of view advocated by the American political scientists Robert A. Dahl and Charles E. Lindblom in their classic study *Politics, Economics and Welfare*. When the boundaries between the public and private sectors

Table 1.1 *Ways of interrelating the public and private sectors*

Organization/ personnel	Public				Private			
Financing	Public		Private		Public		Private	
Production equipment	Public	Private	Public	Private	Public	Private	Public	Private
Public or private sector	Public	Mixed types, hybrids						Private

Source: E. Killand (1986), modified

5

dissolve, it becomes difficult to delimit distinctly public organizations from private organizations. Some public organizations, such as state-owned companies, differ little from private firms. Others, such as courts and governmental ministries, are fundamentally different.

In addition to the problem of drawing clear boundaries between public and private organizations, it is difficult to identify exactly what is meant by *one* organization within the public sector. This is because public organizations are entwined in a hierarchy, implying that it is difficult to know where one organization stops and another begins. Usually individual persons are members of formal organizations. Yet many public organizations are meta-organizations in the sense that they have other organizations as their members. Thus the organizational pattern within the public sector is like a Chinese box, where one organization constitutes a part of another. The picture that emerges is vastly different depending on whether one looks at the lowest level – at offices or sections, local units such as a school, a social security office or a police station – or whether one focuses on national organizations such as government ministries and central agencies, or on governmental services that stand alone, groups of similar governmental organizations or ministerial areas. Within the public sector, it is problematic to decide where one organization's boundaries lie.

While today's administrative policy, to an increasing extent, uses a concept of organizations that assumes the possibility of delimiting each individual organization from other organizations, and specifying its goals and reading its results, the actual organizational pattern moves in a different direction, with a network structure that is increasingly characterized by complex webs of interaction. This entails a blurring of the boundaries between the different organizations, with the accompanying problems of specifying clear goals for each individual organization and of identifying one organization's results separately from what other organizations may have contributed.

CHARACTERISTICS OF PUBLIC ORGANIZATIONS

Despite the considerable grey area between public and private organizations, it is our point of departure that public organizations in representative democracies differ from private organizations in fundamental ways. First of all, *public organizations have leaders elected by popular vote*. Regardless of whether a public organization is close to or far removed from the political leadership, there is a democratically elected political leader at the top to whom the organization is accountable. In contrast to private enterprises, which are accountable to a board originating from the shareholders, public organizations are responsible to a democratically elected leadership that is, in turn, accountable to the people through general elections. Thus public organizations are part of a parliamentary chain of governance and face different challenges to those faced by private organizations. The parliamentary chain of governance implies that all political authority stems from the people. The legislature is elected by the people, the government originates from the legislature, and cabinet ministers are responsible for what goes on in their respective organizations. A parallel, publicly elected leadership is found in the local governments of most democratic societies. Common to all public organizations in representative democracies is that they act on behalf of politically elected authorities and are governed through a written body of regulations and laws.

Second, public organizations differ from many private-sector organizations in that they are *multifunctional*. This means they cope with partly conflicting considerations, such as political steering, control, representation and participation by affected parties, co-determination of employees, sensitivity vis-à-vis users, transparency, publicity and insight into decision-making processes, predictability, equal treatment, impartiality, neutrality, quality of services, professional independence, political loyalty, efficiency and effectiveness. Political-administrative systems in representative democracies are based neither on pure majority rule nor on pure professional systems; they are not dominated solely by affected parties or governed only by rule of law or the market. They combine these forms of governance. Considerations of constitutional values must be weighed against considerations of majority rule, affected parties, professional competence and efficiency. This means that one does not, as is the case in private organizations, face a bottom line or one superior consideration such as profit and economic surplus. This multifunctional organizational model makes public organizations particularly vulnerable to criticism. It is very difficult to balance the different interests against each other in a way that pleases everybody. At the same time, however, this allows flexibility, influence and individual use of judgement by employees. Multifunctional organizations give opportunities for discretionary judgement and degrees of freedom in assessing what considerations to emphasize and, hence, for civil servants to have influence and exercise power.

The challenges multifunctional organizations face may be perceived either as pathological or as inherent features of the system. In the first perception, ambiguities and conflicting goals are seen as problems to be eliminated, and leaders seek forms of organization and control that will help eliminate 'the illness'. This view is typical of the NPM reform movement and is at the root of reforms in many countries' public sectors. In the second perception, unclear and partly conflicting goals are seen as inherent to multifunctional organizations, and one of the core distinctions between public and private organizations. The challenge, according to this view, is to find ways to live with partly conflicting considerations and demands, rather than seeking solutions to them. Public organizations face lasting and insoluble tensions which cannot be easily resolved.

In this book we lean more towards the second perception than the first. Our point of departure is that the public sector constitutes a hybrid system, some of whose principles for management and coordination are inconsistent. Combining these different principles helps balance interests and values. Partially conflicting goals create flexibility and room for manoeuvre, but also problems of responsibility. In practice, there is also often a tenuous balance between various considerations, and tensions arise within and between public organizations over how these considerations should be weighed against each other.

Third, most public organizations differ from private organizations in that *they do not operate within a free and competitive market,* even though increased independence, the forming of state-owned companies and exposure to competition have increased the presence of the market and market-like arrangements in many public organizations. One type of argument for public organizations springs from the idea that the market has a limited capacity to handle problems that require public intervention. An important task for a government is therefore to rectify or counteract problems created by the market, or which the market is unable to handle. The American organization theorist Hal G. Rainey distinguishes between three groups of such problems:

- *Public goods and the free-rider problem*: Once provided, certain goods benefit all. As a result, people have a tendency to behave like free riders and let others pay. The government therefore uses taxation to pay for such goods. National defence can be one example of this, police protection another.
- *Individual incompetence*: Since people often lack sufficient competence or information to make rational individual choices, public regulation is necessary. An example of this is control of food and medicine.
- *Externalities or spillover*: Certain costs can be passed on to other parties that are not involved in market transactions. A company that pollutes the air imposes costs and disadvantages onto others, and these are not calculated into the price of the good. Ministries of the environment regulate these types of environmental externalities.

It is, however, important to note that what is referred to as the *market* often deviates in practice from the ideal typical market presented in business administration textbooks, with free competition between many suppliers and demanders. Summing up these differences, for public organizations a stakeholder perspective is more appropriate than a shareholder perspective.

DELIMITATION OF ORGANIZATION THEORY FOR THE PUBLIC SECTOR

This book is rooted in a research tradition that combines organization theory and political science. An organization theory for the public sector will be based on democratic theory and theories about decision-making in formal organizations. By 'formal organizations in the public sector' we mean, for instance, ministries, agencies, federal banks, courts, state-owned companies, local and regional government administration, military organizations, public universities, public health-care enterprises, public nursing homes, public museums and public foundations. These organizations differ from one another in many respects, but they share characteristics as *formal organizations*; they are established in order to attend to collective interests and special tasks; and they have relatively stable patterns of behaviour, resources and rewards connected to their activities.

A key assumption is that *organizational form will affect the content of public policy*. Organization theory offers a middle road between the legal tradition, which focuses on legal categories and the formal body of laws in order to understand an organization's mode of operation, and an environmental–deterministic approach, which views an organization's mode of operation as mainly reflecting external demands and pressures. Our point of departure is that the focus should be on how a 'living' organization operates in practice, in interaction with formal, structural and legal constraints, external factors, internal traditions and cultures. Moreover, there should also be a focus on leaders' active performance of their management function. This book will make this approach more concrete by presenting an *instrumental perspective*, a *cultural perspective* and a *myth perspective*. The perspectives are mainly treated separately, but there will also be a discussion about how they can interact with and complement one another.

The influence a public policy has on society will depend on what resources the public sector has at its disposal, but also on how these resources are coordinated and how the public sector is organized. The organizational and operational modes of public organizations are not seen as neutral technical questions but as political questions. Our position, in line with that of American political scientist E.E. Schattschneider more than forty years ago, is that organizing will lead to systematic and routine selections of certain participants/actors, problems and solutions. Certain groups, values and interests are taken into consideration while others are ignored or obstructed. Those who participate in public decision-making processes act on behalf of formal organizations, and how they use their discretion is influenced by the constraints and possibilities offered by the organizations they represent.

The starting point is that public organizations are woven into a complex political and social network of organized interests, citizens, user groups and clients. They experience competing logics, loyalties and sources of influence that are rooted in their organization's political and administrative leadership, as well as in its culture and external environment. It is therefore necessary to use different perspectives for analysing public organizations. We need to clarify what each perspective emphasizes, but also the interplay between structural features, cultural ties and myths. Public organizations are characterized by conflicting goals and heterogeneity. They do not function as uniform actors but must live with tensions and disagreements. Decision-makers therefore find themselves in a world where both the present and the future remain diffuse and demand interpretation, and where actors, problems and solutions must – in different and partly unpredictable ways – be selected and linked to decisions.

One important observation is that public organizations do not, in any simple and unproblematic way, change and adjust according to shifting demands from their environment, or from changes in the political leadership. Institutional factors, as expressed through cultural traditions, established rules and socially defined conventions, put restraints on the decisions made within public organizations. This is why instrumental perspectives alone are insufficient for helping us understand how things work.

Institutional factors can, as a cultural perspective will stress, be a result of organizations gradually having grown more complex through the development of informal norms and practices. In addition to solving tasks in an instrumental sense, they have become value-bearing institutions with their own distinct identities and opinions about what the relevant problems and appropriate solutions are.

Organizations can also be institutionalized by adopting models for what are widely recognized as proper or fitting solutions from similar organizations in their environment. This is one of the key arguments of a myth perspective. 'Correct' and modern forms of organization are at the very root of public organizations' modes of operation, and this helps make them more similar, at least on the surface. Such institutionalized environments can represent a form of *fashion* that may impose clear guidelines on how organizations function in reality. At the same time, as institutions render certain types of behaviour possible and hinder others, they gradually change through political initiative.

BOUNDED RATIONALITY, POLITICAL SCIENCE AND ORGANIZATION THEORY

This book is based on a tradition of theoretically oriented and empirically based studies of decision-making in formal public organizations which generally shows that the purely instrumental, rational and economically oriented decision-making models only apply to a limited area. A key assumption is the notion of *bounded rationality*. This assumes that members of organizations and decision-makers have limited knowledge or cognitive capacity and will act on the basis of simplified models of the world. Decision-makers have a limited amount of time, attention and analytical capacity for the tasks and problems they face, and their attitudes and actions are constrained by the organizational structure they are placed in and by the external actors and environment they are linked to. They have neither the possibility nor the capacity to review all the goals, all the alternatives or all the potential consequences of the various alternatives. Hence they face problems of capacity, understanding and authority. This necessitates a process of *selection*. Some aspects grab their attention and focus; other aspects are ignored or neglected.

Bounded rationality implies that organizational structure is vital for channelling attention and decision-making behaviour at the same time as judgement is exercised within a formal framework. Therefore, the set of values and cultural norms that dominate public organizations is critical. Through organization, the ability for rational calculation increases, as does insight into the connection between means and ends through prognoses, planning and analyses. At the same time, however, the ability also increases to exercise social or political control and coordination through the exertion of power and authority, and the ability to influence others to act in a desired manner.

A political science-oriented organization theory implies that the traditional emphasis on internal structures must be extended to include the importance of the environment surrounding a public organization's development and mode of operation. The traditional idea is that a public organization's external relations are dominated by its subordination to political leadership and that it functions as a technical, neutral tool for political leaders and is regulated by rules and laws. This view is insufficient if one wishes to understand how public organizations operate. The same goes for the notion that the internal structure is completely dominated by hierarchy and routines. Public organizations must be seen as political actors with dynamic relations to political leadership and to actors in the society they are a part of. Political organization involves systematic and routine selection. Through the establishment of rights and duties for participants, rules and decision-making procedures, some actors, conflict lines and standpoints are organized *out* of public decision-making processes, while others are organized *into* them.

Economic analytical models have increasingly gained entry into studies of the public sector and the way in which it operates, including in the fields of political science, organization theory and sociology. The new *prima philosophica* is that the market should direct politics, not the other way around. Economic indicators are increasingly accepted as a measure of how well public organizations work. Competitiveness, efficiency and pricing systems are put forth as standards by which all things should be measured. With this book, we wish to challenge a one-sided economic analysis of politics and society by bringing in more central aspects of democratic theory and organizational theory. In doing so, we hope to help clarify the possibilities and constraints inherent in organization as a political tool.

The public sector is justified by its primary mandate: to serve the people. One important task is to solve conflicts and problems using as few resources as possible. A political science-oriented organization theory approach must take into account that one of the pivotal tasks is to secure economy and efficiency within the public sector. This requirement is particularly important when the public sector is large and craves resources, and when access to resources is limited. Meanwhile, seen from the vantage point of an organization theory rooted in political science, it is not enough to concentrate attention on economy and efficiency. The way the public sector operates must be described, analysed and evaluated from a democratic-political vantage point. This means directing the focus towards the sector's basis of values,

11

knowledge and power. A particularly important task will be to clarify what role democratic values and ideas play in the organization of the public sector. A democratic form of governance is built on an optimistic faith in a population's ability to govern itself. It is based on a notion that democracy's stipulation of public transparency, its authorization of criticism and opposition, and its emphasis on popular participation and influence will secure the ability to learn from previous mistakes. It is this learning ability that is the democratic form of governance's primary source of dynamism and development.

Political and administrative organizations in the public sector must be analysed and judged according to how they influence processes of decision-making and implementation. Yet they must also be analysed and judged by how they influence the long-term creation of opinions, beliefs and attitudes in society at large. A democratic form of governance is about being sensitive to people's wishes and having the ability to reflect the will of the people. Yet this is not enough: democratic policy-making should also be discursive and transforming. This means that through public debate governance should help test, modify and develop values and attitudes, as well as expectations and demands aimed at the political community.

Democracy presupposes that the people choose how the public sector should be developed and changed. During the last decade, however, a different view has gained ground. The development of public organizations and institutions has first and foremost been regarded as a necessary adjustment to driving forces that are beyond democratic control – such as globalization, internationalization and technological development. It is important to avoid fatalism as well as idealism. History has taught us that societal development seldom moves in only one direction over a long period of time and that there are great variations in the public sector's development from one country to another. Instead of, on the one hand, assuming the freedom to choose the forms of organization one desires within the public sector, or, on the other, presupposing that this development cannot be influenced at all by political decisions, the task is to analyse the degree of freedom and the room for manoeuvre that exist in a situation where both national and international environments are changing. Our ambition is to help create a more realistic understanding of how the public sector is organized, changed and maintained, and of what assumptions and conditions are necessary in order to use organization as an active tool.

DEPENDENT VARIABLES

How can an organizational theory for the public sector be delimited from general organizational theory? The path we have choosen to focus on is described and explained here. First, an organization theory for the public sector, with its emphasis on the study of public policy and administration, should contribute to generally clarifying the key organizational forms that exist within public administration, but also those that exist between the public administration and various groups in society. What actual forms of organization exist and what changes are happening in them? Second, an organization theory of this kind ought to help clarify the types of selection different organizations make. This means the extent to which they attend to, are neutral towards or opposed to values, situations or interests within society. What are the effects of the different forms of organization? Third, it should help explain the existence of different forms of organization, with an emphasis on examining to what extent such forms are determined by public policy. Why are different forms of organization established and changed?

The three perspectives we focus on have different approaches to these questions, and use different tools to search for answers. An instrumental perspective emphasizes the ability to exert political control and to engage in clear organizational thinking and rational calculation of causal relationships and effects. A cultural perspective challenges instrumental assumptions and their underlying means–end rationality and highlights the constraints and possibilities lying within established cultures and traditions. A myth perspective highlights adjustments to existing beliefs and values in the environment in order to understand how organizational changes occur and what effects and implications they have.

A key dependent variable is the *decision-making behaviour of public organizations*, that is, the authoritative distribution of responsibilities and resources between organizations, actors, sectors and levels in the political-administrative system. The basic question in any democracy is to what extent such decisions are representative, that is, whether public decision-makers act in accordance with the wishes, demands and interests of the population, or at least of a majority of it. Public organizations are seen as integrated parts of the political-administrative system. We therefore focus on political organization as an expression of the dynamic relations between political, administrative and private-sector actors in a democratic context.

Decision-making in public organizations can be of two types. First, decisions directed outwards – towards citizens, user groups and clients. These can be decisions that affect single individuals or enterprises, but they can also affect the distribution of goods and allocation of burdens between groups and persons. Public organizations prepare cases for political bodies and implement decisions, and can therefore be important contributors in shaping policy. How can we explain initiatives in public organizations? Why are some alternatives expounded while others are not? Why are some interests reviewed while others are neglected? And why are some decisions implemented quickly and painlessly, while others are opposed, changed or simply peter out?

Second, decisions in public organizations can be directed towards internal organization. These can be decisions regarding reorganizing the formal structure through mergers, divisions or moving organizational units vertically or horizontally, changes in procedural rules, or relocation and changes in personnel composition through measures directed at recruitment, career advancement or retirement.

Although an organization theory for the public sector is limited by its object of study and by what it is intended to explain, it can apply many different explanatory factors and perspectives in order to understand the decisions being made. A key question is how organizational frameworks – which include internal factors as well as those relating to the environment – influence decision-making processes and their outcome in formal public organizations. We will apply a series of perspectives from organization theory to answer this question. The study of public organizations is confronted with competing theories, unsettled models and conflicting approaches. Organization theory cannot offer political science a finalized paradigm. There is no general consensus as to what theory – or what nucleus of competing theories – is most relevant for the study of public organizations. Empirical studies of decision-making in formal organizations can, however, offer observations and theoretical contributions that may be useful in studying the public sector.

We have chosen to concentrate on three selected perspectives: an instrumental perspective, a cultural perspective and a myth perspective. This structure enables us to focus on three main groups of explanatory factors connected to:

a)   conscious choices and intentions of the political leadership and other actors, and the way these are expressed though formal structures;
b)   the constraints inherent in established traditions and cultures, as they have developed over time; and
c)   dominant values and norms in the current environment, which influence the possibilities for what public organizations can do.

Organization theories for the public sector have grown more complex. This may reflect the increased complexity of the political-administrative system and of public decision-making processes, for organizational patterns are more specialized than before, both horizontally and vertically. New and hybrid organizational forms have sprung up internally in the public sector as well as in the interface between the public and private sectors.

First of all, we will apply instrumental perspectives with an emphasis on the political control and means–end rationality implicit in formal structures – both as a means of analytical, hierarchically based problem-solving, and as negotiations between actors with partly conflicting interests. Second, we will use institutional perspectives that focus on internal aspects of institutionalized organizations, historical legacies and established traditions, but which also look at external institutionalized environments and prevailing beliefs regarding what constitute relevant problems and good solutions. These perspectives will be specified and elaborated on by examining the distinctive characteristics of the public sector.

We will argue against approaches that presuppose one singular dominant organizational model, mainly because these do not succeed in capturing the diversity and range in a large and fragmented public sector. Examples of this can be comprehensive visions such as a Weberian bureaucracy, where the dominant administrative model is based on hierarchy, routines and division of labour; or NPM, with its emphasis on efficiency, market-orientation and management techniques from the private sector; or networks, where lateral linkages and coordination between public and private organizations are stressed. Organizations in the public sector are involved in shaping and enforcing rules and laws, but they also function as political, academic and professional advisers, service providers and mobilizers of resources. They are faced with conflicting logics and identities while acting as rule-driven utility-calculators and problem-solvers. Such a complex organizational pattern can hardly be understood using a theoretical approach that starts from a simple set of universal assumptions about actors, organizations and change. Our approach is to develop three perspectives that, on their own and together, can help increase the understanding of how a complex public sector is organized and how it works in reality.

STRUCTURES, PROCESSES AND TASKS IN PUBLIC ORGANIZATIONS

Politics can be defined as an endeavour that consists of putting a problem area on the public agenda, having it accepted as a binding public responsibility and organizing a permanent problem-solving routine. This implies that processes and structures are crucial components of public policy. By *processes* we mean activities and behaviour that play out over time. These can be decision-making, opinion-forming, implementation or learning processes. By *structures* we mean the frameworks within which processes unfold. The structures set limits as to who can participate. They also limit what are deemed acceptable, reasonable, appropriate or valid perceptions of a situation, a problem or suggested solutions. The organizational structure consists of role expectations and rules for who should or can do what, and how each task should or can be done. Meanwhile, this structure says nothing directly about how an organization's members actually behave; it only provides guidelines and a framework.

A distinction can be made between formal and informal norms. *Formal norms* are often outlined in organizational charts, rules and job descriptions. Such structural characteristics have a central position in instrumental perspectives. They specify procedures, methods, responsibilities, rights and duties assigned to various units and positions. *Informal norms and values* are found in established traditions and organizational cultures that an organization's members internalize or acquire through experience and daily work with their colleagues. These are central to cultural perspectives. Informal norms can also spring from an organization's environment, through ideas about what is deemed appropriate in organizations that are highly esteemed and used as ideals, in the way emphasized by a myth perspective. An organization theory for the public sector must focus on formal and informal norms and thus on organizational structure, culture and myths. This will be described more closely in the following chapters.

In formal organizations there is often a connection between structural characteristics and tasks. This is particularly highlighted in instrumental perspectives. Organizations in the public sector have a wide spectrum of tasks. For instance, distinctions can be made between advising on policy issues, regulation, administration, control and supervision, and the production of services. The organizational pattern reflects the range of tasks. In central government, responsibility for policy advice lies with the ministries, whereas the exercise of power, control and supervision is concentrated in agencies. Service provision and commercial tasks are often placed in various types of state-owned companies. Corresponding distinctions between political, administrative and business-related tasks in different forms of organizations are also found on regional and local levels. In recent years there has been a tendency to further clarify and cultivate the linkage between, on the one hand, tasks and roles, and on the other, formal organizational structure. This is done by transforming integrated agency organizations into 'single-purpose' organizations, where the different tasks are the focal concern of individual organizations, for example by singling out the controlling tasks in specialized supervisory bodies. The government's roles as owner, purchaser, provider, implementer and regulator are more specialized than before, and the ideal appears to be to set up one organization for each task.

Decision-making will also have a pivotal position in the study of public organizations. Here we will apply an *extended decision-making concept*. This involves the need to examine what happens prior to formal decisions being made, as well as what happens afterwards. While the first stage focuses on setting agendas, the possible courses of action and their consequences, the second stage focuses on implementing public measures, feedback and interpreting how the public measures are working. Concentrating solely on decision-making itself, where a choice is made between various courses of action, is only reasonable if the other phases are unproblematic. This is seldom the case in today's complex political-administrative systems.

In addition to decision-making, *opinion-forming* is also central in public organizations. Public policy is just as much about discovering goals, identities and affiliations as it is about finding the best tools to reach given goals. This implies that the symbolic side of public organizations is of great importance. Politics is not merely a question of distributing goods and burdens by making decisions efficiently; it is also about interpreting experiences in such a way that people's goals, values, beliefs, attitudes and opinions are influenced and their sympathies and antipathies shaped. In this way the public sector's legitimacy is also influenced.

OUTLINE OF THIS BOOK

The book follows a matrix structure. First, we will present the main characteristics of each of the three perspectives in individual chapters, using a delimiting approach. Next, we will give an account of four central aspects of public organizations: goals and values, leadership and steering, reform and change, and effects and implications. Each issue is discussed in relation to the three perspectives (see Table 1.2).

The book concludes with a chapter on understanding and design. It discusses relations between the perspectives and points to a development towards a transformative perspective. This approach argues that a complex public sector demands that elements from an instrumental perspective, a cultural perspective and a myth perspective be included. At the same time, emphasis is placed on the processual aspects and dynamic interplay expressed in various forms of translation, revision and adjustment that occur in processes of change and reform within the public sector. Formal organizational structure, organizational culture and societal norms can influence practice, actions and performance in public organizations, which can then bounce back and change the organizational characteristics.

In the final chapter we also discuss possibilities for a wider prescriptive analysis in an organization theory for the public sector, with particular emphasis on what public organizations *can* do. Such a development demands an expansion of solid empirical-descriptive knowledge of what *actually happens* in public organizations, but also the clarification and elaboration of the normative basis for what goals and values these organizations *should* attend to. The chapter concludes by discussing what strategies can be applied in adjustment and change within the public sector, given the

Table 1.2 *The book's matrix structure*

	Chapter 2 An instrumental perspective	Chapter 3 A cultural perspective	Chapter 4 A myth perspective
Chapter 5 Goals and values			
Chapter 6 Leadership and steering			
Chapter 7 Reform and change			
Chapter 8 Effects and implications			
Chapter 9 Understanding and design			

existing knowledge base of how public organizations work, and we discuss potential paths of development for such organizations.

CHAPTER SUMMARY

- Public organizations differ from private organizations by being multifunctional, having a politically elected leadership and by not usually operating in a market.
- To understand how public-sector organizations work in practice, we need to apply an instrumental perspective – including both hierarchically based and negotiation-based variants – and institutional perspectives, specifically a cultural perspective and a myth perspective.
- Organizational affiliation and the organizational setting will influence people's way of thinking and behaviour, and thus also the content of public policy.

DISCUSSION QUESTIONS

1   Explain the differences between a logic of consequence and a logic of appropriateness. Find examples of decision-making processes in a public-sector organization that are based on such logics.
2   What is meant by 'bounded rationality', and how can decision-making processes in public-sector organizations be affected by it?
3   Discuss the statement 'Public and private organizations are fundamentally alike in all unimportant respects'.

REFERENCES AND FURTHER READING

Allison, G.T. (1983) 'Public and Private Management: Are They Fundamentally Alike in All Unimportant Respects?', in J.L. Perry and K.L. Kraemer (eds) *Public Management: Public and Private Perspectives*, Palo Alto: Mayfield.

Augier, M., March, J.G. and Sullivan, B.N. (2005) 'Notes on the Evolution of a Research Community: Organizational Studies in Anglophone North America 1945–2000', *Organizational Science*, 16 (1): 85–95.

Bozeman, B. (1987) *All Organizations are Public*, San Francisco: Jossey-Bass.

—— (1993) *Public Management: The State of the Art*, San Francisco: Jossey-Bass.

Brunsson, N. and Olsen, J.P. (eds) (1993) *The Reforming Organization*, London: Routledge.

Christensen, T. and Lægreid, P. (1998) 'Public Administration in a Democratic Context: A Review of Norwegian Research', in N. Brunsson and J.P. Olsen (eds) *Organizing Organizations,* Bergen: Fagbokforlaget.

Dahl, R.A. and Lindblom, C.E. (1953; new edn 1992) *Politics, Economics and Welfare,* New York: Harper & Row; new edn New Brunswick, NJ: Transaction.

Dunleavy, P. and Hood, C. (1994) 'From Old Public Organization to New Public Management', *Public Money & Management* (July–September): 9–16.

Kielland, E. (1986) 'Offentlige arbeidsplasser på anbud?' (Contracting Out of Public Services?), in S. Kuhnle (ed.) *Det Politiske Samfunn* (*The Political Society*), Oslo: TANO.

Lægreid, P. and Olsen. J.P. (eds) (1993) *Organisering av offentlig sektor* (*Organizing the Public Sector*), Oslo: TANO.

March, J.G. and Olsen, J.P. (1989) *Rediscovering Institutions,* New York: The Free Press.

March, J.G. and Simon, H. (1958; 2nd edn 1992) *Organizations,* New York: Wiley; 2nd edn Oxford: Blackwell.

Olsen, J.P. (1983) *Organized Democracy,* Bergen: Universitetsforlaget.

—— (1992) 'Analyzing Institutional Dynamics', *Statswissenschaften und Staatspraxis,* 3 (2): 247–71.

—— (2004) 'Citizens, Public Administration and the Search for Theoretical Foundations', *PS: Political Science & Politics,* 1: 69–77.

Rainey, H.G. (1991; 3rd edn 2003) *Understanding and Managing Public Organizations,* San Francisco: Jossey-Bass.

Schattschneider, E.E. (1960; reissued 1975) *The Semisovereign People,* New York: Holt, Rinehart and Winston; reissued Hinsdale: The Dryden Press.

Chapter 2

An instrumental perspective

LEARNING OBJECTIVES

By the end of this chapter you should:

- have a clear understanding of the main elements of an instrumental perspective;
- be able to identify the main characteristics of the formal structure of public organizations;
- have some basic ideas about how formal organizational structure affects concrete actions in public organizations.

ORGANIZATIONS AS INSTRUMENTS

Public organizations carry out tasks on behalf of society. In higher education, for example, this might entail preparing study reforms through a government ministry and implementing new study programmes through public universities and colleges. Organizations can thus be understood as tools or instruments for achieving certain goals seen as important in society, such as raising the standard of higher education. In one sense, this can be expressed partly as public organizations and their members acting with *instrumental rationality* in fulfilling tasks and achieving the desired results. This entails members of an organization assessing the available alternatives or tools according to their consequences and in relation to the chosen goals, making wilful choices between alternatives and achieving the effects desired through those choices. Yet instrumentality can also be expressed in the structural design of an organization in accordance with means–ends assessments, which, in turn, determines how its members behave while carrying out tasks. Instrumental rationality can thus involve both the effects of organizational structure and the process whereby that structure is determined and formed.

In the study of organizations, there are many long-standing traditions that view organizations as instruments. Among the classic social scientists, Max Weber has particularly influenced organizational literature through his analysis of bureaucracy as an organizational form. About the same time, a scientific view of management in manufacturing and production organizations developed in the United States, particularly in the work of engineer Frederick Taylor. In this 'Scientific Management' tradition, often called Taylorism, great emphasis was placed on finding efficient organizational forms and work techniques. In the inter-war years several attempts were made to develop a set of general administrational principles, in connection with the development of public organizations in the United States ('Scientific Administration'). A leading figure here was the American political scientist Luther Gulick. In the aftermath of the Second World War, the American political scientist Herbert Simon and his colleagues developed a theory about administrative decision-making behaviour as a critique of the contributions of Taylor, Gulick and others. Simon doubted the validity of the assumptions Taylor and Gulick had built their work on, but he nevertheless emphasized that members of organizations try to act in instrumentally rational ways and that an organizational structure has great significance for what members actually do or can do.

Explanations that start with the idea of organizations as instruments are concerned with clarifying goals and means–ends conceptions of organizations and their members, which choice of action they follow, and whether and how the result of an action accords with what was desired. We shall therefore first outline the elements involved in actions built upon such a *logic of consequence*. By *formal organizational structure* – often merely called organizational structure – we mean a structure that consists of positions and rules for who shall or can do what and which defines how various tasks should be executed. Organizations are composed of a set of positions and subordinated units and can themselves fall under other larger units. In addition, organizational units can be divided up and coordinated in different ways.

In the following account of organizational structure, our point of departure is bureaucratic organizational forms with strong elements of hierarchy, division of labour and routines. We then go on to sketch how structural features of organizations can influence what organizations do and how their members think and act. Instances of several sub-units and divisions of labour also invite a view of organizations as heterogeneous, with coalitions that make room for disparate goals or interests and diverse resources for the articulation of interests. The individual sub-units and their members can act in an instrumentally rational way, but the results here will also depend on the resources others have and what they do. Public organizations and their sub-units can also enter into coalitions with other public and private organizations and in a similar way be dependent on what these do to achieve their objectives. Other organizations of this kind constitute a part of the organization's *environment*, and we will address how these and other aspects of the environment can influence the structural features of an organization.

From an instrumental perspective, *steering* can occur partly through the way an organization's structure is designed relative to the environment and partly through instrumentally rational actions within these boundaries. Organizational leaders can, to varying degrees, influence their own and others' latitude for action. An instrumental perspective assumes that leaders have the ability for rational calculation and for political control, but also that there may be some limitations to these abilities. We return to this point at the end of the chapter.

THE LOGIC OF CONSEQUENCE – INSTRUMENTALLY RATIONAL ACTIONS

As we shall describe more fully in Chapter Five, organizations have *goals* – ideas about what they would like to achieve or realize in the future. Within this context, a *problem* for an organization can be defined as a perceived distance between a desired and an actual state of affairs. For public organizations this can involve problems defined from within the public administration or from outside. Thus, problem-solving implies actions that aim to reduce or eliminate this distance. Another way of describing this is through the concept of *instrumentally rational actions*. The implementation of such actions consists of four elements:

- *Goal or problem*: What does one want to achieve and what is the distance between that and the current state of affairs?
- *Alternatives*: What actions are possible?
- *(Expectations about) consequences*: What future consequences in relation to the goals might follow from each alternative, and how likely are these consequences – assuming that the alternative is chosen?
- *Decision-making rules*: How shall the choice between alternatives be made?

In some cases the point of departure is an organization's goal or perception of a problem. The organization assesses possible alternatives based upon their consequences, and a choice is made accordingly. For example, a public university might fear that its forms of leadership will not provide an adequate basis for achieving professional quality goals, and it therefore assesses various alternatives that it expects to go further towards achieving those goals. In other cases the point of departure is an organization's alternatives for action. The organization assesses how valuable the consequences following from each alternative are, and a choice is made based on this. A university can be faced with several possible forms of leadership, and it chooses among these according to the consequences goal achievement is likely to entail. The actions required to implement tasks are marked, in any case, by their relation to a logic of consequence, where the organization chooses between alternatives, based upon rational calculations of possible consequences.

The concept of *full instrumental rationality* refers to an organization having clear and consistent goals, a full overview of all the alternatives and full insight into which consequences these alternatives will bring in relation to its goals. From this it often follows that the organization chooses the alternative that gives the maximal or the greatest degree of goal achievement. Even so, many empirical studies of how organizations act show that this is realistic only to a certain degree, particularly for complex public organizations where many considerations come to bear. This state of affairs is crystallized in the concept of bounded rationality, to which we will return in Chapter Five. *Bounded rationality* implies that an organization's goals are diffuse, inconsistent or unstable and that the problems it faces are complex. The concept also includes the idea that an organization has incomplete information about alternatives and consequences. An organization knows of only a limited set of alternatives because of limited capacity, and must select information and premises for decision-making even though it probably has unsure knowledge of means–ends relations. It requires time and resources to acquire a better knowledge base, and complete insight will be impossible to achieve. From this it follows that the organization chooses an alternative that yields good enough, or an acceptable degree of, goal achievement. In other words, the organization will have a decision-making rule built upon achieving *satisfactory* rather than *maximum* results, whereby satisfactory, but not necessarily optimal, solutions are chosen. It must be underscored, nevertheless, that even actions based on bounded rationality are marked by a logic of consequence.

In his analysis of decision-making behaviour, Herbert Simon takes as his point of departure the individual's actions within an organization. As the antithesis of 'economic man', motivated by self-interest and with full knowledge of all the alternatives and consequences, Simon outlines 'administrative man', who acts within a determinate structural framework, but who has incomplete knowledge of alternatives and consequences. A specialized organizational structure gives individuals a relatively narrow range of understanding and purview in their roles. This can ease understanding and capacity problems, but it can also cause knowledge problems and difficulty in seeing one's own activity and role in a wider perspective. As we shall see in more detail below, designing an organizational structure may mean that rationality is somewhat reduced at the organizational level compared with the individual level. We shall also return to how possible conflicts of interest between individual members and their organization can be dealt with through organizational design.

FORMAL ORGANIZATIONAL STRUCTURE

Who shall or can act on behalf of an organization by carrying out tasks is determined by which formal roles or positions an organization's members have, which sub-unit they are in and which larger units the organization is a part of. Here we are concerned with the *formal* structure of organizations. This implies that the expectations of those holding positions are *impersonal*. Norms for practices thus exist independently of the personal characteristics of the individual holding a position at any given time. These formal norms may be expressed in things such as organizational charts, manuals, rules and regulations.

Organizing via the design of the formal organizational structure happens, to varying degrees, through *specialization* and *coordination*. How an organization is specialized and coordinated can have an effect on relations between positions and the sub-units the organization is composed of, relations with the larger units of which the organization is a part, and relations with the other organizations it has dealings with.

A *bureaucratic organizational form*, as Weber describes it, is marked by hierarchy, division of labour and routines. *Hierarchy* entails superior and subordinate positions and various vertical levels in an organization. In a government ministry, various sections or offices can, for example, be part of a division, and all divisions will be subordinate to the political and administrative leadership. Someone in a superior position has the right to command and instruct subordinates, and this is achieved through downward channels of communication. In addition, information travels upwards through various forms of case proposals and reporting systems. The hierarchy in a bureaucratic organization is often tied to a *career system*, where members endeavour to rise to higher positions and are promoted on the basis of qualifications, merit and performance.

Division of labour means that an organization's tasks are grouped into different units and tied to concrete positions – in other words, *horizontal specialization*. Various principles can lie at the root of this division of labour within and between organizations, a point we shall return to shortly. What characterizes a bureaucratic organizational form is not the specific principle, but rather that there is a large degree of division of labour. Such an organizational form is also characterized by many *routines*, that is, rules and procedures for who shall carry out tasks and how they should be accomplished. The content of these routines may differ, but will often be codified in written documents, such as regulations, guidelines and manuals.

Through the superior–subordinate relationship between different levels in a hierarchy, there will be a great degree of vertical coordination within and between organizations. In the central governments of many representative democracies, vertical coordination is expressed in the principle of ministerial responsibility, that is, the cabinet minister is responsible to the parliament for activities in his or her own ministry and subordinate agencies. At the same time, the minister, through participation in the cabinet, is responsible for shaping the cabinet's general policy, and this entails elements of horizontal coordination at this level. Hierarchy can also involve vertical specialization, in that different types of tasks are assigned to different levels in the organization or to organizations at different levels. For instance, tasks related to advising political leaders could be assigned to a ministry, while more professional tasks could be assigned to a subordinate agency. Routines can constitute a form of coordination both vertically and horizontally. Procedural rules can be used as tools within an organization but can also be used to coordinate activities in a way that cuts across organizations. For civil service organizations, such as agencies, this can apply, for example, to general rules for casework, financial management and human-resource management.

Horizontal specialization expresses how different tasks are thought to be allocated on a certain level by means of organizational structure. It might, for example, be decided that one and the same unit will deal with transportation and environmental protection issues, or these might be allocated to different units on the same level. Another example is choosing to have ownership tasks and policy advice in the same agency, or allocating these to two agencies, a practice that has become more common now.

Through the influence of administration theorists such as Gulick it has become common to distinguish between four different principles for horizontal specialization. The *purpose principle*, or *sector principle*, distributes cases according to purpose or sector. At the ministerial level, this means having separate ministries for, say, defence, education, health care and various industries such as agriculture and fisheries. The *process principle* distributes cases according to the procedural method or type of process used in order to achieve a purpose. In a ministry or a municipality, there may, for instance, be distinct units for cases concerning financial management, planning, human-resource management and judicial issues. These cases are not goals in themselves, but steps in the process of advancing towards a purpose, such as education. The third horizontal divisional method for classification is the *client principle*. Here all the cases concerning a particular section of the population are gathered into one organizational unit, so that through collaborative expertise a holistic perspective on them can be achieved. In some municipalities, for instance, there might be individual sections for the elderly or for children or youth. The *geographical principle* implies that an organization's structure reflects a territorial division of society. The principle is exemplarily expressed through the four levels of government – the international, the national, the regional and the local level. It may be expressed in a municipality through the existence of several neighbourhood councils that each take on tasks such as schools or care of the elderly.

In an organizational hierarchy, one level may follow one specialization principle while other lower or higher levels follow different ones. This might mean, for instance, that a government ministry with a purpose such as education may have its own sub-units for various processes or courses of action. By allocating issues of concern horizontally, responsibility for coordination will move upwards to a higher level in the organization or to a larger unit the organization is a part of. For example, a ministry's leadership will have responsibility for coordinating activities for several divisions, and the cabinet will have responsibility for the activities of several ministries.

Many types of organizational forms can be thought of as alternative or supplementary to a bureaucratic organizational form. At one extreme is a completely *flat structure*, that is, an organization without superior and subordinate hierarchical ordering, but with several positions and sub-units at the same level. In practice, the concept of flat structure is also used for organizations with two or fewer vertical levels, as a contrast to 'tall' hierarchies. In a flat structure, members of an organization can either always be tied to the same position or sub-unit or rotate among these. In a *collegial structure*, a board of directors or an advisory council can be set up instead of, or in addition to, the top leadership in the hierarchy. For example, cabinet ministers deal with many issues as a collegium, and so do city government commissioners. Many public organizations have a permanent board of directors devoted to leadership, for example state-owned companies and public universities. A collegial structure can also cut across organizations, for example, by establishing coordinating committees that include members from various organizations, for *horizontal coordination* between them. Examples might be coordinating committees a government uses to handle European Union (EU) issues, where different ministries and agencies are represented. Another alternative is a *matrix structure*. Here a position or sub-unit is subordinated to several superior units simultaneously. These superior units usually operate according to different principles of specialization. An example might be a unit for elderly care in a neighbourhood under the jurisdiction of a municipal service for elderly care and a wider neighbourhood administration. In this case, the client principle and the geographical principle would apply for the same unit.

In addition to arrangements such as these without time limitations, public organizations have many *temporary arrangements* that extend beyond the bounds of bureaucratic organizational forms. This is the case for *public commissions* or *task forces* appointed by a government ministry to determine alternatives for accomplishing specific tasks, such as a commission that reviews new or revised laws. Here persons often take on such duties in addition to their regular positions, but these tasks may also be allocated to an individual as a full-time job for a limited period. Pertinent examples include project organizations that are established in order to review and implement specific tasks, such as the building of airports, railway lines and major bridges. Here persons are usually removed from their regular positions and placed in a temporary unit that disbands when the task has been accomplished. This method is frequently used for reorganizations in public administration and for large public construction projects.

Boards of directors, advisory councils, coordinating committees, matrix structures, public commissions and task forces are all various forms of *network structure* that supplement the bureaucratic organizational form. This is not merely the case within individual public organizations but also applies to relationships between public organizations, and with organizations in the private sector, so-called public–private partnerships.

Public organizations can also be distinguished from one another according to whether they have a *simple* or a *complex structure*. While an organization with a simple structure has few positions and sub-units and few connections between these, a complex structure will have many levels, many units on each level and many connections vertically and horizontally. Moreover, connections can be differentiated from each other according to how tight or loose they are, that is, whether they are tightly integrated or consist of more or less independent units. The larger an organization is, measured in terms of the number of members, the greater chance there is that it will have a complex structure. A large organization with a bureaucratic organizational form can nevertheless be relatively simple. Nowadays, complexity can increase by dividing up public organizations, as has been the trend in recent years, through structural devolution, divisionalization and separating independent result units, all of which make public organizations increasingly look like conglomerates.

Public organizations can also be described according to the degree to which they are centralized or decentralized. This normally concerns the levels at which decisions are made in and between organizations. In a *centralized* organization or group of organizations, the final or important decisions almost always are taken at the superior level, and these decisions are expected to be followed up at the lower levels. In contrast, such decisions in a decentralized organization or group of organizations will be delegated to a lower level. The concept of *decentralization* is often used to describe such a condition, but will more precisely concern processes whereby decisional authority is delegated to a lower level. Reforming public organizations through restructuring does not necessarily lead to either centralization or decentralization, but may involve both simultaneously. The Norwegian hospital reform in 2001 illustrates this well. It centralized power by having the central government take over ownership of hospitals from county governments; at the same time, the hospitals were transformed from being administrative organizations into decentralized health enterprises, which entailed decentralization.

STRUCTURAL FEATURES AND CONCRETE ACTIONS

Although the formal organizational structure does not necessarily indicate anything about the actual behaviour of members in an organization, it will constrain how tasks are carried out. One of the ways this manifests itself is through the use of various *specialization principles*. Geographical specialization, for instance, makes it more likely that different sectors will be coordinated within each individual geographical area. The opposite would be a specialization built on the purpose principle, implying that focus is on the lines of demarcation between sectors rather than between territories, and such specialization will probably further the standardization of public policies across geographical areas. Specialization built on the client principle will, to a greater degree, imply policies directed towards sectors seen as related to each other. Specialization based on the process principle is likely to support the development of professional expertise in an organization, for example expertise related to financial management and judicial issues. On the other hand, such specializations may direct attention away from the actual purpose of the organization.

The choice of specialization principle may thus have a strong influence on how problems are dealt with and on the content of public policy. This can, to some degree, also be influenced by different forms of coordination, vertically through hierarchy, or horizontally through structures such as coordinating committees. For example, government youth policy has at various times and in different countries been assigned either to a ministry for sports or culture, or grouped together with child-related issues in a ministry focused on family policy. Important youth issues, such as education and employment, however, normally fall under the jurisdiction of other ministries. Central governments often have coordinating committees for youth policy that cut across ministries. Another example of coordination through formal organizational structure is national security and emergency planning policy. While such issues in many countries were previously allocated to units under several ministries (for example internal affairs and defence), with certain elements of vertical coordination through ministers and horizontal coordination committees, they are now often assigned to one agency or one ministry. For problems concerning a specific group within society (for example, youth), or a specific geographical area (for example, a valley prone to flooding), it can nevertheless be difficult to find good ways to deal with such issues if central government is largely based on the purpose principle.

How tasks are accomplished is also expressed through established *routines* in an organization. Rules and procedures can sometimes relate to participation, that is, who has the obligation or permission to carry out particular tasks. Given that time and attention are limited, an organization and its members cannot participate in all issues under its jurisdiction at any given time. In some instances matters will be handled at a lower level in a ministry, while in other, more important instances the entire hierarchy will participate. What is more, rules and procedures may concern content, for example which goals and problems are viewed as pertinent, which alternatives for action and consequences are assessed and how the choice between the alternatives is made. Through existing routines, known problems can be linked with specific alternatives for action, and the choice of actions will then be based on assessing a pre-existing definition of the problem and relevant alternatives. On the other hand, new and unknown problems, and problems involving uncertainty over which consequences will follow from each alternative cannot be handled using established rules and procedures, and may hence result in ad hoc routines and organizational solutions.

Elements of hierarchy in an organization mean that a superior can command and instruct subordinates. What then causes subordinates to follow injunctions? First, the emphasis on impersonal relationships in formal organizations is designed to make members distinguish between private goals and interests on the one hand and the organization's goals on the other, and to use the latter as the basis for carrying out tasks. The tasks are seen as public obligations or duties. Second, it can be in a member's own interest to comply with organizational norms, since future promotion in the hierarchy is usually based on performance in present and former positions within the organization. An organizational structure divided into different levels can, therefore, function in a disciplinary manner, that is, it will help members to distinguish their individual decision-making behaviour from their personal opinions.

Degrees and forms of dividing up labour, along with routines and hierarchy, also clearly delimit individual decision-making behaviour in public organizations. Some of these limitations are related to the *capacity for action*, which means that organizational members are unable to participate in all the decisions they have the right to participate in. Other limitations are related to the *capacity for analysis*, that is, an organizational member's ability to calculate rationally. The organizational structure provides its members with limited goals and commitments they must attend to, but it also filters which information about alternatives and consequences the members have or are able to acquire. Engrained routines for accomplishing tasks can also cause individual decision-making behaviour to be characterized more by rule-following than problem-solving.

Even though the formal organizational structure poses clear limitations on an individual organizational member's choice of actions, it simultaneously creates the possibility for the organization to realize specific goals. Put differently, rationality at the organizational level can be strengthened through structural features, which both constrain and enable the organization's instrumental rational actions. Thus organization theorists such as W. Richard Scott have developed (on the basis of Herbert Simon's ideas about bounded rationality linked to individual decision-making behaviour and the significance of formal organizational structure) what he calls a *rational organizational perspective*, where organizations are instruments for goal achievement.

COALITIONS AND INTEREST ARTICULATION

Thus far we have viewed public organizations as unified actors and emphasized how they make wilful choices on the basis of agreed or common goals. Different individuals or groups within an organization can nevertheless be committed to different goals and interests, and the organization or its individual parts must relate to other organizations that may have other goals and interests. We call this *heterogeneity* or *plurality*. From a *negotiation-based instrumental perspective*, organizations can be understood as coalitions, where each actor acts in an instrumentally rational way, is motivated by interests and can also enter into coalitions with actors outside the organization who, according to their interests, act in similar ways. Interest distribution may be rooted in formal structures within and between organizations, for example it may be related to actors carrying out specialized tasks. Their resources for articulating their own interests can also to some extent be rooted in the formal structure, for example in elements of super- or sub-ordination of actors and different forms of horizontal coordination.

If we view an organization, or a part of one, as an instrumental rational actor, other actors will in many respects be able to influence its possibilities for making wilful choices based on interests. First, other actors can set limitations on which alternatives for action are relevant. This may concern knowledge about alternatives, but also which alternatives can be chosen. Second, other actors' choice of actions can be significant for which consequences the rational actor's own actions bring to bear. The consequences in relation to an actor's goals or interests will thus depend on what other actors do. Furthermore, these actors may contribute knowledge about means–ends relations. One can clearly identify both situations in cases where governments deal with complex issues. Issues concerning asylum and immigration policy, labour-market policy, environmental protection policy and education policy engage and affect different government ministries, even though in most central governments such policies are primarily anchored in one ministry. Third, actors cannot normally of their own accord lay down decision-making rules, regardless of whether these are based on achieving an optimal or a satisfactory result. These decision-making rules will also be influenced by the distribution of resources among actors.

How, then, can conflicts of interest between organizations be dealt with? As we shall see in more detail in Chapter Five, this can be done in four different ways, all related to formulating and developing goals. First, a *dominant coalition* can, proceeding from rational calculations, choose between relevant alternatives of action and assert its own goals and interests. Second, the actors can negotiate a *compromise* between different interests, which in turn provides the basis for an instrumental rational choice based on knowledge about alternatives and consequences. This is quite normal within central governments. Third, the competing goals can be addressed one at a time, so as not to come into conflict with one another. Such *sequential attention to goals* is an example of what is called *quasi resolution of conflict*, for it de-emphasizes the need for consistent solutions. Fourth, goals in different parts of an organization, or in different organizations, do not always need to be viewed vis-à-vis each other. A great degree of specialization and decentralization can in fact mean that each unit has more limited goals and problems that can be addressed independently of what other units do. This way of handling conflicts of interest is often called *local rationality*, and is another example of a quasi resolution to a conflict. Conflicts of interest can also be dealt with by actors who come to an *agreement on means*. If a certain alternative is acceptable for everyone, there is no need to come to a decision on how potentially conflicting goals should be assessed in relation to one another.

ORGANIZATIONAL STRUCTURE, ENVIRONMENT AND UNCERTAINTY

In the early theoretical contributions that regarded organizations as instruments, organizations were often conceptualized as *closed systems*. For instance, Weber emphasized internal relations in public organizations, such as hierarchical elements, divisions of labour and routines. For him, external relations were mainly limited to how such bureaucratic organizations were subordinated to the political leadership and regulated by laws.

In the post-war era it has been more common to view organizations as *open systems*. An organization's environment will be important, both for how its structure is formed and for how tasks can be accomplished through instrumental rational actions. In organizational literature, a distinction is often made between environments in the sense of the *inter-organizational network* an organization is a part of, the *general environment* and the *international/global environment*. The American organization theorist Mary Jo Hatch also divides the general environment into different types: social, cultural, legal, political, economic, technological and physical. From an instrumental perspective on public organizations, the most important parts of the environment are those that influence an organization's possibility to achieve its goals by accomplishing its tasks. These are called the *technical environment* and may concern parts of an inter-organizational network, some types of general environments and, in certain cases, perhaps also parts of the international/global environment. The *task environment* refers to the actors in an inter-organizational network, whom an organization particularly depends on for supplying resources or for getting a return on the results of accomplished tasks.

As the American organization theorist James D. Thompson suggests, the characteristics of the task environment are crucial for how an organizational structure should be designed in line with instrumental rationality. He outlines two dimensions for the task environment: whether it is *stable* or *shifting,* and whether it is *homogeneous* or *heterogeneous*. These parameters, Thompson maintains, can provide the basis for four different types of organizational structure, as shown in Table 2.1.

The first category craves few resources and often makes it simple to act in accordance with the environment because the environment represents predictability and often stands for similar types of expertise, tasks and interests. An example of this might be the cooperation between a ministry and a subordinate agency, or between a ministry and a special interest organization. The second category demands more of an organization because it needs extra resources, both in order to partition its own organization and to coordinate contact with the environment. An example of this is when a heterogeneous ministry, such as a ministry of the interior, has to engage in dialogue with many different actors in the environment, regardless of whether these other actors are public or private interest organizations.

Table 2.1 *Organizational structures in different environments*

	Stable environment	Shifting environment
Homogeneous environment	1 Simple structure	3 Decentralization to regional sub-units
Heterogeneous environment	2 Several sub-units based on specialization according to the purpose or process principle, which each correspond to homogeneous parts of the task environment	4 Decentralization to sub-units based on specialization according to the purpose or process principle

Source: Thompson (1967), modified

Because of the dynamic environment, the third category represents potentially greater uncertainty and uses even more resources than the first two. This might, for example, be the cooperation between a ministry or agency at the central level and regional sub-units for education, health care or agriculture. The fourth category represents the greatest amount of uncertainty and resources because it requires splitting up the regional sub-units. Examples of this can be the offices of county councillors or regional units of the transportation sector.

The distinguishing characteristics of actors in the task environment sketched above are significant because they create differing degrees and forms of uncertainty for organizations. This uncertainty can be related more directly to the properties of tasks and how they are accomplished. Using central elements in a logic of consequence, we can distinguish between whether or not there is agreement about goals, and whether or not there is agreement/certainty about the understanding of means–ends relations. Such reasoning can provide the basis for sketching four forms of action with their accompanying structural features, as in Table 2.2.

The first category represents a stable form that is relatively unchallenging and needs few resources. It may reflect homogeneity and agreement among the political and administrative leadership. Applied to decision-making in a ministry, this might mean that a division, a section or an individual member has a clear goal and knows the means for achieving it and its consequences. The decision-making process is thus relatively simple. The second category reflects heterogeneity and divergent organizational positions. There may be agreement on a relatively general goal, for example reducing unemployment, while various cabinet ministers, constrained by differing ministerial commitments, may disagree about the means for achieving that goal.

The third category craves more resources, holds greater uncertainty and potentially involves more conflicts. An example would be a cabinet and large special interest organizations; which may disagree over which political goals are the most important but agree on how they should be reached. Thus there are disagreements

Table 2.2 *Forms of action with accompanying structural features*

	Goals	
	Agreement	Disagreement
Causal relations		
Agreement	1 Computation in a bureaucratic structure	3 Bargaining in a representative structure
Disagreement	2 Consensus in a collegial structure	4 Inspiration in a network structure

Source: Thompson (1967) and DeLeon (2003), modified

about political priorities, which may reflect different ideological commitments, different positions and different fields of expertise. The fourth category represents the most uncertainty and conflict, because there is great disagreement about goals, and established knowledge is debateable and uncertain. This is often what one sees in dealings between public authorities and more ad hoc, action-oriented environmental protection organizations.

Nevertheless, an organization is not influenced solely by its environment; it can also to some degree influence its environment. Among other things, the organization can constitute part of the technical environment and task environment of other organizations and thus may affect how these are designed. What is more, many public organizations will be included in what, using Hatch's terminology, are called different types of general environments for other organizations, such as legal and political environments.

STEERING THROUGH DESIGN AND EXPLOITING LATITUDE FOR ACTION

From an instrumental perspective on organizations, steering will involve influencing the relationships that are significant for achieving goals. Seen from the vantage point of organizational leaders, this will happen partly through designing structural features and partly through instrumental rational actions within these frameworks. The formal organizational structure allows leaders to secure for themselves the capacity for analysis and the right to participate, and hence the opportunity to exploit the latitude for action these frameworks provide. The organizational structure allows leaders to regulate other actors' participation and determine which alternatives for action will be relevant for them.

Structural design may include features of bureaucratic organizational forms, that is, degrees and forms of hierarchy, division of labour and routines, but also of other organizational forms, such as boards of directors, coordinating committees and public commissions. For instance, when a new or revised law is reviewed by a commission, the commission's composition determines who has the right to participate in this phase of work while its mandate specifies which goals, alternatives and consequences are deemed relevant. Also, choosing to use a commission to review the law or allowing the work to be done within a ministry indicates who has the right to participate during this phase. Similarly, in the next instance, when a proposed law is sent for a hearing to the affected parties, the question of who is allowed to articulate their views, which problem definitions are used and which alternative solutions are deemed to be particularly relevant are all predetermined by structural features.

As for actions within the structural framework, we have mentioned that an organization's leadership does not have the capacity to participate in all decisions in which it has the right to participate, and this can result in problems of control. Where the leadership does participate directly, it can build upon its means–ends insight and rational calculations to make decisions, or it can build upon its bargaining strength to advance its interests in relation to other actors who have other interests and resources. The organizational leadership can nevertheless also influence decisions without participating directly, for other actors can base their actions on insight into what leaders *would do* without them needing to be physically present. These actors can, for instance, refrain from putting forward an alternative solution, because they know that the organization's leaders will disapprove of it. Instances of such *anticipated reactions* and *autonomous adaptation* are widespread within and between public organizations, and may be rooted in past experiences.

RATIONAL CALCULATION AND POLITICAL CONTROL

We started from a perspective of organizations as tools for achieving given goals determined by leaders or groups in society. The possibilities for achieving these goals by carrying out tasks will be limited, partly by an organization's understanding of means and ends, and partly by its power to influence situations in relation to other actors who have interests connected to the same tasks. The instrumental rational ideal is a situation in which organizational leaders possess a great ability for rational calculation and, through hierarchical authority, exert much control over other actors. As we noted above, however, there are situations when leaders' means–ends understanding is incomplete and where they must negotiate with other actors who have different interests and resources.

Such a view of organizations can also be related to more general characteristics of models of governance and autonomy in public administration. In what the Norwegian political scientist Johan P. Olsen calls 'the sovereign, rationality-bounded state', the foundation for knowledge is seen as problematic because of the limitations on rationality, but he highlights how organizational design can turn public administration into an instrument for political leadership. This sort of *governance model* is marked by instrumental rational actions and hierarchical authority. In what Olsen calls 'the corporate-pluralist state', political control is problematic. Specialization in the public administration provides the basis for developing a range of interests in organizational units, thus enabling organized groups in society to participate in shaping and implementing public policy. In such a model of governance, actors act in instrumentally rational ways, but the political leadership's effectiveness is limited by the power base of other actors.

The challenges facing the public leadership vary according to combinations of rational calculation and political control. To begin with, the ideal of achieving high values for both of these variables puts pressure on leaders to expend great resources in order to develop expertise in organizations, and often to be directly involved and to have a high degree of control over other participants. Second, the combination of placing a high value on rational calculation and a medium or low value on political control can create significant problems for implementing desired changes; in other words, proposed changes risk remaining on the drawing board. Third, the combination of a high degree of control and medium or little insight can result in solutions that are not well reflected or change almost nothing – a situation that immediately calls for new reform processes. Fourth, a mid to low value for rational calculation as well as for political control can easily lead to chaotic or anarchic processes, where few problems in society are solved and conflicts between actors increase.

CHAPTER SUMMARY

- Instrumentally rational actions may come about through the design of the formal organizational structure as well as through exploiting the given structure.
- Many types of organizational form exist in the public sector and may be alternative or supplementary to a bureaucratic organizational form.
- The choice of organizational form depends on the type of technical environment and task.

DISCUSSION QUESTIONS

Choose a public-sector organization with which you are familiar.

1 Identify how and to what extent the chosen organization is based on certain principles of specialization and coordination.
2 Discuss some consequences of its formal organizational structure.

3   Identify its type of technical environment and task environment and discuss how and to what extent its formal organizational structure is contingent on these factors.

REFERENCES AND FURTHER READING

Cyert, R.M. and March, J.G. (1963; 2nd edn 1992) *A Behavioural Theory of the Firm*, Englewood Cliffs: Prentice-Hall; 2nd edn Oxford: Blackwell.

deLeon, L. (2003) 'On Acting Responsibly in a Disorderly World: Individual Ethics and Administrative Responsibility', in B.G. Peters and J. Pierre (eds) *Handbook of Public Administration*, London: Sage.

Egeberg, M. (1999) 'The Impact of Bureaucratic Structure on Decision Making', *Public Administration* 77 (1): 155–70.

—— (2003) 'How Bureaucratic Structure Matters: An Organizational Perspective', in B.G. Peters and J. Pierre (eds) *Handbook of Public Administration*, London: Sage.

Gulick, L.H. (1937; reprinted 1987) 'Notes on the Theory of Organization', in L.H. Gulick and L.F. Urwick (eds) *Papers on the Science of Administration*, New York: Institute of Public Administration; reprinted New York: Garland.

Hatch, M.J. (1997; 2nd edn 2006) *Organization Theory: Modern, Symbolic and Postmodern Perspectives*, Oxford: Oxford University Press.

March, J.G. (1994) *A Primer on Decision Making*, New York: The Free Press.

Mintzberg, H. (1979) *The Structuring of Organizations*, Englewood Cliffs: Prentice-Hall.

Olsen, J.P. (1988) 'Administrative Reform and Theories of Organization', in C. Campbell and B.G. Peters (eds) *Organizing Governance, Governing Organizations*, Pittsburgh: University of Pittsburgh Press.

Scott, W.R. (1981; 6th edn 2007) *Organizations: Rational, Natural and Open Systems*, Englewood Cliffs, N.J.: Prentice-Hall; 6th edn (with G.F. Davies) Upper Saddle River: Prentice-Hall.

Simon, H.A. (1947; 4th edn 1997) *Administrative Behavior*, New York: Macmillan; 4th edn New York: Simon & Schuster.

Taylor, F.W. (1911; new edn 1998) *The Principles of Scientific Management*, New York: Harper & Bros.; new edn Mineola: Dover.

Thompson, J. D. (1967; new edn 2003) *Organizations in Action*, New York: McGraw-Hill; new edn Somerset: Transaction.

Weber, M. (1922; 1997) *The Theory of Social and Economic Organization*, New York: Simon & Schuster (first published in German).

Chapter 3

A cultural perspective

LEARNING OBJECTIVES

By the end of this chapter you should:

■ have a clear understanding of the main elements of a cultural perspective;

■ be able to understand some main concepts about organizational culture such as informal norms and values, the logic of appropriateness, path dependency, critical decisions, integrative processes, and vertical depth/horizontal width;

■ have a basic understanding of how the cultural factors in a public organization may influence attitudes and actions.

THE MEANING OF ORGANIZATIONAL CULTURE

Organizational culture has to do with the *informal norms* and *values* that evolve and become important for the activities of formal organizations. Both a government ministry and a municipal unit can have an organizational culture. In a public organization it is important to distinguish between informal norms and the formal norms presented in Chapter Two. These two sets of norms have differing origins and operate in different ways, yet they also influence each other, as we shall discuss later. According to a logic of consequence, goals are often given a priori, or are agreed on by political leaders, and they are achieved via formal structures and norms. Goals in a logic of cultural appropriateness, by contrast, are discovered in the course of a process, while informal norms, values and identities develop gradually. The classic distinction made by the American organization theorist Philip Selznick is between the *institution* – where informal norms grow gradually, in an organic process – and the *organization* – which has formal norms, associated with the instrumental, tool-like and 'mechanical'. When a formal organization develops informal norms and values in addition to the formal variety, it acquires *institutional features,* and one speaks of *institutionalized organizations*. This makes for a more complex organization, less flexible or adaptable to new demands, but also one equipped with new and necessary qualities that will potentially help the organization to solve tasks more expediently and function well as a socially integrated unit. A good metaphor to illustrate the difference between organizations and institutions is to say an organization is the skeleton, whereas an institution is the flesh and blood. Both elements are crucial.

How can one grasp the organizational culture in a public organization? This is not as easy as finding out about formal norms, where one can take recourse in explicit and relatively easily communicated laws, rules, organizational charts and work manuals. It is often said that an organizational culture 'sits in the walls', and one can only learn about it and internalize it after a certain period of time in the institution; in other words, it has to do with *socialization*. This notwithstanding, when studying organizational culture, one can use various sources in order to grasp it. One method is to interview members who have been in the organization a long time and who know the institutional characteristics well, for example, an experienced administrative leader, a director of an agency with many years in the job or 'the old mayor', all of whom are likely to have accrued a deep, insightful knowledge of their organization's informal norms and values across a wide spectrum. A rather different perspective might be obtained by asking a senior executive officer or a secretary with many years of service. Reading written accounts of a public organization's history and traditions is also a good way of immersing oneself in an organizational culture.

One can also examine what public organizations want to convey through *physical symbols* and find out about institutional characteristics through these, for the symbols are manifestations of the underlying culture. The American political scientist Charles Goodsell has enquired systematically into the relationship between physical symbols, the types of tasks public organizations perform and the culture they represent. His main point is that if public organizations primarily have tasks related to control and regulation, such as the police or courts, they will often adopt authority symbols to signal a coercive culture where 'users' have little leeway and where civil servants are not particularly obliging. At the opposite end of the spectrum public organizations with clear service profiles and in competitive situations will use physical symbols to signal open, user-friendly cultures. Often public organizations will have complex combinations of tasks that result in more compound physical symbols and more complex cultural profiles. This is typical for a number of public organizations such as road, telephone, railway or postal sectors; as a consequence of modern reforms, these are in transition from being internally directed and closed organizational structures to becoming more open structures that stress service and efficiency. A typical example is how the wines and spirits monopolies in some Scandinavian countries have developed. They have traditionally had a rather negative profile, with little openness and almost no product exposure – a profile that reflected norms about low alcohol consumption and the 'shame' of earning money through such an activity. Now, however, the monopolies offer self-service, have friendly, service-minded staff, display their products prominently and provide a lot of information about them, all of which reflect norms of commercialization and market orientation.

If one associates organizational culture in a public organization with the evolution of a set of distinct informal norms and values, this means that one highlights those things that unite and integrate the organization's members. A 'moral framework' is constructed for what behaviour is appropriate – often referred to as ethics. This also creates conditions for a high degree of mutual trust and collective values in the organization.

THE EXPLANATORY POWER OF CULTURAL VARIABLES

In many of the classic studies of organizational culture, particularly within organizational sociology and to some degree in organizational anthropology, there is an internal focus on diverse social variables. One set of these concerns is an organizational culture's strategy for survival. The organizational culture is said to help the institutionalized organization survive through 'pattern maintenance'. For public organizations this is not a particularly central problem because they seldom die; there is, however, an intrinsic value in an absence of conflict and in reducing uncertainty and turbulence in general. More interesting is the general argument that an organizational culture is the 'integrative glue' needed to develop a true collective feeling in public organizations. This argument presupposes an absence of cultural heterogeneity and tensions. If one emphasizes that public organizations must realize collective goals, this can be a crucial characteristic. A third way of gaining an insight into the effects of organizational culture is to describe culture as a goal unto itself, because an organization's members learn and develop as people through the informal norms and values they internalize.

All these social arguments tied to organizational culture can potentially have an instrumental side, that is, informal norms and values can be useful. Employees can feel more loyal and function better because the institutional aspects of their activity are emphasized. The classic Hawthorne studies provide an example of this. Employees were placed in a work situation where light was manipulated. It was found that they became more efficient when the light was stronger at their work place, yet, surprisingly, they remained just as efficient when the light became weaker again. One explanation for this was all the additional attention the employees received in connection with the experiment.

Another example is taken from a large survey carried out in Norwegian ministries and agencies, where the effects of *developmental dialogues* (dialogues between leaders and employees where current work and future career paths, but not salary, are discussed) were studied. It was revealed that those who had taken part in such dialogues, which can be seen partly as social contracts, were less likely to quit the organization. A third example concerns the general trend in many cabinets of emphasizing the significance of a social framework: government-sponsored social events are important because they improve social interaction, with benefits for the working of government. It has therefore become rather common for the political executive leadership to create integrative social arenas for cabinet members.

Political science studies of organizational culture in public organizations bring into stronger focus the effects of culture on decisions. These studies compare culture with other contexts and explanatory factors, based on what one methodologically could call either a *competitive* or a *complementary strategy*. In this way the perspective widens and becomes more instrumentally oriented, thus providing leeway for analysing the effects of organizational culture in relation to other contexts or logics of action governing public employees' actions. Although this is discussed more extensively in Chapter Nine, certain approaches to inter-perspectival problems may be mentioned here. Is it the case, as the theory predicts, that the effects of organizational culture will only be perspicuous if the formal structure is loose and provides few guidelines for decisions? Under which conditions will an organizational culture advance or impede the effects of a formal structure? How significant is the correspondence between the informal and the formal norms that organizational culture and formal structure respectively represent?

THE LOGIC OF CULTURAL APPROPRIATENESS

The foundational logic of action tied to organizational culture is labelled the *logic of appropriate behaviour* or *appropriateness*. This logic means that, when acting in public situations, one will not primarily act rationally according to careful deliberation of pro and contra arguments, or out of self-interest or assessments of possible consequences of actions (as outlined in Chapter Two). Instead, one will engage in *matching*, whereby rules for action are deployed in order to link situations and identities. One will thus ask the following key questions:

1 Which type of situation am I faced with as a public decision-maker? Is it easy to make a decision? Is the decision routine in character or does it constitute a response to a crisis? These are questions of *recognition*.
2 Which identity is (or identities are) most important for my institution and for me? How clear and consistent is my identity and that of my institution? These are questions of *identity*.
3 What are my institution and I expected to do in a situation like this? This is a matter where *rules for action* should link the situation with identity.

The idea is that this matching or linking will occur relatively intuitively and that the organizational culture entails a relatively consistent set of rules and identities, so that such links are simple to make.

What makes an action appropriate is a normative and institutional foundation that may be highly divergent from that found in other organizations, depending on how an organizational culture has evolved and what its dominant informal norms and values are. In some public organizations it may be culturally appropriate to act according to norms and values built on equality and considerations of general practicability, while in others it may be more appropriate to act according to a rational logic and a means–ends orientation. It is worth noting that cultural and informal rules are based mainly on past experience, while instrumental and formal rules are oriented more towards the future.

Matching a situation and an identity may have various origins. It may, for instance, be the result of *learning from experience,* that is, one knows in which situations one should activate various rules and identities. Here experienced organizational members will have a clear advantage over new members, for the former represent an institutional memory and will try to pass it on to others. Yet there is no guarantee that learning from experience gives clear guidelines for culturally based action, particularly when experiences vary and the culture is heterogeneous. Matching can also occur as a result of what might be called *categorization*, which happens when one has developed complex categories or 'mental maps' for rules and identities. Certain cultural norms and values are prioritized more strongly than others, so when they arise, one will intuitively categorize them as desirable and act accordingly. This might happen, for example, in situations where environment-related values are relevant.

A third possibility is *proximity in time*. In other words, recently used identities and rules are reused. This involves biased search processes that save time and resources. When new issues have to be dealt with, civil servants often resort to their own or the organization's praxis, and the recent past is thus given precedence. A fourth possibility is to deploy the *experiences of other actors* and public organizations. This can either happen through the experience of others being generalized and deemed commonly desirable, a phenomenon that might be called *decontextualization*, or else the experience of others is deemed particularly relevant because they are in precisely the same situation as oneself, in other words, *contextualization*. For instance, in working out plans for reorganizations, public commissions often take their lead from the experiences of international organizations or other countries, and these are examined to see whether they are relevant. An organization's leadership gathers experience and models from countries that are culturally related, in other words, they *contextualize*. Another example is private consultancy firms hired to help with public reform processes. These firms often stress that the concepts they themselves stand for and sell are generally accepted, without delving deeply into the culture of the organization undergoing reform. This is a typical example of *decontextualization*.

The cultural attitudes and actions of members of a public organization will crystallize and become systematic according to the logic of appropriateness. Actors will gain experience of an institutional culture by learning what is appropriate. For example, they will learn what it means to be a democratic politician, a responsible caseworker, a good member of a public commission or a friendly supplier of public services. They will be able to act even in highly complex and fluctuating situations because they are guided by a fundamental cultural basis acquired through socialization into informal norms and values. The logic of appropriateness clearly brings benefits because complex action-stimuli are responded to with *standardized*, almost *intuitive actions*. How effortless such matching behaviour is in reality will nevertheless vary.

It is obvious that civil servants with much work experience will be able to act intuitively according to cultural norms and values more easily than new organizational members, who must go through a period of socialization before they can internalize informal norms and values, either through active 'indoctrination' or passive adaptation. This process can be less problematic if the informal norms and values employees bring with them to a public organization are similar to those found there; put differently, employees are *pre-socialized*. Education or professional background may be significant here. If, for example, a civil servant coming from law school takes up an administrative position with clearly judicial tasks in a milieu dominated by lawyers, he or she will, in many respects, already know what kind of conduct is appropriate. By contrast, a political scientist who is given primarily economically oriented tasks and is surrounded by economists and lawyers will have greater problems making the informal norms acquired through his or her education immediately relevant.

Although the rules and identities of a well-developed organizational culture may be pretty consistent, one still cannot ignore the fact that the complexity of public policy and public administration also produces inconsistencies and multiplicity, giving rise to competing definitions of which attitudes and actions are culturally appropriate. Within a central government, for example, the following combination might be found: informal norms and values tied to growth and protection, to efficiency and due process, and to management and participation. The tensions and differences in organizational culture in other organizations be they national or international, may also play a role. In the EU, appropriate actions with regard to, say, alcohol policy, will be defined according to agricultural and market rules, whereas for some countries alcohol policy is largely a health care and social welfare issue – thus there are clearly different culturally based policy definitions.

Cultural inconsistency and multiplicity can create problems for political and administrative leaders, but it may also increase flexibility. Problems may stem from political and administrative control being undermined, either by uncertainty over whether actions are appropriate or by leaders having to battle to get their logic of action accepted. Flexibility here may mean that there are several not so very different possible modes of action; but this may produce a situation that can simultaneously satisfy several interests and objectives. A leader can build bridges between cultural elements and aid integration by allowing a certain amount of cultural heterogeneity and tension, for instance, by using specific symbolic labels. Administrative culture and the definition of administrative leaders' role may constitute a vague blend of different objectives and values. This may be seen as mainly positive, for it produces increased competence, flexibility and the skill to cope with many objectives simultaneously. As a contrast, one might cite some of the underlying logic of the NPM reforms, which demand that clear priorities be drawn between diverse public objectives and clear distinctions made between various premises for action, and that the content of these premises should be clear and the decisions taken unambiguous.

One could say that cultural stimuli will be most complex for leaders in a public organization, because their roles are most complex in this setting and the things they must take into consideration are the most diverse. However, these actors often have a wealth of experience in handling such diversity, for the diversity encountered in leading positions is also great with respect to formal frameworks for action. To people occupying subordinate positions in a public hierarchy, the formal and informal norms will appear less diverse because their work is more specialized and the cultural framework for action therefore simpler.

Finally, the informal norms and values civil servants hold as members of a public organization have to compete with the different roles and status these people have outside the organization. If public employees primarily take recourse in their public organizational culture when they act, and do not heed other formal and informal private considerations, they will score high values on what American political scientist Stephen Krasner calls *vertical, institutional depth*. The institutional role is highly significant, for employees are imbued with the spirit of the institution's culture. If employees are engaged in activities considered to be institutionally integrated with other activities in the organization, they will score high values on *horizontal width*. They feel part of a larger cultural whole and this makes their own activities more meaningful. The strongest institutionalization will be achieved when members of an organization score high values for both vertical institutional depth and horizontal width.

ESTABLISHING AND CHANGING ORGANIZATIONAL CULTURE

The dominant conception of how organizational culture is established is that informal, institutional norms and values gradually develop through *evolutionary, natural developmental processes*, and the organization gradually adapts via internal and external pressure. *Unintended* and *unplanned*, these institutionalization processes create a distinct identity, a '*soul*' or *culture*. Culture is something an institution *is*. A public university, rich in tradition, will always enjoy much legitimacy based upon what it has represented in the past, in addition to what it now is; its academic culture and autonomy enhance its legitimacy over and above what it actually 'produces'. This is also the case for a federal bank, a ministry of finance or a foreign office with time-honoured traditions. This point is clearly illustrated in a study by the Norwegian political scientist Marit Wærness on the implementation of a three-year budget plan in Sweden during the 1980s, in which several public organizations that were subjected to reforms demonstrated their institutional weight, based on their having been in existence since the seventeenth century.

When we speak of *internal pressure* as a source of institutional characteristics, we primarily mean the informal norms and values members bring with them into an organization and make relevant there. These may be an assortment of characteristics from their social background, but also informal norms and values from a specific education or profession. Social processes connected to the activities in which the public organization is engaged may also be significant. Different groups with wide-ranging tasks and backgrounds may, through collaboration, help to develop dominant and comprehensive institutional norms. Or else they may contribute to the emergence of various subcultures. Last, but not least, an organization's culture may develop through a complex blend of informal norms from social backgrounds and task-related contexts.

The term *external pressure* denotes pressure from the immediate task environment. This means that actors in the environment, whom a public organization interacts with regularly or is dependent upon, either for supplying resources or for output, are significant for the institutional characteristics that develop, because what such actors do is critical for the organization. The most classic example of this is Selznick's study of the Tennessee Valley Authority (established in 1933), a federal American organization for regional development, whose activities were influenced in numerous ways through pressure from affected business interests. One can also imagine that the culture of various government agencies will be influenced by the norms and values of parent ministries, that public universities and colleges will be particularly influenced by the cultural norms of a ministry of education and research, or that the culture in municipalities will be influenced by regional civil service units, the regional legislature or dominant local trade and industry.

The significance of an organizational culture often becomes apparent when the public administration goes through reform processes and reorganizations, particularly if these processes threaten dominant informal norms and values. One can see this in internal reorganizations, when new units are set up and personnel are reshuffled, but also when several agencies are involved. A pertinent example is the cultural opposition to reform posed by several transportation services from the 1980s onwards, up to and including modern reforms. In many countries, increased exposure to competition has been accompanied by a desire to change the organizational structure and the physical symbols. Employees have, for example, reacted negatively to logos being changed into so-called modern symbols. Furthermore, in many countries there also seems to be widespread cultural resistance to mergers that threaten administrative cultures developed over long periods of time. These examples, perhaps the latter in particular, demonstrate the 'historical inefficiency', that is, how a partly public organization can function relatively well, in spite of not living up to demands for efficiency, and hence reacts sluggishly to pressure for change and to external demands for reform.

In some studies of organizational culture, notably those connected with theories of leadership at business schools, one often finds a somewhat different perspective on how organizational culture emerges and develops. Here it is often claimed that organizational cultures can be designed or created deliberately, that is, cultures are things organizations *have*, variables leaders can manipulate to achieve desired results. This is a typical instrumental perspective on the development of organizational culture, a perspective that gives political and administrative leaders new managerial tools. Culture is also often connected with simultaneous and deliberate changes in the formal and physical structure of formal organizations. Examples of this are the assorted studies of the period when Jan Carlsson was chief executive officer of Scandinavian Airlines System (SAS). The studies emphasized how Carlsson tried to redesign the formal structure, the basic informal norms and values, and the physical symbols (logo, choice of colours) of the company all at once in order to give SAS a sharper commercial profile.

Studies rooted more strongly in political science also stress the possibility of institutional design. In a large study of the prison systems in the United States and the Netherlands, the Dutch organizational researcher Arjen Boin showed the American federal prison system to be an institutional success story. It has had, and still has, strong leaders who are able to define a clear, strong culture and to transmit this to many parts of the organization. Moreover, through this culture it has also developed uniformity and standardized practices.

THE SIGNIFICANCE OF HISTORICAL ROOTS FOR CULTURAL PATHS OF DEVELOPMENT

A central notion in the professional literature on organizational culture is *path dependency*. This means that the cultural norms and values that make their mark on an organization in its early and formative years will have great significance for the path of development it follows. A public organization is established at a specific point in history and hence is shaped by specific cultural contexts or norms and values that leave a permanent impression on it. Path dependency may be significant for the content of policy in different areas, such as tax or educational policy. An epoch marked by a wave of democratization or strong norms for decentralization will produce formal organizational structures and informal norms and values different from a period where the emphasis is on hierarchy, management and centralization. Organizational forms originating in the 1970s, for example, are marked by a belief in collegial structures. When Denmark joined the EU in 1972, the organization, through its special commissions, reflected a corporatist tradition, where special interest organizations had a strong position. This characteristic mark has been retained. However, when Sweden became a member of the EU in the 1990s, special interest organizations were barely included in the equation. In this new epoch the corporatist tradition was much weaker.

The types of goal established from the beginning of a public organization's life have great significance for its subsequent development and they are not easy to change, not even when environments and contexts change. This is also the case for the kinds of group an organization aims to address, or the type of expertise it aims to build. The cost becomes too great if such things are changed too often. This may reflect what we earlier called historical inefficiency. From the vantage point of instrumental logic, the institution is intrinsically inefficient because it cannot quickly adapt to changed conditions for action or new problems. Yet from a cultural perspective, one could argue that it is perfectly possible for an institution to live with such historical inefficiency over time.

Path dependency, as outlined for the cultural development of many public organizations, can have clear benefits but also drawbacks. The benefits of path dependency are that it lends stability and depth to informal values and norms in a public organization. Path dependency makes it easier for civil servants to determine appropriate behaviour and to grasp what cultural framework they should operate within. The matching between known identities and situations is easier, and one could say that institutional rules of action can thus function effectively and efficiently. On the other hand, this historical bias may cause the institutional features to render the organization and its actors inflexible. This can be particularly problematic if the environment undergoes rapid change and a large gap emerges between external problems and internal culture. An example of this is the oft-heard claim, during reform processes, that public organizations are too resistant to change and that there needs to be a cultural revolution in order to equip them to face the future. From this perspective, institutional characteristics and rules for action function as obstacles to change. Path dependency is thus a double-edged sword that both offers possibilities and imposes constraints.

James G. March and Johan P. Olsen illustrated some of these major dilemmas in a study of the reform programmes of US presidents. When US presidents are elected they very often propose a reform programme for the public sector. Ronald Reagan and Jimmy Carter are cases in point. The implementation of these programmesis often problematic, partly because the administrative apparatus opposes them and partly because the presidents shift their attention and support to other policy areas. In the short run, therefore, these programmes often fail, and one major reason is path dependency, that is, administrative traditions, norms and values are stronger than the political will to change. Yet the proposed reforms often represent a potential new path in opposition to the old one. Thus, short-term failure may be followed by long-term success for the proposals, because political and administrative actors, as well as public opinion, may eventually warm to the thought that some of the reforms are needed and this ultimately results in implementation. Such successes represent a type of 'civic education' on the part of the actors affected by reforms.

A second example is a comparison made between public reforms in Australia and New Zealand. These countries' reform paths shared similarities and differences from the 1980s through the two following decades. The similarities were obvious. They both attended to some central elements of NPM, such as structural devolution, market solutions, contracts and competitive tendering. However, Australia's more centralized tradition meant that when NPM was implemented, certain centralizing features were retained: a strong Prime Minister's Office, more coordination among central ministries, larger central units and an overall strong core. In New Zealand, by contrast, there was more fragmentation. When post-NPM reforms got under way in the late 1990s, Australia was able to use this centralized tradition to redress the balance in favour of central control and coordination.

A third example concerns the implementation of 'Next Step' reforms in the United Kingdom from 1988 onwards. These were reforms intended to move a lot of service-producing and regulatory agencies away from the core ministries and give them more autonomy. In the meantime, the long tradition of centralization has meant that these reforms are actually less geared towards autonomy than was initially intended. The agencies became only semi-autonomous, formally as well as in practice, because the central ministries had problems relinquishing control, and, just as in the United States, legislative select committees are used to scrutinize these agencies.

ORGANIZATIONAL CULTURE AND LEADERSHIP

What role do leaders play in institutionalized organizations? What is typical for culturally based leadership? In many respects leaders have a double role. On the one hand, they must be administrators of 'historical necessities', in other words, traditions place constraints on their work, and they must ensure that the established informal norms and values have good conditions for growth and are developed and protected. On the other hand, inasmuch as leaders protect the organizational culture's core, swift and comprehensive change will be thwarted. Leaders thus contribute to change, albeit in a limited way, and this allows a certain degree of independent, intentional or instrumental action.

Selznick emphasizes that, whether they are engaged in protecting, developing or changing the organizational culture, leaders help shape a public institution's identity through *critical decisions,* as distinct from the more *routine decisions* that are made. There can be many types of critical decisions. One is when leaders define or redefine their institution's mission and roles, which will often involve a cultural operationalization of what the institution is capable of doing, based on its abilities and expertise, that is, what should it be good at being? This limits the many possible sets of cultural norms and values. A second type of critical function for leaders is the institutional embodiment of the purpose or the roles selected, for they must express, in different ways, which institutional values and norms the organization stands for. A leader wants to show, particularly through symbols, whether the institutional culture stresses expertise, representativity, effective decision-making or due process. Third, leaders clarify cultural norms for recruitment to the organization, emphasizing, say, expertise or loyalty. Fourth, leaders can help create an institutional identity through training, attitude shaping and 'indoctrination'. This enhances the socialization of the organization's members and their integration in the institutional culture. Furthermore, through critical decision-making, leaders defend their organization's integrity by making systems representative, resolving conflicts and setting up coordination and collaboration arrangements, all of which are critical to counteract cultural tensions and conflicts.

Cultural leadership does not necessarily need to fuse with formal leadership, even though it is often easier to practice cultural leadership in hierarchically superior positions. Cultural leaders can also be ordinary members of an organization, who exercise strong informal leadership in a variety of ways. They may be leaders of vigorous social groups in public organizations, or they may draw attention to themselves as a result of their professional status, or else their personal qualities mean that they stand for particular cultural values.

DEMOGRAPHY AND CULTURE

Members of institutionalized public organizations stand in a dynamic and reciprocal relation to their organizational culture. On the one hand, individual actors can influence institutional norms and values by making relevant those specific informal norms and values they carry with them from their social background or acquire through their functions or tasks within the organization. Individual demographic features, such as age, tenure, education, sex, work experience, and ethnic and geographical background, can all be significant for the organizational culture. On the other hand, such links between demography and culture may also be related to groups or collectives. An organization's members may rally round informal norms and values because they as a group have experienced the same things and thus developed common norms over a period of time and thus helped to shape the organizational culture. This occurs most systematically if *cohorts* or groups of employees are recruited simultaneously into administrative positions and if they stand for strong professional norms and values. For this reason public organizational cultures in parts of the public administration may overlap with professional cultures. This will depend on whether specific professions dominate specific organizational units, or whether employees' professional backgrounds are more mixed.

Historical examples of this are the dominance of jurists in the central civil service of Scandinavian countries and some Central European countries over an extensive period of time and the strong inculcation and persistence of their informal cultural norms and values. After the Second World War, the jurists' 'golden age' and dominance were challenged by the professional norms of economists, and in the last two to three decades by political scientists and Masters of Business Administration (MBAs), who have established themselves as strong professional groups within public administration.

The institution also influences individual and group identities through socialization towards common informal norms and values. This occurs via the mechanisms described under the definition of *critical decisions*. One could say that there is a type of social contract for internalizing common cultural norms and values. Organizational members are taught to adopt attitudes about what is culturally appropriate and to act in accordance with them. If they do this, they will in return be treated fairly and appropriately by the institution's leaders. Hence socialization towards institutional values and norms is based partly on reciprocity.

Individuals in a public organization will have a certain amount of freedom to choose between different identities and rules. Although this will presumably weaken their chances of influencing common cultural norms, they themselves will still be influenced by such norms. How much choice there is depends on the degree of heterogeneity in internal cultural norms and on the balance between internal and external cultural norms and role elements, such as, for example, when a civil servant in central government participates in EU commissions and needs to strike a balance between his or her own national identity, professional identity and European identity. In reality, there will be individual variation, for socialization into institutional norms does not mean that a civil servant in central government is programmed to act in a certain way.

CHARACTERISTICS OF A POLITICAL-ADMINISTRATIVE CULTURE

The organizational cultures in the political-administrative systems of various countries reveal clear commonalities and differences. One of the common characteristics concerns the informal norms and values that determine the balance between *loyalty* and *neutrality* in the relationship between the political leadership and the administrative apparatus. An underlying norm here is that non-elected public administration staff must at all times be loyal to the political leadership in power but simultaneously maintain a neutral attitude to the ruling party's political orientation. Too much loyalty creates difficulties when the political leadership changes. But too much neutrality is also problematic, because it may lead to a degree of political insensitivity that hampers the political leadership in implementing its policies.

Second, administrative culture must strike a balance between what Herbert Simon labelled *loyalty* and *professional norms*, meaning that a civil servant must be politically loyal to the political leadership but simultaneously make decisions based on a solid professional foundation. At the same time, too much emphasis on one's own professional field may lead to an insensitive technocracy or management by professionals. Third, administrative staff must strike a balance between premises of *professional value* and premises of *fact*, meaning that they must take into account normative, value-related ballast, which may have evolved in a profession over a long period of time, but also of basic facts and contexts they themselves are specialists in. Other common features of organizational culture in public organizations may be procedural conditions, such as due process, predictability, equal treatment, transparency and information.

As well as these basic similarities, there are also differences between and within countries, with regard to such things as promoting the values of equality and community, focusing on weaker groups, protecting individual rights, etc. One can clearly see this if one compares Norway with the United States. The cultural norms for equality and community are stronger in Norway than in the United States and reflect differences in the size of the country as well as in the degree of cultural and ethnic homogeneity. In the United States cultural norms are more centred on individual rights and legal processes, inequality is more acceptable and cultural ideals about competition and markets are more prominent. The cultural differences between Norway and the United States illustrate the distinctions made by the Dutch organization theorist Geert Hofstede between collectivistic and individualistic cultures and between egalitarian and elitist cultures.

Within a political-administrative system there will always be a number of subcultures, without these necessarily undermining the more general common culture. Subcultures may be based on goals and policy areas, such as the cultural differences between the fields of health care, education and law. Alternatively, subcultures may be established around specific tasks or professional groups, such as those dealing with budgeting, lawyers as a professional group or social workers in municipal welfare offices. Working with specific actors and groups in the environment may also spawn subcultures, for example in working with the elderly, youth or people with behavioural difficulties.

INSTITUTION AND ENVIRONMENT – CULTURE IN THE CONTEXT OF A WIDER POLITICAL SYSTEM

As mentioned above, professional literature within the field of organizational culture is primarily concerned with the task environment of a public organization and the dynamic and reciprocal relations within it. Few of these studies show organizations becoming trapped in their own environment, so-called *environmental determinism*, nor is it very common nowadays for an institutionalized organization to form its own task environment to any large degree. Rather, the central mechanism is a process of *mutual adaptation*. This view has a certain instrumental 'shadow', because the task environment is often defined as those actors in the 'technical environment' with whom one often deals regarding decisions, services and products. Yet one might also see the task environment as defined by those actors who mainly influence an institution's informal norms and values. An occupation's professional organizations or higher-educational institutions may, for example, strongly influence the cultural features of a public institution without them having any strong formal influence over it.

March and Olsen have put some of the basic arguments in the literature about organizational culture into a wider political context. They underscore that political processes and institutions shape and develop different societies and citizens, different public policies, different political and administrative actors, and different kinds of decision-making behaviour. They draw a distinction between *aggregative* and *integrative* political processes and institutions, with an emphasis on the latter culturally oriented type. In aggregative political processes, which can be related to a competitive-democratic ideal, people are a category of 'qualified', 'atomistic citizens', who have no common, natural social attachment or affinities. The will of the people emerges through processes of negotiation and competition between citizens who aim to advance their own vested interests within the bounds of certain rules. The political order is based on rational exchange and market analogies, where powerful actors dominate the field. Political leadership acts as the mediator, with leaders facilitating the negotiations. The distribution of resources is the most salient result of the decision process, while features such as procedure and process are less significant. According to this model, actors must have incentives to act on behalf of the community, and they are characterized by calculation and strategy rather than by vocation or a sense of belonging to a specific group – in other words, they are more concerned about pay-off than propriety.

In integrative political processes, which can be associated with the ideals of democratic discourse or democratic participation, people enter into a community with a past and a future where path dependency is important. Political institutions create individual attitudes and interests and give actors a normative context to relate to and from which to develop meaning. The will of the people is expressed in an attempt to find a general will within the framework of shared societal values, and emphasis is placed on creating and maintaining common goals. The political order is based on historical roots, duties and collective reasoning, and it is critical to create an awareness of this. Leaders in integrative processes should have educative roles, they should point out a certain normative path, nurture social traditions and emphasize obligations and those things that bind the community together. They should help limit the realization of private interests and values that may potentially

51

undermine collective values. Integrative traditions, obligations and rights should be a normative guide, independent from political decisions, and should provide standards for judging institutions, actions and responsibilities. Politicians and public servants alike are responsible for loyalty, authority and professional integrity, for they are all involved in managing and administering public interests.

March and Olsen question how easy it is to bring into being the primary cultural characteristics in integrative processes and institutions. Addressing this problem highlights the contrast between integrative and aggregative processes and institutions. They ask how one can engender support for developing the common good in a political system or, put differently, how one can ensure integrity and common interests and make private or vested interests subordinate to these. They maintain that the institutional answers to these problems are to be found in socializing the role of citizen, in the socialization, discipline and control of public employees, in a high level of social awareness among political representatives and in a strengthening of political institutions' symbolic roles.

They also point out that integrative processes can be manipulated for the benefit of specific leaders and groups. Imbalances become engrained when certain cultural values and norms are systematically repressed and conflicts are obfuscated through 'idealization'. Furthermore, March and Olsen question how easy it is to ensure debate about institutions and to develop deliberative features: to develop competence, community and consensus, to ensure wisdom and hinder rhetoric, to balance transparency and exclusivity, and, not least, to give institutions and individuals autonomy within the community.

Johan P. Olsen sketches a model of governance that lies very near to the integrative model, namely 'the institutional state'. According to this model, a state is a moral community built on traditions reflected in value systems and institutions that provide rules for correct and good behaviour. A state guarantees the moral and political order, which, among other things, is tied to citizens' rights and obligations; such norms and values are ranked higher than values related to majority rule and should not easily be changed by such rule. According to this model, certain parts of the public administration have a special identity or 'mission' that grows gradually through natural developmental processes. These parts thus acquire the role of bearers and defenders of values and are not merely neutral instruments for the political leadership.

POSSIBLE ADVANTAGES AND DISADVANTAGES OF A WELL-DEVELOPED ORGANIZATIONAL CULTURE

There are diverse views on whether a well-developed organizational culture in public organizations involves advantages or disadvantages. Those who underscore the advantages view the institutional or cultural characteristics of public organizations primarily as a means to increase the government's legitimacy. Institutional characteristics make a public organization into something appreciated and a significant element in society. When a public organization has cultural norms and values that are generally accepted and deemed desirable, it is generally positive. This is also the case when public organizations are led by institutional entrepreneurs who embody cultural characteristics in such a positive way that they provide examples for society at large, for, in witnessing them, people are inclined to believe in the reason and rationality of the public system. Institutional characteristics may help citizens to understand better the events happening around them each day and affect their actions.

Strong institutional features in a public organization may also have clear internal effects. Feeling part of an institution with a clear mission and direction, where what one does is meaningful and is in tune with what others do, can be a source of personal growth. What is more, it improves the quality of the organization, with supervening external effects. Feeling competent and combining personal growth with being useful to society may be regarded as an ideal situation. Institutional features may also aid the smooth functioning of large and complex public organizations, for a strong organizational culture saves resources, in the sense that given rules enhance expediency, or that, without using too many administrative resources, employees may be induced to think and act in similar ways within the bounds of allotted freedom, even though they are in organizational units that are physically distant from each other. Several studies of American governmental authorities demonstrate this, for example, national forest rangers or the federal prison system.

Those who support institutional features concede that they may entail an inherent conservatism, yet their advocates point out that public institutions very often are in a process of gradual change and are not overly rigid. They emphasize that good institutional leaders manage to balance the status quo with innovation and preserve traditions while meeting contemporary demands. Organizations with clear institutional features are often said to achieve their goals more easily than those with weaker ones. It is also claimed that strong institutional features safeguard individuals, for example users of public services, against abuses of power. Where formal safeguards are not sufficient, cultural norms can bridge the gap.

Critics of institutional characteristics point out that overly strong institutional characteristics create public organizations that are often too rigid and too inwardly directed, that is, they think mostly about themselves. They are not concerned enough about adapting to the environment and they resist democratic control. Institutions have a tendency to exist for themselves, not for the environment, partly because their members are 'indoctrinated'. It is stressed that strong authoritarian leaders create strong institutional characteristics, but that these are often negative for the internal environment, and even more so for the external one. One example is Adolf Hitler in Germany during the Second World War. A quite different example from the world of public administration might be J. Edgar Hoover in the FBI during the 1950s and 1960s. Critics claim that public organizations with strong institutional features lack plurality, debate, constructive conflicts and adaptable structures that can change according to the changing environment. Centralized missions, tight procedures and rules are old-fashioned concepts for some critics. Strong institutions are also said to be vulnerable to 'moral capture', that is, they can become tools for unwanted norms and values advanced by determined leaders.

There is a long research tradition in some countries, mainly in sociology and political science, which draws its impetus from the negative aspects of the 'tight society', that is, institutions with strong organizational cultures. This has been discussed in relation to schools, prisons as institutions, police violence and child protection institutions. Studies have also shown how social welfare during the 1950s and 1960s was influenced by institutional features marked by the judgement of laymen on social commissions or advisory boards, and as such could have negative effects for clients. This stands in contrast to the subsequent more rule-oriented social apparatus, but this is not problem-free either, because social workers develop a culture marked by their becoming 'quasi-lawyers'.

A middle position would be to say that strong institutional features in public organizations potentially have both positive and negative aspects, as do bureaucratic organizational forms. Put differently, there is nothing inherently good or bad about institutional characteristics. The critical question is their content and what they are used for. Charismatic personalities or entrepreneurs are often necessary in order to create and maintain institutional features. This can be positive in itself, yet not all aspects of such a person's activity need necessarily be positive, for such actors can also, with time, be damaged by their own success; they may, for example, develop norms intended to protect themselves and their activities from being controlled. Institutional cultures based on professional norms can help individuals develop and can be important factors in improving the quality of public services. At the same time, however, they may contribute to professional dominance and regrettable inequality in services for certain client groups.

CONTEXTUALIZATION, ETHICS AND TRUST

A general theme in this chapter about organizational culture is the significance of informal norms and values that develop gradually, but are then challenged in the face of internal and external pressure. Through a process of institutionalization a distinct culture, mission or soul develops in each organization. This creates a multiplicity of public organizations each of which acquires it own value profile. The informal norms and values developed through processes of institutionalization create a moral or ethical framework for organizational members and furnish them with a normative guide to appropriate attitudes and actions. This can also be an important factor in building mutual trust between the political and senior administrative leadership on the one hand, and the administrative apparatus on the other. Members of organizations come to trust their leaders through shared values, and the leaders develop confidence in their employees via various relationships and contexts based upon a common normative foundation.

CHAPTER SUMMARY

- Cultural norms and values develop gradually, through adaptation to internal and external pressures, and they are influenced by the critical decisions leaders make.
- People in public organizations act according to historical norms, values and what is seen as appropriate.
- An organizational culture will interact with a formal structure in influencing attitudes and actions in public organizations.

DISCUSSION QUESTIONS

Choose a public-sector organization that you know something about.

1 Try to identify some of its main cultural values and norms, and discuss different ways to identify these cultural features.
2 Try to imagine that you are a leader in this organization, and discuss the cultural constraints you may have in acting appropriately.
3 Identify a high-profile media case this organization has been involved in and discuss the relative importance of cultural and formal norms and values in this case.

REFERENCES AND FURTHER READING

Boin, A. (2001) *Crafting Public Institutions: Leadership in Two Prison Systems,* Boulder: Lynne Rienner.

Christensen, T. and Lægreid, P. (eds) (2001) *New Public Management: The Transformation of Ideas and Practice,* Aldershot: Ashgate.

—— (2007) *Transcending New Public Management: The Transformation of Public Sector Reforms,* Aldershot: Ashgate.

Christensen, T. and Peters, B.G. (1999) *Structure, Culture and Governance: A Comparative Analysis of Norway and the United States,* Lanham: Rowman & Littlefield.

Goodsell, C. (1977) 'Bureaucratic Manipulation of Physical Symbols: An Empirical Study', *American Journal of Political Science,* 21 (1): 79–91.

Hofstede, G. (1980; 2nd edn 2001) *Culture's Consequences,* London: Sage.

Hood, C. (1998) *The Art of the State: Culture, Rhetoric, and Public Management,* Oxford: Oxford University Press.

Jacobsen, B., Lægreid, P. and Pedersen, O.K. (2004) *Europeanization and Transnational States,* London: Routledge.

Kaufman, H. (1960) *The Forest Ranger,* Baltimore: The Johns Hopkins Press.

Krasner, S.D. (1988) 'Sovereignty: An Institutional Perspective', *Comparative Political Studies,* 21 (1): 66–94.

March, J.G. (1994) *A Primer on Decision Making,* New York: Free Press.

March, J.G. and Olsen, J.P. (1983) 'Organizing Political Life: What Administrative Reorganization Tells Us About Government', *American Political Science Review,* 77 (2): 281–96.

—— (1989) *Rediscovering Institutions: The Organizational Basis of Politics,* New York: The Free Press.

Olsen, J.P. (1988) 'Administrative Reform and Theories of Organization', in C. Campbell and B.G. Peters (eds) *Organizing Governance: Governing Organizations,* Pittsburgh: University of Pittsburgh Press.

Peters, B. Guy (1999; 2nd edn 2005) *Institutional Theory in Political Science,* New York: Pinter; 2nd edn New York: Continuum.

Selznick, P. (1949; reissued 1984) *TVA and the Grass Roots,* Berkeley: University of California Press.

—— (1957; reissued 1984) *Leadership in Administration,* New York: Harper & Row; reissued Berkeley: University of California Press.

Stinchcombe, A. (1965) 'Social Structure and Organizations', in J.G. March (ed.) *Handbook of Organizations,* Chicago: Rand McNally.

Thelen, K. (1999) 'Historical Institutionalism in Comparative Politics', *Annual Review of Political Science* 2: 369–404.

Wærness, M. (1993) 'Implementation and Institutional Identity', in N. Brunsson and J.P. Olsen (eds) *The Reforming Organization,* London: Routledge.

Chapter 4

A myth perspective

LEARNING OBJECTIVES

By the end of this chapter you should:

- have a clear understanding of the main elements of a myth perspective;
- be able to identify the main characteristics of popular organizational recipes (myths), their content, how they are created and 'packaged', and how they spread;
- have some basic ideas about how popular organizational recipes may affect the way public organizations operate.

MEANING OF MYTHS

We have chosen to call the book's third main approach a *myth perspective*. In organization theory it is often referred to as the New Institutional School, and is founded on classic works by American researchers such as John W. Meyer, Brian Rowan, Paul J. DiMaggio, Walter W. Powell and W. Richard Scott. A key conception is that organizations operate within institutional environments where they are confronted with socially created norms for how they should be designed and how they should function. Organizations must try to incorporate and reflect these norms outwardly, even if they do not necessarily make the organization's activities more effective. Through this process organizations become more similar to one another, at least on the surface, in stark contrast to the multiplicity described by a cultural perspective. Socially created norms in institutional environments are called *myths*. They can be broad and are often referred to as *superstandards*, or standards with a more limited scope. Myths can spread quickly, through imitation, and they can be adopted by public organizations without producing instrumental effects, that is, they may sometimes function as 'window dressing'. Leaders of public organizations can, for instance, talk about reforms in a way that makes people believe they are putting reforms into practice while in reality the leaders do little to make this happen. The Swedish organization theorist Nils Brunsson has labelled the discrepancy between talk and action hypocrisy; however, in some cases popular organizational recipes might be implemented and translated into practice.

The American sociologist Talcott Parsons was one of the first to formulate the insight that organizations cannot survive 'merely' by striving to be efficient. They also need legitimacy from the environment. Organizations seeking legitimacy from institutional environments must demonstrate that they live up to the fundamental Western norms of modernity, such as continuous growth, innovation and rationality. These norms are reflected in a wide repertoire of general ideas and more precise recipes for how modern, and thus legitimate, organizations should look, which structural components they should have and which procedures and routines they should prioritize. These general and popular ideas and trends often become fashionable, that is, they acquire the status of something 'all' public organizations should adopt at a certain point in time, until they go out of style and new fashions arrive. *Myths as fashions* also illustrates a central point made by March and Olsen in their 'garbage-can' model, whereby solutions seek problems rather than the opposite, as is the case for instrumental perspectives.

The institutional environments public organizations have to cope with are complex. Different parts of an organization strive to obtain legitimacy from a range of external actors, such as the mass media, intellectuals, professions, banks and institutions of accreditation, and become dependent on this. An organization is therefore confronted with many different, often inconsistent and changing ideas and recipes for legitimate structures and procedures. Popular recipes from institutional environments may also be called 'institutionalized standards' or 'rationalized myths', that is, institutionalized and widely spread ideas for what kinds of formal structures, technologies, processes, procedures and ideologies an organization should adopt. A myth is thus a socially legitimated recipe for how to design part of an organization. It is an idea which excites, grabs attention and has achieved exemplary status in several organizations.

Rationalized myths have two important hallmarks. First, they are presented as effective tools organizations can use to achieve goals. When a myth is *rationalized* this implies that the members of an organization have become convinced – by apparently scientific arguments – that it is an effective tool for achieving specific organizational goals. Despite this, organizations often experience situations where the instrumental effects of adopting a popular recipe do not match expectations and are therefore disappointing. A rationalized myth may be defined as a non-scientifically justified conviction that an organizational recipe is grounded in scientific research and rationality. Second, independently of whether myths result in expected effects, they are still institutionalized in the sense that for a period of time it is taken for granted that they are timely, efficient, modern and thus 'natural' ways of steering and organizing. In this chapter we address five questions about rationalized myths, as they are expressed in institutionalized organizational recipes:

■ *The contents of institutionalized recipes*: What are they about, and what kind of organization do they prescribe?

■ *The relationship between recipes*: How do different institutionalized recipes compare with one another, to what degree do they compete and to what degree do they harmonize?

■ *The form of recipes*: What is it about institutionalized recipes that makes them so 'elastic'?

■ *The formulation and diffusion of recipes*: Where and how do institutionalized recipes come into being and how are they spread?

■ *The adoption and implementation of recipes*: What happens when an organization attempts to adopt and implement rationalized recipes and apply them to local conditions?

A myth perspective is often seen either as stemming from natural and cultural perspectives or as a category of the institutional perspective. In our conclusion, however, we will also attempt to interpret rationalized myths in the light of an instrumental perspective, for this elucidates the extent to which myths should be understood as symbols for enhancing organizational efficacy.

Since the end of the 1980s a myth perspective has increasingly been deployed as a theoretical frame of reference for studies of reform processes in the public sector. This has partly to do with political science generally having become more attentive to the symbolic aspects of public politics. This, in turn, reflects the fact that public organizations are increasingly becoming *expressive organizations*, in the sense of being concerned about their image and reputation in the environment, for example with regard to the mass media, the public and top political executives. Notwithstanding, the most important reason for increased deployment of the myth perspective is probably that, since the early 1980s, the public sector has become more exposed to external ideas and recipes circulating in institutional environments. This is particularly the case for the massive attempts to transfer ideas from the private to the public sector. Myth perspectives have shown themselves to be particularly useful in accounting for these types of private-sector-inspired reform processes in the public sector.

CONTENT OF MYTHS

Myths are more or less clear recipes for how to design an organization. But what kind of organization do they provide recipes for, and what does the organization the recipes prescribe look like? The definition above emphasized that each recipe merely prescribes how a part of an organization should be designed. A single institutionalized recipe is not at all a complete solution for how an entire, complex organization should be designed. It would be more appropriate to describe them as institutionalized form-elements or components. An assortment of recipes exists for how to shape all aspects of modern organizations, for example leadership, formal organizational structure (formal coordination and specialization), the execution of various activities (recipes for processes, procedures and routines), organizational culture, auditing systems, etc. Altogether, the supply of ideas and recipes has increased considerably in the past twenty-five years. This means, among other things, that actors attempting to establish new public organizations or to reform existing ones have access to an exceedingly wide assortment of legitimated and popular organizational recipes.

Each institutionalized recipe usually has its own distinct literature, that is, publications that present it and promote it. The individual recipes are usually identifiable through abstract concepts known as *linguistic labels*. What follows is a limited selection of these, classified according to which aspects of an organization the recipes are for. A distinct literature exists for each of these and, although most are derived from the private sector, we have now entered into a period where these recipes are actively sought out and implemented in the public sector:

- *Recipes for management and leadership*: Team-based management, change management, transformative leadership, service management, Total Quality Leadership (TQL), knowledge management and value-based management;
- *Recipes for designing the formal organizational structure*: Divisionalized structure, flexible structure (including matrix structure and project organization), flat/collegial structure and single-purpose organizations;
- *Recipes for human resource management*: Motivational initiatives, colleague-training programmes, career planning, competence mapping, HRM Scorecard, performance appraisals, developmental dialogues, headhunting, downsizing and empowerment;
- *Recipes for organizational culture and work environments*: Customer and service culture, citizens' charter, tribal culture and learning culture;
- *Recipes for organizing work processes*: Value Process Management (VPM), Business Process Re-engineering (BPR), Total Quality Management (TQM), time planning, quality assurance systems, Six Sigma, lean production/lean management, benchmarking and assorted internal control systems;
- *Recipes for financial control*: Management by Objectives (MBO), Management by Objectives and Results (MBOR), balanced scorecard, Activity-based Costing (ABC), Activity-based Management (ABM), Economic Value Added (EVA) and contract management.

Nowadays a wide array of rationalized recipes for management, leadership and organizational design are in circulation. These spring up and spread quickly to many highly diverse organizations, including public organizations, and 'have their day' for a while. Several of the recipes listed above clearly have already *had* their day. Others are still popular and current reform recipes. This is the case, for example, for MBOR, which many public organizations have tried to implement since the turn of the millennium. MBOR may be defined as a system in which specific performance objectives are determined, progress towards objectives is periodically reviewed, end results are evaluated and rewards are allocated on the basis of the results. Also current are ideas concerning the so-called flat structure and independent units, entailing, among other things, that public services led and politically controlled by senior leadership are turned into units with greater responsibility for their own expenses and income and for quality of service and prices. These are some of the ideas and recipes currently informing the many comprehensive reform initiatives in public administration units across the world.

RELATIONSHIP BETWEEN DIFFERENT RECIPES

Our own times are marked by a tremendous supply of popular organizational ideas and recipes. But what is the relationship between these recipes? What are their similarities and differences?

Taking the similarities first we can say that they may be grouped into families, depending on which part of the organization they are directed towards. Particularly closely related are recipes that arise from a commonly held ideology or philosophy. For example, one set of recipes is claimed to have risen from administrative philo-sophies such as managerialism. The most well-known organizational recipes in the public sector today are those that fall under the heading of NPM. NPM is a family of business-inspired recipes for the public sector derived from the private sector. At its core are ideas about professional management (i.e. leaders with knowledge about how to manage and much autonomy to make decisions), increased competition and the use of contracts as tools for political management.

One can also focus on what differentiates recipes. Often leaders and others adopt *competitive recipes,* for example divergent ideas for how to design a formal organ-izational structure, a process or a procedure. This can be illustrated by two popular and widely spread ideas: MBO and TQM. While MBO may be said to focus attention on effectiveness and efficiency, TQM is a strategy aimed at embedding awareness of quality in all organizational processes. It provides an umbrella under which everyone in the organization should strive to achieve quality and customer satisfaction. Rendered in their pure form in the history of organizational ideas, these two recipes appear almost contradictory. To take one example, let us imagine that a public service agency is instructed to implement MBO. The agency will most likely be asked to outline a set of disambiguated and operationalized goals to be achieved within a fixed time period. The leadership will supply resources (personnel, money, etc.) to be used to achieve the goals. Local managers will be given greater autonomy to decide for themselves how resources are to be combined and used in order to achieve the goals. Now let us imagine that the same agency is also instructed to implement a quality-control system such as TQM for the services it provides. This will usually entail the agency planning a quality-assurance work process, for instance by deciding who should do what and in which order and how to discover, report and avoid deviations, etc. This quality-control work process will then be outlined and inscribed in rules (a quality system) to be followed. While the former recipe provides a large degree of freedom for local leaders to decide how to use resources and organize work processes in order to achieve goals efficiently, the latter recipe theoretically limits that freedom, because it prescribes the trajectory of work processes in great detail. Thus, there are contradictions between the recipe for management by objectives and the recipe for quality assurance.

ELASTIC RECIPES

Some popular organizational ideas, for example MBO and TQM, can be interpreted as conflicting, indeed, even inconsistent. We know that many organizations, not least those in the public sector, have tried to implement both these recipes, often simultaneously. How can organizations introduce – and live with – concepts and models which appear inconsistent when juxtaposed? In large organizations with numerous units, connections may not be drawn or comparisons made between different ideas. Inconsistencies may therefore go undiscovered or be concealed on purpose.

A second reason is that rationalized myths in the form of institutionalized organizational recipes are not physical objects but *immaterial ideas*. In contrast to physical objects such as cars, airplanes and televisions, ideas do not have a final form when they arrive from the 'producers'. Hence, organizational recipes can be compared with semi-fabricated objects that need to be finished locally in the individual public organization. Rather than building elements with fixed forms, which may or may not interlock with other elements, modern organizational recipes may be said to consist of rather 'elastic materials' that give individual organizations much autonomy to eventually develop their own version and to find new ways of adapting the recipes to one another. This is just one explanation for why apparently inconsistent ideas can co-exist in organizations. The concepts are interpreted locally and ways found to adapt them, along with local solutions for how the recipes can be spliced together.

Even so, the elasticity of organizational recipes varies. Some clearly spell out and prescribe in great detail how certain structures, procedures and routines in organizations should be formed. In such instances little freedom is given for local interpretation. Usually, however, organizational recipes are capacious enough to offer considerable possibilities for local interpretation and adaptation. One example of this is the attempt to implement a so-called 'flat' organizational structure in Scandinavian municipalities over the last two decades. This recipe has shown itself to be very elastic, and a great many local versions now exist.

DEVELOPMENT AND DIFFUSION OF MYTHS

Where do rationalized ideas about, say, leadership and organizational design come from? How are they developed and how do they spread? Such ideas usually have a clouded history. Often it is difficult to date them or to find out where and when they first emerged, even if popular management literature often presents them in narratives about their origin and history. What is fascinating is that *alternative* stories are often told about how and when one and the same concept originated. This is the case for MBO and TQM, two of the most widely spread contemporary concepts. One possible explanation might be that the various provenances actually refer to slightly different variations of the same idea 'whose time has come', and which therefore arise in different contexts and at different places simultaneously, just as when mushrooms appear in different places in the woods in the autumn. One specific cause for the provenance problem is that popular recipes are often timely systematizations and conceptualizations built on more general, *timeless* ideas. For example, as regards the design of rational organizations, the idea that organizations should have clear goals is relatively universal and timeless, as is the idea that activities and resources should be directed towards goal achievement. At various times and places these general ideas have provided the basis for a great many attempts to hammer out slightly different local versions. In principle, each of these attempts can be dated and their source located, and they may have their own local history. Some attempts are patently better known than others and provide the basis for histories of idea that has been disseminated almost globally. A case in point is the story about Peter Drucker and the origin of MBO. The story goes that Drucker, while working for General Electric, was inspired by routines used there and hence developed the popular concept in the early 1950s. But there are also local versions of the origins of the idea, for instance about actors who coined and spread local versions of MBO and TQM in the United Kingdom, Sweden and the Netherlands, etc. Thus, several alternative stories may circulate about the origin of popular recipes without any of them necessarily being wrong.

Although the ideas that popular organizational recipes are based on are often rather general and timeless, it is nevertheless possible to identify groups of actors who are intensely involved in the development and diffusion of specific recipes. There are roles for producers as well as for mediators, and also for authorizers, that is, those who, by virtue of their position and status, have the ability to endorse specific recipes and enhance their popularity and capacity for diffusion. Newer research has identified five groups of actors who play particularly important roles as producers and mediators.

The first group is a set of actors – or agents – who specifically contribute to developing and spreading recipes to the public sector. Some of the most important are *international organizations*, among others the Organisation for Economic Cooperation and Development (OECD), the European Union, the United Nations (UN), the International Monetary Fund (IMF), the World Bank and more recently the World Trade Organisation (WTO). As authors of organizational recipes, these actors can almost symbiotically collaborate with important member countries whose claims to have been successful help promote ideas and initiatives for reform. These actors make their assistance to individual countries contingent on certain conditions, including the proviso that the country in question accepts and adopts certain recipes or concepts. Such international actors are also increasingly collaborating with international private actors, and national agents are also engaged in developing and spreading recipes for national public organizations. Now and then these agents formulate recipes, but their main concern is to redesign existing concepts to fit better with specific parts of their nation's public sector. The concepts are often inspired by the international organizations and by those who certify them, which makes it more appropriate for individual public organizations to follow them up.

The second group of producers and mediators is *consultancy firms*. Over the last twenty years this group of actors has played an ever-increasing role on the supply side of popular organizational ideas. There are two main reasons for this. First, there has been a vigorous growth in the number of large resourceful consulting firms. In the course of the 1990s, the largest companies have grown far stronger in economic resources, have increased the services they offer and have opened offices worldwide. They have therefore become exceedingly influential and one of the dominant actors on the supply side. Second, while the traditional role of consultants was to mediate knowledge to clients that the consultants had not necessarily developed themselves, in the course of the last twenty years the largest firms have invested great resources in their own research and collaborated with research institutions for the strategic purpose of not only being 'transporters' but also producers of organizational knowledge. This has made them even more important actors on the supply side.

The third group is made up of organizations in *higher education*, especially business schools, but also universities. Through their research and education of candidates these schools, particularly those in the West, have moved into central positions in the development and diffusion of organizational ideas and recipes. Several of the most popular recipes today are claimed to have sprung from research at well-respected business schools in the United States (e.g. Business Process Re-engineering and Value-chain Management). Just as important is the spread of organizational ideas and recipes through graduates, notably those with international, standardized Master of Business Administration degrees. Since the late 1970s, this has been one of the world's most popular academic degrees.

Between these last two groups of actors – consultancy firms and business schools – there are often close connections that speed up the development and diffusion of organizational ideas. The spread from business schools to consultancy firms happens when graduates are employed by consultancy firms. Another kind of transfer occurs when theorists from business schools collaborate with consultants and publish articles or books that launch organizational recipes. This is quite common and it often increases the recipe's legitimacy and capacity for diffusion.

Mass media of various types are the fourth important group of mediators for organizational recipes. Noteworthy are the many publishers and newspapers specializing in topics such as economics, organization and leadership. Among the most well known are the *Wall Street Journal* and the *Financial Times*. Another influential mass media group consists of highly respected international business periodicals, such as the *Harvard Business Review*, *Business Weekly* and *The Economist*. These regularly publish popularized portrayals of various organizational recipes and, by virtue of their prestige and distribution, are important media for the spread of ideas. Also worthy of mention are the numerous books on management and leadership. This type of publication was established as a distinct genre in the late 1970s. Between 2,000 and 3,000 books are published yearly in Western countries, in one or several categories of management, business and organization. Consultants author a significant number of these, either alone or together with academics from business schools and universities. There are many instances of new ideas and recipes being developed, presented and spread through such books. MBO, for example, was initially spread through Peter Drucker's book *The Practice of Management*, first published in 1954. Other cult books by management gurus are Peters and Waterman's *In Search of Excellence* from 1982, and Osborne and Gaebler's *Reinventing Government* from 1992.

Large multinational companies are the fifth group of actors. Since the end of the nineteenth century, when the first of such organizations emerged, they have grown in number and are now important symbols for and the prime motor behind economic globalization. Although these organizations are usually perceived as being clients and users, they also frequently function as developers and mediators of organizational recipes, for they often develop their own recipes and devices based on their experience and research efforts. In practice they are important mediators because they are represented throughout the world and thus distribute ideas worldwide via internal channels. Moreover, because of their size, visibility and prestige, large multinational companies often become strong models for other organizations.

There is a widespread perception that a division of labour exists among these last four groups of actors concerning their roles in the development, mediation and use of organizational recipes. Business schools and other research institutions are typically perceived as developers and producers of knowledge; consultancy firms and the mass media then package and popularize that knowledge in the form of recipes, which are then offered to large multinational companies and other organizations. These companies and organizations adopt and implement the recipes. In practice, however,

65

the boundaries between these groups are becoming blurred. There are many examples of this: large consultancy firms try to emulate academic organizations when they spend large resources to build up their own research units; universities and business schools encroach on the territory of consultancy firms when they are hired to create specially tailored education and training programmes for specific organizations and when their research staff act as paid consultants for businesses and public organizations. What is more, the mass media do not merely play the role of passive mediators of popular organizational ideas – powerful publishers often take the initiative in conducting research. They organize book projects on recipes in the making and hire various academics and consultants to author them. Finally, many large multinational companies exceed the bounds of their role as 'passive' customers and users when they invest in research and development. As a consequence of these overlapping activities, it becomes difficult to assign the roles of producer, mediator or user of organizational knowledge and recipes to specific actors.

The groups mentioned can be said to create and mediate technical solutions to problems of efficiency in the public organizations of different countries. If these technical solutions seem similar, it may be because the problems in different countries are similar too. From a myth perspective, however, the disseminated solutions are for the most part recipes with significant symbolic power. One way of describing the ongoing dissemination is to compare it with the spread of clothing fashions: just as the fashion world makes certain clothing popular for certain seasons so, also, in the world of public organizations, certain recipes are popular for certain periods. If we employ this metaphor for the groups described above we can say that the authors and mediators of organization recipes are 'fashion merchants', while the countries and public organizations that adopt them are 'followers of fashion', who are pressured into conformity by peers, although individual organizations may have more independent attitudes about using whatever is in vogue.

ORGANIZATIONAL IDENTITY AS A CONDITION FOR THE SPREAD OF ORGANIZATIONAL RECIPES

An important but often ignored condition for the establishment and spread of organizational recipes is that there are many organizations asking for such ideas. Just as important, however, is that, in spite of their differences, organizations are perceived to have much in common. More specifically, organizations must be transformed from the concrete level (e.g. a ministry, a subordinate agency, a municipality, a publishing company, an army unit, a hotel), where they appear to be completely different, to a more abstract level where they can be perceived as fairly similar. It is via this more abstract system-identity as a *formal organization* that disparate enterprises, firms and public administration units can appear to be alike. And it is precisely the notion of such diverse units sharing an identity as organizations that has gained wide acceptance in the last twenty years. This suggests that a worldwide common system-identity for different units – that of being an organization – is about to emerge. This is expressed by entities increasingly understanding themselves and presenting themselves outwardly as 'organizations'.

The spread of a worldwide organizational identity – also increasingly adopted by public organizations – has created the basis for the conception of a world of relatively similar systems consisting of mostly the same components, such as goals, leadership, formal structure, organizational culture, procedures for dealing with personnel, quality systems, auditing systems, etc. This has helped generate a huge and rapidly expanding market for the creation and diffusion of organizational recipes.

CHARACTERISTICS OF THE MOST WIDELY SPREAD ORGANIZATIONAL RECIPES

The ability of recipes to spread and their actual dissemination varies greatly. Some barely garner attention and interest beyond a limited group of cognoscenti, while others spread rapidly between countries and continents and precipitate reorganization processes in a wide spectrum of organizations, including public ones. The most widely spread recipes also have their own distinct literature, called 'concept literature', that is, publications, often in several languages, that argue for the adoption of recipes by organizations.

How, then, can we explain why certain recipes are so widely disseminated? The Norwegian political scientist Kjell Arne Røvik has illuminated this question in a study of the background to the diffusion of three popular recipes, MBO, TQM and *developmental dialogue* (a dialogue between two 'equal' actors, a manager and employee, which does not include discussions about traditional areas of conflict such as salary negotiation). Røvik has studied how these three superstandards are presented and how attempts are made to justify them through concept literature. From an instrumental perspective, one would expect the most widely spread recipes to be those that organizations have found most effective in achieving results. One would thus expect the literature to be characterized by documentations of these recipes' effects and effectiveness. Strangely, though, this is hardly ever the case. Instead, research shows that the most widely spread concepts have the following seven things in common, and these are assumed to be important reasons for their wide distribution:

- *Social authorization*: Recipes acquire spreading power as a consequence of being objects of emphatic social authorization. This means that in the concept literature, attempts are made to link the recipes to well-known and successful organizations and/or individuals, for example well-known leaders. Social authorization occurs partly through stories about the origin of recipes. One common feature is that they are presented as having been invented by visionary leaders or pioneers who work as consultants. In addition to these stories of origin, the literature frequently contains stories about previous users – organizations and individuals that have adopted and used the recipes successfully. Authorization happens when large international and well-known actors, either public or private, are given pride of place as successful users. It is rare, however, to find attempts to authorize recipes that describe how they have actually functioned in public organizations.

- *Universalization*: Another important common feature in the way recipes are presented in concept literature is that they are often seen as panaceas, tools that work successfully in all types of organizations, independently of location, purpose, size, cultural context, number of employees, type of work force, or private or public sector. It is presupposed that the recipes can be used everywhere and by everyone. A crucial precondition for this is what we earlier characterized as the fundamental and overarching identity of *formal organization* applied to what are in fact highly divergent units, for only when a large assortment of units are perceived as similar can standardized products be mass-produced, in this case, recipes for all organizations. Universalization takes several forms in the concept literature. One of these is the claim that the recipes are founded on universally valid causal connections, in other words, cause-effect relations are assumed to work identically in all organizations. One is led to expect that if recipe *a* is implemented in public organizations *x, y* and *z* (e.g. an agency, a nationalized company and a municipality), it will produce the same effects provided that the required steps for implementation are followed. Attempts to make people believe recipes operate in accordance with a universally valid causal logic – independent of time, type of organization, location, etc. – are important elements in the effort to increase their dissemination.

- *Commodification*: From the early 1960s a profound and systematic development towards a more comprehensive commodification of ideas about organization and leadership has been observable. Recipes have been transformed into products or wares to be bought and sold on a market, and this market increasingly includes public organizations. In the West this development can be explained in terms of the logic of the *market*. Accordingly, specific roles have emerged for producers, mediators and buyers of managerial and organizational ideas. Competition is stiff for potential customers' attention and buying power, and therefore different prices are set for different recipes. 'New' ideas and recipes are constantly being introduced, while 'old' ones fade and fall out of use. In many respects this phenomenon resembles modern consumer society. Therefore, the likelihood that a new organizational recipe will spread depends partly on the degree to which it is successfully commodified – that is, transformed from a general idea into a product, which, in competition with other products, captures attention and creates demand. Based on studies of the way the three superstandards (MBO, TQM and developmental dialogue) are presented, we can confirm that the following four elements are important in a successful strategy for transforming an organizational recipe into a sellable product:

a)   the recipe should be formulated into an easily communicable message;
b)   information about the recipe should be easily available to potential customers;
c)   the recipe should be presented in a user-friendly form; and
d)   potential customers should be genuinely promised that the returns will exceed the effort and cost of acquiring the product.

This is particularly important for the public sector just now, where the focus is on effectiveness, efficiency and economy.

■ *Timing*: A frequently noted but imprecisely defined notion is that an organizational recipe must capture the spirit of the times in order to become popular. Interpreted from an instrumental perspective, a recipe must be developed and launched at the point when it successfully matches the dominant problem-definitions for organizations within the given time period. According to a myth perspective, however, it is more important that a recipe be *presented* and *defined* as a timely solution. In other words, a recipe is a social construction made to appear a successful match for an organization's given problems at a certain time. Indeed, much of the concept literature presents the three super-standards in a timely, developmental context, so that they will be perceived as new, modern and directed towards the future.

■ *Harmonization*: Many academics have described public organizations as arenas for exercising power, negotiating, building alliances and coping with conflicts. The most frequently discussed conflict dimensions exist between leaders and employees, parallel sub-units, different professions and occupational groups, the sexes and individuals. With a view to addressing this problem the concept literature contains a number of common features in how it presents MBO, TQM and developmental dialogue. There are, for instance, numerous attempts to harmonize the recipes by defining and presenting them in ways that do not provoke or challenge any of the above-mentioned conflict dimensions. The majority of publications emphasize that the *entire* organization is the target for the recipes rather than specific internal units. When specific groups are mentioned (such as leaders, professions, ministerial divisions, agencies or women), the recipes are seldom described as 'weapons' one group can use against another to gain advantages. Care is taken to avoid the pitfalls of recognized conflicts. This is another vital factor in making recipes spread. For example, MBO is often justified by arguing that leaders will gain more clout and strengthen their capacity to manage, while frontline personnel simultaneously gain more freedom to make decisions. Such bridge-building through harmonization

69

descries elements of decontextualization, that is, that the myths should fit all organizations and all groups of actors and therefore must be general and flexible.

- *Dramatization*: A conspicuous feature of how superstandards are presented in concept literature is the stories about their origin and diffusion. These stories contain many dramatic elements. Central to the dramaturgy is that the stories should be exciting and feature a basic contrast or, even better, a conflict between ideas presented by high-profile actors. Such dramatic elements are easily recognizable leitmotifs in the literature on MBO, TQM and developmental dialogue. Here the stories feature personalities with a strong profile, such as Peter F. Drucker. The concept entrepreneurs are presented as determined individuals with a strong conviction or belief, and they are portrayed battling against established ideas and characters in order to get their new ideas heard. Such stories also contain dramatic turning points where the 'correct' nature of an insight and idea is suddenly recognized and ultimately wins out. Dramatic messages are more easily spread than others because they are exciting and therefore capture public attention. The dramatic points are easy to remember and can be retold and communicated easily. In this way a dramatic message acquires a life of its own and often spreads quickly without costing very much.

- *Individualization*: Another feature MBO, TQM and developmental dialogue share is that they are individualized concepts. This means that the message, to a significant degree, is directed towards individual members of an organization. The recipes thus constitute appeals not only to leaders and the organization as a system, but also to each individual. This form of individualization makes it easier for organizational recipes to spread, because it coincides with some of today's strong social undercurrents regarding individualism. Recipes spreading thus also depends on the degree to which they are individualized and on whether they are designed to appear as tools for individual development, growth and career advancement.

An analysis of the three superstandards reveals that they have seven characteristics assumed to contribute to their wide dissemination. If recipes are to spread successfully they need to be socially authorized, universalized, commodified, well timed, harmonized, dramatized and individualized.

HOW RATIONALIZED RECIPES ARE ADOPTED AND IMPLEMENTED

We shall now turn to what happens when rationalized myths 'meet' organizations. A recipe's journey into an organization can be called an *adoption*. This is a journey that often has neither a distinct beginning nor an end. It usually begins when someone in an organization (often in management) becomes aware of an organizational recipe and gets excited about it. If it looks like a promising solution to local problem-definitions in the organization, the likelihood increases that implementation will be attempted. The trajectory usually begins with an official decision to adopt a recipe followed by attempts to interpret and adapt it to make it capable of influencing some of the organization's activities.

Theorists are usually concerned with the two following questions in relation to the meeting between ideas, recipes and organizations: why are organizations motivated to adopt popular organizational recipes and what happens when organizations try to implement such recipes? The first question has been addressed by Paul DiMaggio and Walter Powell, who have identified three different reasons for organizations to adopt recipes. The first is *coercive adoption*. This happens when an organization, perhaps via laws or regulations, is instructed to implement certain recipes. In such a situation the organization has no other choice. This applies, for instance, to the EU-based instruction to implement various forms of internal control in public organizations. The second is *normatively based adoption*. This refers to the kind of dissemination and adoption that arises from the common norms, values, knowledge and networks held or engaged in by various professional groups. Examples of this can be the contribution of economists to spreading some of the basic ideas associated with NPM, or physicians spreading ideas about 'evidence-based medicine'. The third is *mimetic adoption*, which often occurs when organizations in situations marked by great uncertainty, try to emulate others which are perceived to be successful and prestigious. Usually this takes the form of imitation without much preliminary calculation and analysis. Consultancy firms often persuade public organizations to engage in this kind of adoption:

- *From ideas to practice*: Taking a formal decision to adopt popular organizational recipes does not necessarily mean they will be implemented. Different research traditions offer three possible processes and outcomes when organizations attempt to implement recipes. These can be expressed as theories about *quick coupling, rejection* and *decoupling*. The theory of *quick coupling* is mediated exemplarily in popular management literature. Usually an optimistic scenario is presented: the popular idea or recipe can be implemented relatively quickly and will render the expected positive effects. This requires, however, that the implementation processes are carried out deliberately and according to rational plans and principles. Popular organizational recipes are for the most part presented as fully developed and tried-and-tested tools, ready for use and relatively easy to implement.
- *Rejection*: Within a cultural perspective, one finds a more sceptical and pessimis-tic scenario for what may be the outcome of attempts to implement popular organizational ideas. In this tradition organizations are complex, value-based institutions generally able to successfully resist reforms, especially attempts at rapid change in structures and processes. The recipes are accordingly presented as vague ideas, simplified and popularized, stripped of their original contexts.

71

When an attempt is made to implement them in complex organizations, they will often be revealed as incompatible and unsuitable. Sometimes they will clash with the values an organization cares about and is committed to. This may explain why hospitals and health-care units have generally had problems adopting recipes directed towards achieving greater efficiency. Popular organizational recipes are also frequently revealed as being too *unsophisticated* to handle the complexity of the organization's work processes. If the recipes do not fit in these ways, they risk being rejected and attempts at implementation come to a halt.

- *Decoupling*: Although popular concepts may be too vague or unsophisticated in relation to the complexities of an organization's tasks, or else perceived as out of step with basic values and norms within an organization, modern organizations will nevertheless experience pressure from the institutional environment to incorporate them because they are seen as up-to-date and legitimate ideas and recipes. This is a key argument of New Institutionalism. According to this theory, modern organizations must deal with the following dilemma: on the one hand they must be efficient, which often requires adhering to tried-and-tested solutions, and on the other hand, they must adopt the ideas and recipes perceived to be modern at the time, not least because these recipes have the potential to give the organization external legitimacy. One way of tackling this dilemma is to adopt modern concepts, but to deliberately keep them decoupled, so that they have little effect on activities, or at any rate the activities that are significant for the organization's ability to make decisions and to produce goods and services effectively. From this perspective, myths or recipes are ideas that lie on the surface of organizations like *varnish* and function as a kind of window dressing intended to convince the environment that the organization is modern and efficient, without it actually changing very much on the inside. Research on reforms in public organizations has shown, for example, that political and administrative leaders frequently over-sell new reforms; they promise more than can be delivered, which often intensifies the symbolic character and decoupling of reforms.

However, although the theories of quick coupling, rejection and decoupling may explain some variance, several empirical studies indicate that they do not sufficiently cover the spectrum of possible outcomes of attempts to implement popular organizational ideas. These theories pay too little attention to the adoption and implementation processes that unfold over a relatively long period of time. We shall briefly present two theories that take the *time* aspect into consideration and which partly modify, partly supplement, the above-mentioned theories. The *virus theory* addresses the possible long-term effects of adopting ideas and the *translation theory* addresses to what degree and in what way organizations can manipulate recipes:

- *The virus theory*: When an organization first adopts new ideas and recipes, it may notice a *new language* being spoken, in the form of new concepts and lines of argument. Popular organizational recipes are actually well-codified ideas. The decoupling theory maintains that attempts to change organizations through new recipes will often be limited to just such a linguistic change, for example, leaders in a public service agency may talk about balanced scorecards, human resource management, ethical accounting, etc., without actually turning those ideas into new routines and practices. There is, however, some evidence that new terminology may, over time, also give rise to new routines and practices, in other words, talk and action may be coupled in the long run. The term 'virus' is used metaphorically to describe new recipes that come into an organization like a sort of 'linguistic infection', and which usually, after a relatively long period of 'incubation', express themselves in changed routines and practices. How new terminology can eventually influence practices is demonstrated in several studies. A Swedish study by Bengt Jacobsson showed that when hospital employees began to talk about and conceptualize their organization as a kind of 'business', they gradually became more like economic actors, for instance by trying to avoid 'bad customers'.

- *Translation theory*: Put simply, one could say that while the virus theory tries to account for what recipes can do to organizations, the translation theory tries to account for what organizations can do to recipes. This is a theory initially developed by the French sociologist Bruno Latour. The point of departure is simple: organizational recipes are ideas, not physical objects, hence, they do not have final forms. When recipes spread, they are continually translated and are therefore constantly mutating into ever-new local versions. This occurs, for instance, when recipes from the EU are translated into transnational networks.

Yet why are organizational recipes translated and reshaped when they spread to new organizations? Sometimes this happens as a result of *rational calculation*. In constructing the local version by calculating what will be the most useful variant for the organization, the useful elements are culled and the rest discarded. At other times recipes are adapted to local situations so as to avoid conflicts. This was what happened when American-style *performance appraisals* were tentatively introduced in the Nordic countries towards the end of the 1960s. Labour unions felt provoked because they thought this kind of evaluation was a way of introducing a much more differentiated system based on each employee's performance and therefore constituted an attack on Scandinavia's collective bargaining tradition. This led to efforts to translate the American-inspired performance appraisal systems into what we know today as *developmental dialogue*. Translation of organizational ideas can also happen *unintentionally*, that is, simply because those responsible for implementing it in a local context have insufficient knowledge of the concept.

Where, then, are recipes translated and who does the work? Often actors outside the individual organization function as translators. Various governmental agencies have translated a series of general recipes, anything from MBO to service declarations for civil servants. Translation also takes place internally in individual organizations. Leaders but also staff members (particularly those involved in personnel and organizational issues) are among those most involved in translation.

How are the recipes translated? In principle, organizations have great freedom to translate, and hence to transform ideas, to make as many local versions as they deem necessary. Translation happens partly by transforming ideas into more concrete terms. Popular organizational recipes are, as mentioned, often general ideas (remember the metaphor of semi-fabricated objects) and they must therefore be interpreted and made explicit if they are to be used in specific organizations. Translation can also occur as *partial imitation*, that is, only certain elements of a popular recipe are adopted and the rest discarded. *Combination* is another method – some elements from one recipe are joined with parts or the whole of another. And in other instances, the term *remelting* more readily captures the transformation happening through the translation process. Recipes are thus radically reshaped, often so comprehensively that the local version has the character of an innovation – something quite new. This is a theme we will return to in Chapter Nine.

The idea of organizations translating and thus redesigning rationalized recipes has many implications. It challenges 'the great homogeneity scenario', a position held by key organization theorists such as DiMaggio and Powell, together with Meyer and Rowan, in classic studies from the late 1970s and early 1980s. Briefly, the scenario is that institutionalization and globalization, which increasingly exert an influence over great distances, are forces that work in the direction of increased *structural isomorphy* among the world's organizations, ergo the escalation of homogeneous organizational forms. One of the insights communicated in this chapter – that organizations translate and manipulate ideas and recipes from institutional environments – helps to modify the idea of an inevitable homogenization process taking place among the world's organizations. Recipes that spread are interpreted and reinterpreted so that new and differing versions of them are continually emerging. This becomes an intermediate and pragmatic argument – situated between the argument of isomorphy and convergence (typical for a standard interpretation of the myth perspective) and the argument of divergence and multiplicity (typical of the cultural perspective).

RATIONALIZED RECIPES IN INSTRUMENTAL AND INSTITUTIONAL INTERPRETATIONS

Many organization theorists have a rather equivocal attitude towards the pheno-mena presented in this chapter, namely the creation, diffusion and adoption of popular organizational recipes. This is because the phenomena can be understood in different ways, in light of an institutional approach (the approach taken in this chapter) or from an instrumental perspective (see Chapter Nine).

If seen instrumentally and rationally, popular recipes are tried-and-tested tools leaders can use in trying to make organizations more effective. There is a strong belief that they spring from practices that have worked well in one or, better still, several other organizations. The most popular and widely disseminated recipes are therefore perceived to have spread because they have shown themselves to be exceptional tools for increasing efficiency, ideally in a large number of organizations. When attempts are made to adopt recipes in individual organizations, this often happens as the result of a problem-driven search for solutions. According to this view, the organization first experiences problems and is motivated to search for solutions to match. Several potential solutions (recipes) are therefore usually assessed before one deemed good enough is chosen. Thereafter, efforts are made to thoroughly organize the implementation process in order to establish new routines and activities. If the choice is made to translate and change the chosen concept, it is done deliberately by calculating what is needed and what can be ignored.

From an institutional vantage point, however, organizational recipes appear as meaningful symbols. They have been interpreted and ascribed contents that extend beyond merely being tools for effective problem solving. Institutionalized recipes are not 'just symbols', they are *rationalized symbols*. This means that emphasis is placed on defining and presenting them as tools for enhancing efficiency and modernization. The claim is that popular organizational recipes have acquired legitimacy and the ability to spread because they have become symbols of basic rationalistic values in modern society, for example reason, efficiency, democracy and science, and, as such, they are associated with the traditional Western ideal of continual progress, that is, the movement forwards and upwards towards some ever-better state of being. Yet with that, this symbolic perspective also ties in with the instrumental-rational tradition in a complex way and makes it difficult to imagine popular organizational recipes either only as symbols or only as effective tools.

When a recipe is established as a model, this concerns much more than the extent to which it has proven able to function as a tool for efficiency or effectiveness. As mentioned earlier, a recipe is more likely to spread if it is successfully linked to authoritative actors, such as progressive and modern countries, companies, academic organizations and leaders. Moreover, modern society celebrates continuous renewal and change, not least actors and organizations representing technical innovations. Recipes therefore also acquire spreading power if they can be presented as symbols of *the new* —anything that breaks with older habits of purveying goods and services.

Recipe adoption, from an instrumental perspective, happens through search processes conditioned by a problem, yet a symbolic interpretation also allows the possibility that just the opposite may be the case. First, someone in an organization becomes aware of and excited about a rationalized recipe and only then does he or she 'discover' a local problem that can be adequately solved by implementing the recipe. Yet even if a recipe is formally adopted, this does not ensure that it will be put to use (according to the theory of decoupling between ideas and practice). And while translation, interpreted instrumentally, appears to be an attempt to turn general recipes into tools well-adapted to local conditions, in the institutional-symbolic interpretation, translation appears as a possible device for ensuring decoupling between myths and practice, namely a recipe can be redesigned such that it poses no threat to existing practices in the organization.

CHAPTER SUMMARY

- Organizations – private as well as public – are located in institutional environments where they are confronted with socially created norms and recipes for how they should be designed and how they should function. These norms and recipes are called myths.
- There is a wide range of popular recipes for shaping all aspects of modern organizations, for example leadership, formal organizational structure, organizational culture, processes, etc. Popular organizational ideas usually spread rapidly. A number of institutions and individuals function as producers and mediators of such ideas.
- The formal adoption of popular recipes by public organizations can have numerous outcomes (quick coupling/implementation, rejection, decoupling or the 'slower' process of translating ideas into practice).

DISCUSSION QUESTIONS

1   Identify and discuss factors that may cause organizations to adopt popular organizational recipes (myths).
2   Choose a public-sector organization with which you are familiar and try to identify which popular organizational recipes this organization has adopted during the last five years.
3   Identify and discuss factors that may aid or hinder the implementation of popular organizational recipes, that is, the translation of such ideas into practice in public organizations.

REFERENCES AND FURTHER READING

Brunsson, N. (1989; 2nd edn 2002) *The Organization of Hypocrisy*, Chichester: John Wiley; 2nd edn Oslo: Abstrakt.

Cohen, M.D., March, J.G. and Olsen, J.P. (1972) 'A Garbage Can Model of Organizational Choice', *Administrative Science Quarterly*, 17(1): 1–25.

Czarniawska, B. and Joerges, B. (1996) 'Travels of Ideas', in B. Czarniawska and G. Sevon (eds) *Translating Organizational Change*, Berlin: Walter de Gruyter.

DiMaggio, P.J. and Powell, W.W. (1983) 'The Iron Cage Revisited: Institutional Iso-morphism and Collective Rationality in Organizational Fields', *American Socio-logical Review*, 48 (2): 147–60.

Drucker, P.F. (1954) *The Practice of Management*, New York: Harper.

Hatch, M.J., Holten-Larsen, M. and Schultz, M. (2000) *The Expressive Organization: Linking Identity, Reputation and the Corporate Brand,* Oxford: Oxford University Press.

Jacobsson, B. (1994) 'Reformer och organisatorisk identitet' ('Reforms and Organizational Identity') in B. Jacobsson (ed.) *Organisationsexperiment i kommuner och landsting* (*Organization Experiment in Local Government*), Stockholm: Nerenius & Santerus.

Latour, B. (1986) 'The Powers of Association', in J. Law (ed.) *Power, Action and Belief,* London: Routledge & Kegan Paul.

March, J.G. and Olsen, J.P. (eds) (1976) *Ambiguity and Choice in Organizations*, Bergen: Universitetsforlaget.

Meyer, J.W. and Rowan, B. (1977) 'Institutional Organizations: Formal Structure as Myth and Ceremony', *American Journal of Sociology*, 83 (2): 340–63.

Micklethwait, J. and Woolridge, A. (1996) *The Witch Doctors: What the Management Gurus are Saying, Why it Matters and How to Make Sense of it,* London: Heinemann.

Osborne, D. and Gaebler, T. (1992) *Reinventing Government: How the Entrepreneurial Spirit is Transforming the Public Sector,* Reading: Addison Wesley.

Parsons, T. (1956) 'Suggestions for a Sociological Approach to Theory of Organizations', *Administrative Science Quarterly*, 1 (1): 63–85.

Peters, T.J. and Waterman, R.H. (1982) *In Search of Excellence,* New York: Harper & Row.

Røvik, K.A. (1996) 'Deinstitutionalization and the Logic of Fashion', in B. Czarniawska and G. Sevon (eds) *Translating Organizational Change*, Berlin: Walter de Gruyter.

—— (1998) *Moderne Organisasjoner* (*Modern Organizations*), Bergen: Fagbokforlaget.

—— (2002) 'The Secrets of the Winners: Management Ideas That Flow', in K. Sahlin-Andersson and L. Engwall (eds) *The Expansion of Management Knowledge,* Stanford: Stanford University Press.

—— (2007) *Trender og translasjoner. Ideer som former det 21. århundrets organisas-joner* (*Trends and translations. Ideas that form the 21st century's organizations*), Oslo: Universitetsforlaget.

77

Sahlin-Andersson, K. (2001) 'National, International and Transnational Constructions of New Public Management', in T. Christensen and P. Lægreid (eds) *New Public Management: The Transformation of Ideas and Practice*, Aldershot: Ashgate.

Sahlin-Andersson, K. and Engwall, L. (2002) 'Carriers, Flows, and Sources of Management Knowledge', in K. Sahlin-Andersson and L. Engwall (eds) *The Expansion of Management Knowledge*, Stanford: Stanford University Press.

Scott, W.R. (1987) 'The Adolescence of Institutional Theory', *Administrative Science Quarterly*, 32 (4): 493–511.

Chapter 5

Goals and values

LEARNING OBJECTIVES

By the end of this chapter you should:

- have a clear understanding of how goals and values are defined, how they develop and what implications they have in public organizations;
- understand how goals and values are viewed according to instrumental, cultural and myth perspectives;
- have a basic understanding of the use of Management by Objectives and Results (MBOR) in public organizations.

MEANING OF GOALS AND VALUES

A usual definition of *goals* in formal organizations is that they are concepts or definitions of something one wants to achieve or to realize in the future. Organizations are collectively oriented towards achieving goals, and this is especially true for public organizations. Goal achievement requires specialized as well as coordinated activities. Goals are meant to influence how formal organizations are structured or organized and thus provide guidelines for their activities. In reality goals will, to varying degrees and with varying clarity, be tied to specific ways of organizing a formal structure. Goals will also to some extent influence decision-making behaviour and social interaction in organizations. Goals can be important for leaders in choosing between alternatives and in evaluating what their organizations have achieved. Goals can either be deliberately unclear or unclear because they reflect disagreement and complexity – something quite typical for public organizations. Unclear goals can provide leaders with more flexibility and can ease decision-making, but they can also make it difficult to assign responsibility in a public administration system. Goals will often be linked to an *instrumental* perspectives – as something purposely rational – but they may also have cultural and symbolic aspects.

Values are often associated with a cultural perspective on organizations or institutions. They represent informal norms and considerations that have grown gradually over time and that provide the foundation for the development of historical institutional characteristics or traditions in organizations (as described in Chapter Three). Values are normative guidelines for appropriate attitudes and actions. They provide a 'moral' framework for goals and activities. In public institutions values may pertain to principles like majority rule, rule of law, the participation of affected parties or professional administration. In other words, they develop in connection with formal goals and structures. One view is that values develop gradually through natural processes, while the opposite view is that it is possible to shape values through deliberate design and institutional change. In addition, they may be the result of a tug-of-war between actors with differing interests.

DEFINITION OF GOALS

There are many different kinds of goals. As the American organization theorist Charles Perrow asserts, goals can be *visions* or so-called *official goals,* characterized by an exceedingly high level of abstraction and meant to be general guidelines for actions. Examples of goals of this kind could be 'a better society', 'social equality' or 'better understanding between different ethnic groups', or, on a slightly less general level, 'reduce unemployment', 'reduce pollution' or 'help reduce inflation'. Such goals will often provide a broad framework for the activities of the public administration and, as we learned in Chapter Four, can be regarded from a myth perspective as symbols. Official goals can be utopian visions of things such as 'a good society' or 'just society'. They can be geared towards winning broad legitimacy and support for a public organization from internal and external actors, but they can also be typical for recently established public organizations, before they 'settle down', or for organizations that are reorienting themselves or having problems with the knowledge base for their activities.

Goals can also be *operational*, meaning that they are instrumental, concrete, specific, explicit and standardized. Leaders can use goals as tools in designing organizations, and members of organizations can use them to choose between alternative and specific courses of action. Within the framework of broad official goals, an organization can also have many different operational goals and activities, but since resources are limited, it must make a selection. This is what the instrumental perspective calls *bounded rationality*: in order to deal with a complex world, public organizations and their members must choose things or people to focus on, otherwise they encounter problems of attention and capacity. In addition, the operationalization of official goals offers insight into a formal organization's domain or area of activity. When goals are specifically defined, it becomes clearer which tasks, target groups, expertise or personnel an organization will want to prioritize.

This specific definition of goals in public organizations has traditionally led to some overlap in their activities, even though political and administrative leaders usually seek to avoid this. The overlap may be due to expansionistic ambitions, or it may simply imply that certain tasks or groups should be deliberately treated in a more comprehensive way by several different organizations and according to several different perspectives. Immigration policy is a good example of an area where many public organizations are involved and where each deals with different aspects but pertaining to a similar target group. This is reflected in different yet partly overlapping operational goals, and these may be rather loosely coupled to official goals, causing *goal displacement*. The latter occurs either when official goals become outdated as a consequence of substantial social change or when internal and external actors press for a reorientation of goals and activities.

A third way of defining goals is to emphasize that they may be *informal*. This can be elucidated through the cultural perspective. According to this view, goals are not formally fixed but are signalled obliquely by leaders. Gradually they are adopted and endorsed by different groups in the organization. Informal goals can help foster integrative or cultural features in organizations and can work in tandem with formal goals; they may also, however, contribute to internal tensions and undermine formal goals. There may, for instance, be informal signals about prioritizing specific public tasks or client groups or informal pressure to exercise greater judgement in the treatment of certain cases according to regulations. Powerful groups in a public organization may want to reorient their own organization and may assume that official goals will eventually be adjusted to the new informal goals. We can perceive this as a cultural process of change.

Goals can also be characterized according to whether they are *simple* and *one-dimensional*, or else *heterogeneous, multiple* or *complex*. Increasing the number of personal computers for school children in a municipality is a very concrete goal, whereas fostering individual growth as the official goal of education is obviously more nebulous. Goals for environmental protection policy that involve participation from other countries and international organizations with many national actors can be exceedingly complex. And so can goals such as reducing inflation. The often multifarious pro-cesses through which such goals have arisen intensify this complexity. Goal complexity can reflect the degree of specialization within a public organization or, more generally, whether or not the organization has specialized within a particular policy area. It may also reflect how much of its activity connects with that of other organizations. Public organizations with many tasks, large resources and many civil servants will usually have more complex goals than small organizations with only one task. There are tremendous differences in the complexity of goals between, say, a ministry of the interior, which has responsibility for a number of central tasks within municipal and regional government – immigration policy, housing and building issues, minority policy, etc. – and a public metrology service, or an agency which controls weights and measures.

Herbert Simon makes a distinction between *individual goals* and *organizational goals*. Individual goals might, for example, concern individual actors' decision to join an organization or to remain in it (career-oriented goals), while organizational goals control the decisions members make individually but on behalf of the collective, that is, decisions made by virtue of a particular member's position in the formal structure. This distinction – between individual and organizational goals – is disputed by a number of institutional theorists, who point out that there are often links, albeit rather ambiguous ones, between individual preferences and organizational goals.

A final distinction worth mentioning is that between *long-term goals* and *short-term goals*. Long-term goals are usually called strategies and are often marked by being relatively general, visionary and symbolic in orientation. This leads some theorists to distinguish further between long-term goals as stated intentions and long-term goals that are 'real'. Short-term goals will often be operational and ranked lower in a more comprehensive goal-structure. While long-term goals address sustainability issues, short-term goals tend to be more efficiency oriented.

The British sociologist David Silverman claims that there are at least four methods for defining goals in an organization. The first method is to look at the *original goals*, which are often formulated in formal written documents. This can provide a good insight but may also be problematic if goals change in the course of the organization's history. The second method is to look at which goals the present leadership of an organization aspires to. This gives a good overall picture of an organization's goals but may be misleading because leaders and organizational members further down in the hierarchy may have different goals, or leaders may deliberately construct goals with a symbolic character. Third, one can take as a starting point the activities an organization actually carries out and draw conclusions about what the relevant goals are. The challenge lies in being able to see general patterns and goals in a complex set of activities. A fourth method for identifying goals is to look at what the complex demands are for each individual's role, and in this context Silverman limits his focus to clear role-related demands and excludes more personal or informal demands. Here the challenge is to distinguish between various goals in a complex goal structure and to recognize the relative significance of formal and informal goals. These methods are inspired mainly by an instrumental perspective on organizations, but they also bear features derived from a cultural perspective.

FORMULATION AND DEVELOPMENT OF GOALS

Theoretically speaking, goals can be established, formulated and developed in many different ways. An instrumental perspective encompasses several different versions, but common to these is that they often emphasize cognitive or knowledge-based aspects of goals. Rational Choice Theory, associated with 'economic man', seldom sees establishing and developing goals as problematic for it presupposes that goals are externally given, clear and consistent and relatively unproblematic to pursue and fulfil. This analytical approach focuses on the connection between goals, means and consequences, but it considers the goal-formulation process irrelevant. This way of thinking is reflected in certain aspects of NPM reforms, where it is often presupposed that what is important is to choose the right means to fulfil clear and given goals. Few questions are asked about the underlying process of establishing goals or their implementation, particularly with regard to the balance between different considerations and the involvement of different actors; and few questions are asked about 'doing things in the right way' according to a process perspective. Neither does this way of thinking make much allowance for the difficulty of formulating goals or for the idea that goals may be discovered and developed gradually in the course of a decision-making process.

Such a way of thinking is often found in the ideal of rational public planning and was common in Western Europe after the Second World War, when new professionals entered central public administration – the economists. According to this mindset, politicians should define and furnish goals and it is up to civil servants, or rather technocrats, to use their professional knowledge and models to find the right means of fulfilling them. A critical question is whether politicians are willing or able to formulate clear public goals, or whether such goals are actually the result of what the technocrats want – in other words, are politicians' goals merely a reflection of technocratic will. In a complex public system there is a danger that an individual sector or public organization will be primarily concerned with its own goals and means of achieving them, what one might term *local rationality* and institutionally determined goals. These do not guarantee comprehensive or collective goals; on the contrary, they may make it more difficult for these to be formulated. We will address this problem more closely in our discussion of MBO later in the chapter.

A second instrumental conception of goal-formulation and goal development is the theory of bounded rationality and 'administrative man'. According to this theory, goals in an established public organization will be based on the constraints imposed on decision-makers by formal structures and by capacity problems: in other words, an organization and its members have to be selective in choosing considerations and premises for decision-making, because they cannot cope with an excessive degree of complexity. The behaviour of members is characterized by being 'biased and narrow', and they thus learn which problems and solutions to concentrate on, which goals they should set and how these should be developed. This means, for instance, that if a public administration system or one of its units finds that its goals cannot be achieved, or else that they are achieved too easily, ambitions must be adjusted accordingly and new goals must be established. These are sought in close proximity to the previous goals and based on experience with those goals. This helps save on resources, since it avoids engaging in a broad search for alternatives.

Goals will normally be formulated by senior executives in an organization rather than by the lower echelons of the hierarchy. This is particularly the case for more general goals, which originate from internal situations or from changes in the environment, that is, when the internal organizational structure is out of step with the external situation, such as when hospital waiting lists increase or when a municipality's treatment of social welfare cases has major flaws. Leaders can simplify decisions for civil servants by providing them with narrower goals. Such goals are the basis for *chains of means and ends*, where means eventually become ends, ends one must find new means to achieve. According to this theory, goal structure reflects authority relationships within the formal structure and cognitive limitations. Goals are promoted top-down, while their fulfilment is contingent upon organizational members' ability and will to follow them up and on whether the structural framework around them is sufficiently clear.

A third version of an instrumental perspective is based on the notion that to formulate or change goals, one must recognize that the political-administrative system and its environment are *heterogeneous*. This means that negotiations between different internal and external interests are critical. The established goals provide insight into negotiations and compromises between different interests, all of which can render greater legitimacy but not necessarily clear goals. The multiplicity of goals is most often based on organizational units and positions having different perspectives and interests – what one might call *interest-based* goals. When goals change, this often reflects renegotiation of coalitions and the establishment of new coalitions, because the composition of interests changes and the environment is in constant flux.

According to a seminal work by Richard Cyert and James March, it is possible to distinguish between the determination, development and selection of goals. They stress that decisions about goals are informed by heterogeneity and based on diverse mechanisms. First of all, goals can be a result of successful coalitions, which may yield goal clarity, but they can also result from conflicts related to minority influence. Second, goal formulation can be marked by compromises between a number of different interests. This often bestows great legitimacy on the goals and decisions, but potentially renders them less clear. Third, there can be sequential attention to goals, resulting in so-called quasi-resolution of conflicts. This means it is agreed that different and partly conflicting goals will be realized at different points in time and that goals and the focus of attention will shift over time. Such a solution means that goal structure is likely to be less consistent, but it solves disagreements and conflicts in the short term, thus allowing public leaders more flexibility. Sequential attention may also reflect goals being determined according to the current situation.

There are many examples of negotiation processes forming the basis for goal formulation and coalition change. In the early years of oil production there was a great emphasis in many countries on technology and economy, and goals tended to be defined in these terms by both public and private actors. With the establishment of public administration units for regulating oil production, environmental protection goals have gradually gained in importance, regard for safety has increased, coalitions have changed and the complexity of the corresponding goals has burgeoned. Ad hoc environmental protection groups have added to the complexity of problem-definition and the structure of negotiations in this policy field. Decision-making processes concerning oil and other energy sources around the world also show that negotiation processes are often based on long wish lists, and the compromises reached between different considerations are characterized by 'flexible wording'.

A second example of negotiation processes as the basis for goals is when several ministries or agencies are involved in the same policy area and have different interests that must be adapted to each other, as is the case with immigration policy, for instance. We also see this when special interest organizations participate in public commissions and make public leaders enter into compromises on legislative goals. The US Congress provides numerous examples of complicated negotiations aimed at resolving different states' or individual politicians' interests within a collective system. Such negotiations often result in the quasi-resolution of conflict, that is, legislators agree to disagree and to fulfil different interests at different points in time.

Local rationality reflects the heterogeneity of public organizations. This means that within different sectors, public organizations and individual actors pursue their own interests in a rational way, without paying attention to the interests of other actors. This can often lead to a fundamental lack of rationality at the collective level since actors pursuing their own interests does not guarantee good results for the community. In his book on the Cuban missile crisis in the early 1960s, an impasse involving the discovery of Soviet nuclear missiles, the American political scientist Graham Allison writes about how the CIA and the individual branches of military defence followed their own interests for handling the potential threat. This led to the missiles being discovered later than they otherwise would have been.

From a *cultural perspective*, goal formulation and development is seen rather differently. Goals are a source of motivation and identification for internal and external actors alike. The main point, according to this perspective, is that goals do not exist a priori, they cannot be designed or negotiated, and formal goals either have or do not have significance for action. Such a view is clearly at odds with various versions of an instrumental perspective on goals. Here goals are more informal; they are discovered and developed gradually over time, in an *evolutionary* and *natural process* whereby the public organization adapts to internal and external pressure simultaneously. These informal goals arise through collaboration between and within social groups in a public organization. They emerge gradually, through interaction with formal goals. According to a functional mindset, certain needs or functions (informal goals) must be satisfied so that an organization can survive, and these goals will not have any primary instrumental objective or be output-oriented but will instead be

85

supportive, *integrative* and *maintenance-oriented* goals that may either promote or hinder formal goals.

Informal goals that develop in close relation to formal goals – that is, they are clearly task-related – may be intended to support a discretionary decision or assessment. In public social services, for example, social workers may develop informal goals relating to how different types of clients should be treated. Thus the objectives of street-level bureaucrats might differ significantly from the goals of their political or administrative executives. However, informal goals grounded in interaction and the establishment of social groups may be tied to learning or developing social integration and, as such, they may not be directly connected to formal decisions. What is more, there are often differences between official goals and actual goals, a phenomenon known as *goal displacement*. A classic example of this is Robert Michels' study of the German Social Democratic Party in the early twentieth century. Party leaders eventually turned the organization into a goal unto itself, with *oligarchic features* and lacking internal democracy – both clear departures from its original goal. This may also be viewed as a case where informal and cultural goals undermined formal goals.

According to a *myth perspective*, goals will be determined and developed according to the current situation or as a result of pressure from the environment. This perspective tends to see the goals as more *fluctuating* and *unstable* than the other perspectives do. Here, goals are primarily symbols, ideas and visions, reflecting a theory that the world is easier to talk about than to deal with. Symbolic goals might be formulated to mark the occasion of a new government, for instance, or to draw attention to a specific political party. Examples are concepts for public reform that tend to exert strong symbolic pressure on public organizations but seldom last long and are constantly being replaced by new concepts. Administrative leaders may also deliberately use symbolic goals to increase the status of a public organization, for example by emphasizing that it stands for something modern or that it is giving high priority to improving its expertise.

Symbolic types of goal can result from natural developmental processes that put pressure on a public organization from the outside, without the organization being able to do very much about it. Such pressure, however, may also result from a desire to imitate reforms espoused by international or national organizations that proffer symbolic goals with a certain authority. This explanation, combining elements from an instrumental and a myth perspective, can also be applied to situations where public leaders deliberately create and spread myths and symbols, either because they are thought to have an intrinsic value or because they aid other instrumental changes.

TYPICAL FEATURES OF GOALS IN PUBLIC ORGANIZATIONS

Typical for public organizations is that they generally have complex and vague goals and want to prioritize many different concerns and activities simultaneously. This distinguishes them from private market-based organizations, which are often more one-dimensional, particularly with regard to their main goal: profit. From an instrumental perspective, this hallmark of public organizations can be understood as a reflection of a complex society and a complex political-administrative system where many actors and concerns must be addressed. This is a genuine feature of political processes. What is more, different policy areas overlap and are relevant to one another, and this increases the complexity of goals, structural solutions and public initiatives. The complexity also increases because decisions are appealed and thus prolonged, and the conditions for decision-making change in the course of the process. There will, however, be variations in complexity between different types of public organizations and policy areas. Environmental protection policy is a typical area where goals are complex and many factors are involved, while more technical areas are less complex (such as municipal tasks like renovation, snow-removal and custodial tasks).

If goals are vague, it may be because they are meant to be. Goals can be deliberately constructed to build bridges between conflicting interests and thus function to reduce the amplitude of conflicts. Unclear goals also provide leaders with considerable flexibility in how they should be presented and implemented. Unambiguous goals may bind leaders to targets which they know are difficult to achieve and which may eventually prove to be their undoing.

Complex, vague and mutable public goals can also be viewed in the light of a cultural perspective. They can be expressions of a *culture of political compromise,* necessary in order to achieve solutions acceptable to the whole community. Such a decision-making style may be marked by a desire to achieve unifying solutions and consensus through collaboration and processes of political partnership. Citizens make many demands on their politicians, and expectations often conflict. Political parties must formulate goals that can embrace a wide range. Hence government under complex and shifting conditions does not always result in sharp, clear goals; it engenders a culture of compromise where many considerations and actors are included. This may often be seen as a cultural advantage, but it will appear more problematic in the light of demands by modern reformers for clarity and accountability.

Public goals can also be understood from a myth perspective. Public organizations will always have a number of visions and official goals for they are political organizations with genuine symbolic features, although the conditions for developing such features have become more difficult in a period when covering expenses and balancing budgets often have a higher priority. Visions can be expressed in many different ways, for example at a national level, particularly during political campaigns, but also in a parliament when legislation on major issues is being decided, or in the actions of cabinet ministers when cases and decisions are presented. It is appropriate for political leaders to have visions, at least within certain limits. Visions have always been central to political processes because they seem to stake out a course and hold out the hope of a better future in various policy areas. Visions also provide politicians with flexibility for, instead of circumscribing a definite goal, they are rather vague statements about what one could imagine doing *if* conditions allowed, which probably they seldom do. This may endow politicians with *increased legitimacy*, because it makes them look energetic and capable, and apparently dynamic politicians often appeal to voters. A good example is British Prime Minister Margaret Thatcher during the 1980s. Meanwhile, the excessive use of vague and symbolic goals can create problems, because politicians, civil servants and regular citizens may experience problems in dealing with the discrepancy between symbols and action. This is particularly the case if the distance between visions and actions is very great and if groups of actors interpret symbols as concrete action. Such a scenario may eventually lead to cynicism, among the public, among civil servants and even among politicians themselves. Nevertheless, a balance between symbols and actions may be possible. Moreover, politicians often start out with genuine good intentions but then find their plans more difficult to put into practice than imagined, so they compensate with symbols and talk.

The extent to which official goals are put into operation in public organizations often indicates how politically and administratively ambitious an organization is. If operationalization is wide and realizes much of the potential contained in official goals, an increased use of public resources often follows and can reflect clear priorities. Nevertheless, operationalizing also entails taking into consideration other public organizations that work in adjacent areas and deciding whether it is desirable for these areas to overlap. Putting goals into operation also requires a clear internal design, that is, having a clear idea of internal organization and of how the various tasks are to be prioritized. According to the purpose principle, the basis for specialization in a formal structure is the operationalization of goals and when the purpose changes, this leads to an internal reorganization. This can be understood from an instrumental perspective. The operationalized goals and corresponding specialized structure are meant to prepare civil servants for the tasks they will be engaged in. The Norwegian-American sociologist and economist Thorstein Veblen calls this *trained incapacity,* meaning that there are a number of roles and positions in which civil servants are supposed to work in a highly specialized way with just a few tasks assigned to them, and the coordination of such activities is the responsibility of leaders higher up in the hierarchy. Therefore, a hierarchy of operationalized goals also exists, where the main goals are broader than the sub-goals, the main goals are result-oriented effect-goals and also performance indicators (to use the official terminology of MBOR).

Informal goals in public organizations can emerge in different ways. They can be a reflection of formal goals not being comprehensive, for if they were the organization would be excessively rigid and would not allow civil servants the necessary degree of freedom. In other words, leaders must, from time to time, give signals to their staff and communicate informal goals and values that can influence attitudes and actions within the degree of freedom allotted. These informal goals can help to further tighten hierarchical control, for they socialize and discipline, but they can also slacken and modify the effects of formal goals if the latter are problematic and need to be modified. Informal goals often have their origin in historical and cultural traditions and can be linked with the development of 'worker collectivity' in public organizations. They may reflect informal social norms and values in groups, subcultures and professions and eventually help to undermine formal goals. Informal goals can thus be defined by leaders in a so-called 'top-down' process, but they can also come from lower down in the organization – that is, from the bottom up.

MANAGEMENT BY OBJECTIVES AND RESULTS

The complexity of goals in public organizations presents itself in different ways. In many Western countries complexity has traditionally been more implicit than explicit, but this has changed in recent years, primarily through the growth of a performance management concept called *MBOR*. This concept entails a redoubled attempt to operationalize goals for government and to use these goals more actively both in choosing between alternative actions and in evaluating results. Since the 1980s governmental organizations in many countries have been required to have an annual activity plan with one overriding goal, other more specific goals, specified accountability for achieving goals, mechanisms for reporting results and performance, and a system of rewards and sanctions. For a government ministry this principle entails formulating a set of overriding goals for the activities related to the main goal (education, defence, agriculture, etc.); specifying separate objectives for each division that can be internally directed (administrative) or outwardly directed (professional); and outlining objectives for each administrative unit that are tailored to specific issues under deliberation (e.g. legal issues). Finally, MBOR envisages objectives for making casework more effective and goals for the development of internal expertise and coordination. MBOR is also used by ministries to steer regulatory agencies and other agencies.

MBOR is associated with NPM reforms, but its roots lie back in the 1970s, in attempts at programme budgeting. This system for planning and steering can be a useful tool for public organizations and is seen by many as a clear improvement over more traditional administrative systems. At the same time, it is controversial in many respects. Questions have been asked about whether it is possible to develop and use clear public goals in a world that is increasingly complex and difficult to understand and whether such systems will lead to problems of knowledge and implementation or to an increased use of symbols. Another question is whether such systems are even desirable, for many hold that more traditional systems with general goals give politicians more flexibility to deal with several different concerns simultaneously. Moreover, questions are asked about what the consequences are likely to be of an increased emphasis on concrete action and operationalization, for there is a tendency to measure what is easy to measure while other more qualitative factors are overlooked or their priority demoted. An example of this is the increased emphasis on quantification through the DRG system (diagnosis-related groups) in Western health enterprises (with its ancillary rewards and sanctions), which is being pushed forward at the expense of qualitative care.

A governance model of MBOR is ideally based on goals formulated by politicians, and these should reflect the needs of the people at large. Politically defined goals should thus be realized through an administrative implementation process, the administration should report on the results achieved and, from this information, a reward and sanction system should be used to rectify behaviour. Such an ideal has not been easy to achieve in practice. Goals politicians set are often developed further down in the administrative apparatus. These are often *activity goals* and result indicators that have a tendency to aggregate into political goals and therefore are more technical than the ideal dictates. Another problematic characteristic of this system is that it increases fragmentation in the public administration, because the formulated goals, rather than being generally applicable, are usually related to sectors, organizations or units and as such represent 'tunnel vision'.

Structural devolution in the public sector in many countries also influences, to a great extent, the formulation and use of public goals, and this reflects a qualitative shift in government policy. In traditional *integrated government systems*, overriding society-related goals and sector-oriented goals were dominant, while more commercially oriented goals played a secondary role. In a *disintegrated* or *fragmented government model* inspired by NPM (which became widespread in many countries during the last decade), broad political goals have been consigned to the background and commercial goals have come to the fore. In many of the structurally devolved state-owned companies, the focus is now largely on narrower economic objectives such as profit, while some of the traditionally important socio-political and sectoral goals are more often seen as special interests and non-commercial considerations, which citizens must pay extra for because it is unlawful to cross-subsidize. An example of this is the transformation of postal services in many Western European countries. Traditionally postal services in cities have been profitable, while those in peripheral areas have not. Profit made in the cities was often used to subsidize sparsely populated areas, and this fulfilled goals of regional development. NPM has changed this system completely. Now all postal services must earn a profit, cross-subsidization between central and peripheral areas is not allowed and unprofitable postal services are defined as non-commercial and therefore cost extra. This illustrates how NPM results in more one-dimensional and economically oriented goals and policies.

When MBOR was introduced it was stated that this sort of management was radically different from *Management by Rules* (laws and ordinances) and that it was important to break with the latter. MBOR was supposed to be future-directed, have a clear means–ends orientation and be focused on consequences, while Management by Rules was seen as rigid and regressive, even though there were also inherent goals in laws and rules. One could say that in practice this distinction has not been all that apparent and that a number of performance indicators for MBOR are not all that different from the traditional rules. We are also now seeing more hybrid combinations, often characterized as 'Objective-Oriented Management by Rules' or 'Rule-Oriented Management by Objectives'.

VALUES IN PUBLIC ORGANIZATIONS

At the root of public goals lies a complex set of public values and norms for what are thought to be desirable and acceptable attitudes and actions in government and public life. These values can be a result of natural developmental processes and long historical-institutional traditions and can be understood from a cultural perspective. As mentioned in Chapter Three, from this perspective Johan P. Olsen calls the state a 'moral community', for its values provide a normative-moral framework for collective action. Yet values can also be implicit and arise through decisions about laws and rules, goals and formal structures, regardless of whether these are established through hierarchical steering or through bargaining. Modern reforms entailing structural devolution and increased competition are underpinned by implicit values about efficiency and individual choice.

We readily assume that some main categories exist for values in governmental activity. First, in their goals public administration systems should reflect a *principle of majority rule* based on the electoral or parliamentary chain of governance, but they should also attend to the diverse concerns of minorities. Thus public goals must necessarily reflect a wide spectrum of different interests and groups in society. The principle of goals being representative can partly be understood from a pluralistic angle in an instrumental perspective, but also from a cultural vantage point. Social and cultural pluralism should be reflected in pluralism in the public administration. It is not easy to formulate such goals, because society is complex and constantly changing, and one needs to achieve a balance between majorities and possibly permanent minorities. Thus, increasingly, the people's representatives have an *uncertain mandate*, rather than just a mandate of the sort that is *bounded* (to follow public opinion or party programmes) or *independent* (in the sense of administrators sometimes having a prerogative to use their ability to make their own judgements, in the spirit of trusteeship).

Another important component of the principle of majority rule is that the people's elected representatives – the politicians – not only steer according to the will of the people through a hierarchically ordered administrative apparatus but must also influence and cultivate public opinion and preferences. This means that governmental goals should reflect representativeness as well as the will to engage in hierarchical steering, regulation and control. Hence governmental goals can simultaneously reflect

91

and deviate from the will of the people, with regard to anything from tax relief or punishment for drug-related crimes to attitudes about genetically modified food. Political leaders therefore have an independent responsibility to influence and educate people and hence to influence values, rather than merely passively reflecting them.

A further aspect related to majority rule is that public organizations should be marked by a certain *effectiveness of political steering*. They must have the ability to gather information, deal with casework, make decisions and implement them effectively. If they do not, the political leadership will incur problems of legitimacy. These types of value primarily line up with an instrumental perspective but they may also be imbued with symbolic aspects. In NPM efficiency-related goals have a prominent position, whether this means effective decision-making as a form of technical efficiency or cost-related efficiency and the improved use of resources. There will always be a certain complexity about values because there are also values related to participating in the decision-making processes of democracy, regardless of whether it is wide or specialized participation.

Second, public goals must reflect the values inherent in the *principle of affected parties*. Particularly affected stakeholders, for example special interest organizations, should be included in decision-making processes in the public sector. Government representatives must be sensitive to signals from society, but they must also be able to influence the whole range of societal goals and interests. The principle of affected parties is primarily related to a negotiation-based version of an instrumental perspective (a system of dialogue and exchange), but it is also connected to a cultural perspective, for it reflects the fact that the government can be selective in its objectives in various policy areas. This gives increased attention and advantages to certain stakeholders, but it also increases the possibilities for their governmental regulation and control. It is not always readily apparent who the affected parties are, particularly in complex policy areas. Therefore a political process takes place in which some stakeholders are engaged in dialogue while others are excluded, according to what the government's goals and values are. Powerful special interest organizations or lobbies will attempt not only to be regular participants in governmental decision-making processes, and thus to enjoy exclusive participation rights, but will also try to get their special problems and interests taken account of in joint solutions in various areas of public policy. Organized groups therefore want public goals to be directed towards them specifically, but they also want broad goals that generalize their interests. Even so, the principle of affected parties should not be practised on too wide a scale, otherwise groups with strong resources will enjoy special advantages, which would run counter to the government's responsibility to take into account groups with weaker resources.

Third, values related to *professional knowledge-based steering* are reflected in public goals. It is vitally important that public decisions and activities are underpinned by a strong professional knowledge base. It is difficult for politicians to have the necessary specialized knowledge in all the various policy areas, so they need to be able to rely on the professional expertise of the public administration. Therefore governmental goals will also often reflect the values and evidence-based knowledge of professional groups, and this can be understood from a cultural as well as an instrumental perspective. On the one hand, professional groups will have a number of normative premises and values that have been inculcated over a long period of time; on the other hand, they will also have many concrete, means–ends-oriented fact-premises. Such premises are, according to Herbert Simon, typical for low-level civil servants in public administration, whereas value-premises are more prominent in leadership role-enactment, where more general goals related to principles are important.

A fourth type of values in government are those related to *rule of law, rights* and *politically autonomous areas*. These can be termed *fundamental rights* and may be understood from a cultural perspective. This may mean that the most basic and collective rights are expressed in governmental goals, but there are also rights for special groups, often minorities. These include such things as freedom of speech, freedom of the press, the right of peaceful assembly and fundamental guaranties of due process and human rights. It is also important to have openness and transparency in public administration, and this is ensured through laws and statutes securing the right of public access to government information. A core catalogue of rights will be common to many countries, but there are also great variations. For example, some countries guarantee everyone's right to education, social services and health care, while other countries, such as the United States, instead emphasize a number of individual rights in their public goals. The concept of politically *autonomous areas* implies that some areas of society and some aspects of people's lives are not directly subject to governmental control, and this can be a precondition for citizens' endorsement of governmental control in other areas. Through goals and institutions, governmental authorities are not only the *foremost guarantors* for such autonomous areas but also a *potential threat* to them. This is exemplified in the American debate on terrorism after 11 September 2001 or in the debate over homosexual marriage rights.

Related to this fourth principle, mention should also be made of *voices of the past and present,* for these voices are core aspects of what Johan P. Olsen calls 'the institutional state', as seen through a cultural perspective. Such values explicitly emphasize that historical and institutional traditions should be expressed in present and future considerations and goals. One will always be able to claim that the past is over-represented in the present, through existing formal and informal norms. Nowadays, there is always pressure to break with, tone down or redefine the past, as modern reforms illustrate. Typical values of this kind concern areas such as senior citizen policy, social welfare and social security policy, that is, values that explicitly respect stability, predictability and tradition – things previous generations have built up. In short, this principle relates to culturally oriented values with appurtenant goals, as revealed in debates on pension reforms in some countries.

An additional aspect of this is that the present generation must think about future generations and avoid making irreversible decisions that tie up or undermine resources future generations will need. This discussion is particularly relevant for goals relating to oil and gas extraction and diverse energy and environmental protection issues, where various *self-imposed restrictions* are being placed on the use of resources now.

Olsen points out that, based on the principle of fundamental rights, institutional features are often expressed in the setting up and growth of independent public organizations designed to take care of concerns related to culturally oriented values. More structurally devolved advisory boards are examples of this. They include ombudsman-like institutions for children and consumers, or for dealing with administrative malpractice, and are designed to keep politicians at a distance. Nowadays, democratically based objections sometimes arise over allowing such considerations to be too independently organized.

A number of values in public organizations are more specific than the general values discussed here, but they will reflect the general values in a number of ways. They may be specific policy areas, either for a sector or for specific organizational units, time periods or situations. They may be values pertaining to *procedures,* courses of action and aspects of casework, governing how, by whom and in what way cases should be dealt with, and emphasizing predictability, equal treatment and impartiality. Specific values may also be *substantial values,* where concrete goals are specified and must be achieved within a specific time period. In modern terminology these could also be called effect-oriented performance goals, for example goals for how many cases a public organization should process, or for the amount of time each case is supposed to take, but also goals related to improving the quality of water or air, recruiting more science teachers or putting more unemployed people in jobs.

EFFECTS OF GOALS AND VALUES IN PUBLIC ADMINISTRATION

An instrumental perspective regards goals and underlying values as highly significant for controlling actions and anticipates that effects and results will closely reflect goals and values. Attempts haves been made to make this mindset more widespread in public organizations, through MBOR and through the introduction of per-formance indicators. A central element in this mindset is that governmental goals and their accompanying values should be clear and consistent. But there may be internal as well as external resistance to goals and values, and the conditions for putting them into practice may change over time. This can lead to goals and values being displaced. Also central to such a mindset is that a tight connection must exist between clear values and goals on the one hand, and (re)organization of the public administration on the other; in short, formal structures must reflect changes in goals and values.

Attempts to steer according to goals in a complex world often run into knowledge-related problems. The goals may turn out to be too vague, inconsistent and complex, and thus be difficult to fulfil. As such they may not provide a good enough framework for the various actors. As critics of NPM often point out, goals cannot provide clear guidelines for how to organize public administration and it can be difficult to quantify and measure results in relation to them. An overstated example of scepticism about performance management would be to ask rhetorically how one should formulate clear goals for peace in the Middle East, and then to try to measure whether the goals have been met. Sometimes an organization may have a mixture of general and specific goals without these necessarily having any explicit connection with one another.

A cultural perspective would focus on the internal social effects of informal goals and would be sceptical about the instrumental effects of formal goals. In this view, the maintenance of social networks, learning and self-realization will be more important values than achieving formal goals. Informal goals and values can in principle hinder as well as promote the achievement of formal goals, but few studies have delved deeply into the effects of informal goals on formal decisions.

A myth perspective emphasizes that formulated goals are primarily symbolic in character and are not meant to be instrumentally effective. Goals will be part of a symbolic meta-structure and used to bolster legitimacy, while the underlying structure, be it formal or informal, will steer actual decision-making behaviour. Such symbolic goals can work together with formal and informal goals and either hinder or enhance the effectiveness of these. Various actors may aim to operationalize goals, either because they deliberately want to use them instrumentally, or because they do not recognize the duplicitous nature of the goals and believe them to be directed towards concrete actions.

CHAPTER SUMMARY

- Viewed from an instrumental perspective goals are intentional and formal; cultural and myth perspectives see them as informal and symbolic features.
- In an instrumental perspective goals are defined by top-down decisions or negotiations; in a cultural perspective they develop gradually.
- Goals and values are often complex and ambiguous in public organizations, but modern reforms such as NPM try to make them clearer and more instrumental.

DISCUSSION QUESTIONS

1   Define and give example of some of the following distinctions: formal/informal goals, official/operational goals, complex/simple goals, long-term/short-term goals, individual/organizational goals.

2   Discuss what is typical for goals and values in a public organization you know.
3   Discuss some of the advantages and disadvantages of using MBOR in a public organization.

REFERENCES AND FURTHER READING

Aberbach, J.D. and Christensen, T. (2003) 'Translating Theoretical Ideas into Modern State Reforms: Economic-inspired Reforms and Competing Models of Governance', *Administration & Society*, 35 (5): 491–509.

Allison, G.T. (1971; 2nd edn 1999) *Essence of Decision*, Boston: Little, Brown; 2nd edn (with P. Zelikow) New York: Addison Wesley Longman.

Bouckaert, G. and Halligan, J. (2006) 'Performance and Performance Management', in B.G. Peters and J. Pierre (eds) *Handbook of Public Policy*, London: Sage.

Cyert, R.M. and March, J.G. (1963; 2nd edn 1992), *A Behavioral Theory of the Firm*, Englewood Cliffs: Prentice-Hall; 2nd edn Oxford: Blackwell.

Etzioni, A. (1964) *Modern Organizations*, Englewood Cliffs: Prentice-Hall.

Lægreid, P., Roness, P.G. and Rubecksen, K. (2006) 'Performance Management in Practice: The Norwegian Way', *Financial Accountability and Management*, 22 (3): 251–70.

Lipsky, M. (1980) *Street-level Bureaucracy*, New York: Russel Sage Foundation.

Michels, R. (1915; new edn 1999) *Political Parties: A Sociological Study of Oligarchic Tendencies of Modern Democracy*, Glencoe: Free Press; new edn, Somerset: Transaction.

Olsen, J.P. (1988) 'Administrative Reform and Theories of Organization', in C. Campbell and B.G. Peters (eds) *Organizing Governance: Governing Organizations*, Pittsburgh: University of Pittsburgh Press.

Perrow, C. (1972; 3rd edn 1986) *Complex Organizations: A Critical Essay*, Glenview: Scott, Foresman; 3rd edn New York: Random House.

Scott, W.R. (1981, 6th edn 2007) *Organizations: Rational, Natural and Open Systems*, Englewood Cliffs: Prentice-Hall; 6th edn (with G.F. Davies) Upper Saddle River: Prentice-Hall.

Selznick, P. (1957, reissued 1984) *Leadership in Administration*, New York: Harper & Row; reissued Berkeley: University of California Press.

Silverman, D. (1970) *The Theory of Organizations: A Sociological Framework*, London: Heinemann.

Simon, H.A. (1947; 4th edn 1997) *Administrative Behavior*, New York: Macmillan; 4th edn, New York: Simon & Schuster.

Veblen, T. (1904; reissued 1994) *The Theory of Business Enterprise*, New York: Scribner's; reissued London: Routledge.

Chapter 6

Leadership and steering

LEARNING OBJECTIVES

By the end of this chapter you should:

■ have a clear understanding of the different ways the instrumental, cultural and myth perspectives define leadership and steering;

■ have an insight into different types of political and administrative leadership roles in public organizations;

■ have an understanding of leadership functions, leadership on different levels, leadership and responsibility, leadership styles and traits, and leadership and context.

MEANING OF LEADERSHIP AND STEERING

As mentioned in Chapters One and Two, *steering* can denote a leadership's attempts to make collective decisions and to influence behaviour through a set or system of formal steering and control instruments. According to an instrumental and formal definition, *leadership* means to plan, decide, coordinate and control according to a set of formal goals and a range of operations leaders want to realize. In public organizations, this means that the people, through democratic elections, give political and administrative leaders a mandate to steer according to a set of formal statutes, laws, rules and forms of organization. The Swedish political scientist Lennart Lundquist states that leadership has not been a central issue in political science and that there has been little linkage between research on democracy and studies of leadership. We will therefore attempt to examine these links in this chapter.

Diverse perceptions of leadership are deployed in the various fields and in the literature of management, although the more *cultural perception* seems to dominate. A cultural way of defining leadership is to say, as Philip Selznick does, that it is akin to 'statesmanship'. This presupposes leeway or discretion within a formal framework for various institutionally based and informal processes to play out. In this view, *leading* is associated with interpersonal relations and processes – how people are treated within formal systems. Based upon the distinction between steering and leadership presented above, one could say that modern developments in private and public organizations have brought about a certain shift in emphasis, from steering to leadership, from steering *of* to steering *in*. In other words, hierarchically based, formal leadership is being rejected in favour of decentralized leadership with a certain degree of freedom and stronger participation from organizational members.

In our initial definition leadership more or less merges with steering. Different leadership theories combine and balance a whole series of elements in different ways. Thus, leadership can be based on formal positions and steering tools, including how various leadership roles are defined and how they work in practice. It can also be related to the consequences of leading. Last, but not least, it can, as is often the case in management studies, be defined in terms of leadership qualities or styles and according to context – that is, how different situations are linked with different types of leaders.

Bearing all this mind, the notion that informs this chapter is that of leadership as *organizational behaviour*. Enclosed within a framework, leaders use the formal structure that surrounds them, but they are also influenced by the cultural-institutional context they have been moulded into, with its ancillary informal values and norms. This view combines *steering of* – instrumentally steering an organization – with *steering in* – management and professional leadership in which interpersonal aspects are critical. Steering is a more centralized, directive-related influence enacted indirectly through formal structures, procedures and routines, while leadership is more decentralized, direct and dialogue-based.

The structural and cultural contexts in which leaders operate provide channels for action, but also guidelines and limitations. This is demonstrated later in the chapter, using as an example the roles played by cabinet ministers, where the complexities of ministerial leadership are revealed, not only through different structural guidelines, but also through the fundamental cultural traditions and values cabinet ministers must take into consideration.

Leadership and steering can also be understood from a myth perspective. We will therefore also discuss their symbolic aspects. Steering subordinate levels, institutions and civil servants presupposes the acceptance of public leaders' authority, and symbolic factors can play a supporting role here. Myths and symbols have an even greater role to play in leadership from a cultural perspective, for leadership in the cultural sense does not make much use of formal steering instruments.

In the following pages we will present leadership and steering according to the three main perspectives and, in so doing, will show how combinations of the three can provide insight into the dynamics surrounding these phenomena. Our main intention is to illustrate the usefulness of the different perspectives on leadership and steering using a series of examples from public organizations. Less emphasis will be placed on reviewing the traditional concepts associated with leading, leadership styles and leadership traits or qualities. The reason for this is that the literature is marked by multiple and rather unclear analytical approaches and by highly divergent empirical studies, all of which diminish the usefulness of such studies for public administration.

MORE STEERING THAN LEADERSHIP – AN INSTRUMENTAL PERSPECTIVE

From an instrumental perspective, steering means making collective decisions and putting them into effect. This happens in public organizations when political and administrative leaders and their subordinates act within determinate formal frameworks that channel thinking and action. Public administration is structured so that leaders have the strongest formal means for steering as well as responsibility for coordinating organizational units and members with specialized roles and functions. Leaders are also able to strengthen their own position and to increase the possibilities for policy implementation by changing the formal framework, that is, reorganization. Leaders can steer 'in advance' in the sense that they can exert influence by regulating behaviour through a formal framework, but they can also steer 'retrospectively' through various formally organized mechanisms of control, audit and scrutiny.

From an instrumental perspective, leadership seems largely to conflate with steering. Actors in senior positions perform leadership functions and use formal organizational structures systematically to achieve collective goals. The conditions for such instrumentally oriented leadership are that the leaders have control over subordinate actors, based on formal legal conditions, and that the subordinates accept these, but also that the leaders are able to engage in clear organizational thinking. The ideal is for leaders to have clear goals and insight into diverse means and potential effects, including the ability to learn from experience, but also the ability and means to get subordinate actors to realize goals. This entails focusing primarily on the formal aspects of organizational members' roles, and presupposes that these aspects dominate their actual behaviour. To lead thus involves the exploitation of hierarchical ways and means.

As we mentioned earlier and shall address more fully in Chapter Nine, one can imagine various ways of combining an instrumental and a cultural perspective in order to understand steering and leadership. From an instrumental perspective, one could say that political and administrative leaders attempt to design or shape an organizational culture that will support formal, hierarchical steering. This is to view culture as something one *has* and which one can manipulate, rather than as something that *is* – something which grows according to natural developmental processes (an important point for the cultural perspective, see Chapter Three).

MORE LEADERSHIP THAN STEERING – A CULTURAL PERSPECTIVE

In his comprehensive book on leadership in public and private organizations, the Norwegian organization theorist Haldor Byrkjeflot discusses whether there has been a development from steering to leadership over time, both in terms of language and in the daily activities of organizations. He indicates that leading can be seen as an *alternative form of coordination* in relation to traditional steering. Byrkjeflot emphasizes six tendencies as possible reasons for leadership gaining in importance. The first tendency is that trade and industry have become more exposed to competition and more oriented towards global markets. This has undermined the significance of traditional hierarchical forms of work and aided the growth of more active 'leadership on different levels'– increasingly using more flexible forms of organization and harnessing the competence of public servants and clients. Also worth noting is that the tendency for public organizations to imitate private organizations may have contributed to this. This is reflected in the second tendency, that of increasing decentralization and structural devolution in the public sector, which ties in with the transition from hierarchical steering to leadership and performance management systems. Some have claimed that this leads to a *withering of political and administrative authority* for, instead of instructing and controlling, public leaders must now spend more energy supporting, stimulating and motivating units and actors at lower levels.

The third tendency can be called *de-hierarchization* and *value pluralism*. People are more critical of leaders than before and do not accept their authority as easily, a phenomenon which may reflect an increased level of education. Instead, people evaluate leaders according to the attitudes and values they stand for, and whether or not they can enlist solidarity and confirm identities, rather than for what they actually do or for their steering function. The fourth tendency is an increasing critique of mechanical and technocratic steering ideals, while the idea of *indirect normative steering* is becoming stronger. A fifth tendency is a changed understanding of the concept of democracy, in the direction of more participation by citizens and more typical *communicative leadership* or *deliberative features,* in which public arenas are created for debate and the exchange of ideas. Connected to this is a greater emphasis on non-material values and value-multiplicity. The sixth and final tendency is the growth and stronger institutionalization of *a distinct field of leadership competence,* such as one sees in public and private organizations of higher education, in the public and private sectors more generally and in the increased significance of consulting firms, etc.

These tendencies point to leadership from a cultural-institutional perspective, along the lines of Selznick's statesmanship mentioned above. Leading is viewed as more important than instrumental steering, indeed, as something that limits steering. As mentioned, Selznick associates leadership with value-leadership, with being visionary – that is, defending, promoting and communicating traditional values and norms; fleshing out institutionally determined values and norms; helping integrate organizational members through socialization and training; and helping to resolve conflicts and facilitate participation. In this view actors in formal positions need not always be the ones who exercise leadership, though they often do. Leaders should maintain and promote specific historical traditions and informal norms and values through a gradual process of adaptation, whereby internal and external circumstances and pressures contribute to the process of institutionalization. The aim of leadership is not primarily instrumental; rather, it is directed towards non-instrumental conditions that aid social integration and socialization based on historical traditions and community, survival, learning and personal development. Leading, therefore, becomes primarily *informal interaction with people* within the framework of a formal organization. It is easy for tensions between steering and leadership to arise: between, on the one hand, formal goals and attempts to discipline and control organizational members, and, on the other hand, social interaction and developing a social community within the organization. Yet steering and leadership can also overlap, such as when leadership supports steering due to an overlap of norms and values, or because formal structures parallel informal structures.

SYMBOLIC ASPECTS OF LEADERSHIP AND STEERING

From a myth perspective, leadership can be interpreted in at least two ways. It can be passive – a consequence of natural processes where events in the environment are decisive and leave little room for exercising instrumental and cultural leadership. 'To lead' would then mean to accept and put into effect the myths and fashions pressed upon one's organization by external forces. It would also mean continuously coping with new myths coming from the environment. All in all, rather turbulent conditions for action.

Alternatively, a myth perspective might construe leadership as something more active. According to Nils Brunsson, leaders can use various strategies to try to separate myths and actions. This separation can be enhanced by allowing leaders deliberately to help import, implement and spread myths in organizations. Although myths can be disseminated via natural processes, more emphasis is usually placed on the instrumental aspects of leading. This means that public leaders will be conditioned by myths and cultural constraints or contexts, and consequently their choices of instrumental action limited.

If public leaders deliberately use myths and symbols, these may have an educative function for public employees as well as for the population at large. Leaders may emphasize visions and ideas symbolically in ways that inspire internally, while still providing direction and profile outwardly. The myths and symbols can be interpreted as a theory of action by those whose job it is to act, rather than as precise enunciations of action per se. As a result leaders may strengthen their legitimacy because they are seen as dynamic, rational and effective, while other actors may experience the myths and symbols as general guidelines for action.

TYPES OF POLITICAL AND ADMINISTRATIVE LEADERSHIP

In his analysis of governmental modes of operation, Johan P. Olsen's point of departure is that political leaders are 'organizational people' and that they use and are framed by formal structures, yet he also highlights the significance of institutional and other factors for steering and leadership. To lead, therefore, is understood as getting large organizations to function. Olsen describes leaders according to two dimensions: first, whether the political leader's actions have consequences for the way society develops; second, whether the leader is bound or restricted by non-leaders or other conditions. 'The leader as an agent' belongs to the first type. This is a leader who exercises great influence, but who is also bound. Such political leadership reflects the electoral or parliamentary chain of governance, that is, the leader receives authority from the people and those who are politically elected, but must also be sensitive to their views. Thus the leader is restricted by democratically elected assemblies, interest groups, the mass media, international circumstances, etc., but simultaneously has an organizational apparatus at his or her disposal, which renders great influence and power. This type of leadership combines structural and cultural features.

'The leader as a hero' is the second type. Exercising great power and influence while having few constraints is typical of an instrumental leader. He or she is powerful and able to form public institutions and societies from his or her own ideas. This kind of leader also has a solid educative effect on citizens and strong charismatic abilities and has achieved statesmanship through a long process of learning and development. Cultural and symbolic elements are combined in such leadership, and it is easy to overlook the political-organizational context within which such a leader acts – namely, the need for popular endorsement and to make compromises.

'The leader as an opportunist' will, to a large degree, be bound by other actors and circumstances and not exercise much influence themself. He or she may be a populist who is responsive and sensitive but who changes policies according to swings in popular opinion and who lacks an independent standpoint or does not use public administration in an independent or potent way. The last category is 'the leader as an anti-hero', a 'Don Quixote' who neither has influence nor is influenced to any significant degree. This may be a political leader who is swept along by powerful historical forces, unable either to seize hold of or significantly influence them.

Byrkjeflot divides leadership into six ideal types. The first type according to Weber is 'traditional leadership', where the leader is appointed from above, by a king or queen or by God. Because such a leader's authority is built on long traditions, citizens respect it and endeavour to cultivate good relations with him or her. One could call this culturally based *patrimonial leadership*. The second category is 'bureaucratic leadership', which is based on laws and rules; the leader shows solidarity with collective interests and with the formal organizational framework and the office he or she is appointed to. Career development is determined by formal criteria of seniority and competence. This is also a typical Weberian model of leadership. The third type is 'layman's leadership', reflecting a leader who is the people's representative and the first among equals. The person in question is expected to behave in a popular, crowd-pleasing way and to look after local interests. This type seems to combine features from an instrumental perspective and a cultural perspective.

'Knowledge-based leadership' emphasizes evidence-based decision-making and in-depth learning in a specific field of study and loyalty to the expertise of that field. In relation to public organizations, this will be a skilled or expert leader who fulfils instrumental aspects of layman's leadership and bureaucratic leadership, but who may also be defined along more cultural lines. 'Negotiation-based leadership' emphasizes that a leader has strategic abilities in the sense of asserting and promoting a certain group's interests. These can be critical for a heterogeneous political-administrative system, but also in relation to actors in the environment such as special interest organizations. Olsen captures this phenomenon with the concept of the 'corporatist-pluralist state model'.

The last type of leadership, which most genuinely captures the transition from steering to leadership, is 'professional leadership'. This emphasizes generic leadership and leadership expertise. The leader is highly educated, has a lot of experience, attends to the organization's interests in a professional manner, and is able to stimulate action and enlist solidarity by communicating the organization's purpose internally as well as externally. In the heydays of NPM there was a greater emphasis on professional leadership, while bureaucratic and knowledge-based leadership was abating. This trend seems to have changed in the post-NPM era and the ability to communicate with organizational members is emphasized more than before.

LEADERSHIP FUNCTIONS AND ROLES

A leader's roles and tasks are many and diverse, and their descriptions vary throughout the professional literature. Moreover, the view of leadership functions varies according to which of the three main perspectives we use. There are numerous ways of classifying these functions. One of the oft-used categorizations was coined by Luther Gulick while studying the American federal administration in the 1930s. Gulick's categorization, called POSDCORB (an acronym derived from the first letters of each function), primarily ties the functions to instrumental aspects: planning, organizing, staffing, directing, coordinating, reporting and budgeting. One could perhaps augment this list with initiating, deciding, evaluating, controlling, giving feedback and accounting. Leaders also have responsibility for various aspects of the personnel function – everything from recruiting and training to what happens when employees quit an organization. Leaders should ensure that all these functions are carried out, regardless of whether they do it themselves or not. The American organization theorist and business executive Chester Barnard has outlined a theory about the complex and dynamic relationships between formal and informal factors in organizations and the importance of communication in informal systems. He points to the fact that leaders often have to develop incentives to prevent or modify dysfunctional behaviour by organizational members.

Political and administrative leaders have complex functions and tasks. Cabinet ministers in many countries are often leaders of political parties, but they are also members of a governmental collegium – a cabinet – and take on the functions this entails. In this latter role they must focus on the community as a whole. Third, they are leaders of a ministry and a sector. This necessitates making decisions and sending signals to the administration, helping to steer the ministry and its subordinate agencies and companies but also being responsive to the environment, which includes international actors, the legislature, special interest organizations, the mass media, etc. Parliamentary representatives must represent a constituency, a political party and the policy area they are linked to through membership in a standing committee. Administrative leaders, such as secretary-generals and director-generals, have an important advisory function to perform for cabinet ministers and other political leaders. They must head up the organizing and steering of the ministry and its underlying units but also help implement statutory laws and policies in the environment.

It is difficult to clearly distinguish what is typical for culturally conditioned leadership functions, other than that they are to a greater extent non-instrumental. One way of approaching this is to state that culturally oriented leaders help preserve the historical traditions and informal norms and values tied to formal and instru-mental functions. Such leaders should have an institutional memory of how their organization has planned, organized, made decisions, controlled and recruited previously. This can help modify the present practice of exercising these functions, but it can also promote understanding and acceptance of them on the part of organizational members and the community at large. Another way of viewing institutional leadership functions is to emphasize that they are explicitly oriented towards non-instrumental aspects; to lead means helping to integrate new organ-izational members in the organization, maintaining the informal foundation of norms, nurturing socialization in order to develop the social community, and strengthening competence and personal development. Many governments will emphasize a social framework around cabinet meetings in order to develop a sense of community. A ministry's administrative leaders may set up a programme or initiative with a cultural character in order to change informal values, or they may emphasize the informal aspects of formal initiatives, such as training and development dialogues.

Symbolically oriented leadership functions can also be understood in different ways. On the one hand, all the individual functions mentioned can have symbolic aspects, and leaders are in a position to manipulate these. They may be symbols that present plans as well considered, steering and control as strong, evaluation as thorough, or cultural initiatives as edifying. On the other hand, the complexity of many functions, or ambiguity over what the functions are, may compel leaders to use symbols, even to do so deliberately. These can be symbols directed internally towards organizational members, in order to 'rally the troops' and to strengthen morale or symbols, not necessarily the same ones, directed outwards and geared towards giving an organization a particular profile in relation to its environment. A government can, for example, emphasize internally a united stance vis-à-vis parts of the environment, such as the parliament or mass media, particularly in times of crisis. Meanwhile, outwardly that government will emphasize openness or partnership with these same parts of the environment.

One question organization theorists are concerned with is how leaders actually use their time to carry out various functions. Empirical studies of leaders have revealed that their weekday is exceedingly fragmented and they dash from task to task in a superficial way. This is surely typical, particularly in large, complex organizations, regardless of whether they are private or public, but there is reason to believe that it varies greatly, depending on the type of organization, task composition and internal and external pressures, etc. Studies of governmental organization and function in general, and of cabinets in particular, show that different cabinet ministers in fact emphasize different functions, even though there is a core of common functions they must fulfil.

This leads to the theme of *leadership roles*. Generally speaking, leadership roles are linked with a hierarchically superior and systematically formal, informal or symbolic responsibility, or aspect. Formal public leaders are placed in a hierarchy and have, for instance, senior responsibility for organizing decision-making processes, coordinating initiatives, or implementing resolutions and policies. Institutional or culturally oriented leaders will systematically focus on integrative roles, while symbolically oriented leadership roles are linked with using symbols and myths. One can also assess roles for how they are expressed through the many different functions. Numerous studies have attempted to categorize these roles in different ways. Administrative studies, for instance, often emphasize whether or not a leader is a typical administrator, mediator, integrator or one who emphasizes information, and whether he or she makes decisions or leads the production of services. Studies of local communities and public organizations, often inspired by various fields of social science, readily stress that a mayor or local business leader can be an important entrepreneur and network builder.

LEADERSHIP AND LEVELS

On the basis of research by James D. Thompson, we can draw distinctions between leadership on different levels. We can call the top level the *institutional leadership level* – senior public, political and administrative roles. On this level the functions and obligations are greatest and most complex. They can be formal, informal or symbolic. The challenges are great, but so are the opportunities for contributing to the organization and influencing the environment. Leaders at the institutional level must cope with a whole range of formal demands and constraints, often inconsistent frameworks that cause problems of attention and capacity, in spite of great opportunities for steering and influence. Moreover, when we consider that formal obligations work in concert with cultural and symbolic obligations, it is clear that this level of leadership is complex and challenging.

Leadership at the intermediate level is called *administrative*. Leaders at this level mediate the top leadership's formal decisions and help implement them at the lower level, but their role can also be to mediate and adapt informal norms, values and symbols from the institutional level. At the same time, leadership at this level also helps mediate and adapt standpoints, demands, norms and values from the organization's grass-roots level up to the top level. Leadership at the intermediate level faces cross-pressure from above and below. This cross-pressure will, however, differ in composition over time, implying that roles will change: some intermediate leaders will primarily be the top leadership's messengers to lower levels in the organization, while others will defend the grass-roots level vis-à-vis the top leadership.

Lowest in an organization is the *operative level*. According to Thompson's characterization, role-players have little latitude and are programmed in what they do. Derived from the instrumental perspective, this view also presupposes relatively unambiguous roles. On the one hand, it is abundantly clear that formal roles on the operative level are far narrower than at the institutional level. On the other hand, role clarity at the operative level varies in relation to the type of task. Hence, leadership at this level might mean leading a smaller public service unit, and such leaders do not merely concern themselves with formal steering but also engage in cultural integration and the manipulation of symbols.

Large investigative studies of political leaders and bureaucrats in several countries have clearly revealed different conditions for leaders and roles at different levels in public organizations. Administrative top leaders have the greatest access to political leaders, they put the strongest emphasis on political signals in their resolutions, and they perceive themselves as having the fewest rules controlling their behaviour. Top leaders also have the greatest contact with leaders in other ministries, in agencies and subordinate service units, in special interest organizations and internationally. Finally, top leaders are the strongest advocates of modern reforms. Intermediate administrative leaders have better access to political and administrative top leaders than the grass-roots level; they participate most often in ministerial and inter-ministerial task forces and project organizations; and they need to take more into account in their decision-making, for they must balance political signals and professional premises, affected parties and client interests, etc. Caseworkers in central government definitely have the least access upwards to the political and administrative leadership and they place the greatest emphasis on the interests of affected parties and clients. With narrow networks of contact – horizontally, internally and externally – they are subjected to the largest number of rules, and their behaviour is steered into relatively narrow, specialized roles. What is more, these civil servants, particularly those with law degrees, are most sceptical towards modern reforms.

LEADERSHIP AND RESPONSIBILITY

The meaning of leadership and responsibility seems to be in a state of flux, for private and public organizations alike. In public organizations the conditions of power seem to be changing more rapidly than the conditions of responsibility. Within ministries and sectors it has become less clear who should be held responsible: in some cases it is the cabinet minister; in others there is a stronger focus on the ministry's administrative leadership; while in yet other instances the chief executive officers and the boards of state-owned companies are criticized and sometimes have to step down.

Traditionally, leaders are held to have relatively *overarching responsibility*. This has been typical for political leaders holding executive power, and it means they have a widely defined *institutional* or *cultural responsibility*, with a moral flavour, for what goes on in an organization. Such responsibility consists in leaders acting on the basis of *trust* granted to them, and what they do with this trust is the core of a formal system of superior and subordinate ordering. When voters, through elections, delegate popular sovereignty to political leaders, central aspects of this relationship will be built on trusting the politicians to responsibly exercise their delegated authority. This is sometimes referred to as an *independent mandate*. The delegation of power and authority from the parliament to the executive branch will also be based on this type of responsibility. Parliaments and national auditor's offices can, to varying degrees, exercise active control over their government and administration and trust that delegated power and authority will be executed in a correct, responsible way. Furthermore, politicians traditionally delegate internal power and authority to administrative leaders, and so on, down the hierarchical line. They trust public administration to conscientiously execute responsibility without needing close supervision and surveillance. The responsibility central governments assign to municipalities for implementing aspects of public policy can be seen in a similar way.

Another more 'modern', instrumental and administrative understanding of responsibility is more formal and narrow, and may be referred to as *accountability*. Here, anyone who is assigned formal responsibility must also account for it by systematically *reporting* on how that responsibility has been exercised. This is because informally based trust is not sufficient: the relationship between superior and subordinate levels must also entail elements of mistrust and formality. It is assumed that subordinate leaders and actors will try to avoid being controlled by top-level leaders, and thus leaders deploy various control strategies, believing that formal reporting and control will help solve the problem, for example through steering contracts. If necessary, reporting is supplemented with a system whereby good performance and observance of responsibilities are rewarded and their opposites sanctioned. Today this more formal and narrow definition of accountability operates among professional administrators at various levels.

The accountability mentality is perspicuously represented in the NPM wave of reforms and, as a result, relations between parliament and the executive branches in several countries have changed. Parliaments have revitalized their control and scrutiny committees, begun holding open hearings, increased the use of investigative commissions, and introduced spontaneous question and answer sessions, all of which signal more aggressive control of central government. The national auditor's office has been strengthened in many countries, particularly with regard to performance audits of whether executives have implemented the intentions and goals of the legislature in certain policies and programmes. Furthermore, the traditional financial audits are now more formally controlling than before. Both these last features have heightened tensions between various governmental authorities and made control activities more political. Internal reporting to the executive branch is also more formalized and is built more on distrust than was previously the case. Central political and administrative leaders have at their disposal a more extensive formal apparatus of reporting and control, particularly as regards subordinate administrative units. Finally, individual leaders are now more formally controlled, through leader contracts with performance requirements and reporting and evaluation, all partially linked to salary levels.

Studies have revealed several problems with such a system. First, many leaders have problems making the adjustment from more culturally based responsibilities to more formalized responsibilities, and this creates conflicts. Second, there are problems in defining responsibilities, goals and results clearly enough. Often loose formal ties between a political responsibility and an administrative responsibility result in political leaders being blamed, despite the fact that they lack information about cases that have been delegated, and their ability to intervene has been curtailed. Increased autonomy might change power relations more rapidly than responsibility relations, and this creates legitimacy problems for political leaders. In other words, they tend to become responsible for things they have little control over. But there is also an increasing tendency for administrative and commercial government leaders to step down as a result of conflicts with political leaders. In practice, therefore, combining enhanced autonomy with increased control is difficult.

There are also problems with the *pulverization of responsibility*, that is, there are many different actors involved in processes at lower levels, which makes it difficult to assign responsibility. A new formalized control system, intended to clarify responsibility, seems, in practice, to have created a larger control apparatus and increased conflicts and ambiguities over the responsibilities of leaders. The problems of controlling delegated responsibilities are also linked with problems of defining clear objectives by which to steer, and from which to report. Finally, it is difficult for intermediate level leaders and others who answer to senior leadership to have an overview of what goes on in autonomous public service units.

LEADERSHIP AND THE PUBLIC

Changes in public-sector organizational forms lead to changes in relations between citizens and public organizations. This has implications for political and administrative leaders alike. Responsibility relations between political leaders and citizens have become more complicated and in some respects more transparent. On the one hand, politicians must be sensitive to citizens' wishes via the electoral or parliamentary chain of governance, even though modern reforms have made this more problematic. On the other hand, citizens as users and clients can, to a greater degree, hold politicians directly accountable for providing services, where the focus is more on results and less on processes. Inasmuch as users have highly diverse interests and needs, and politicians are often rather loosely linked to the service-production level, this creates tensions and conflicts as to where to place responsibility, particularly when problems and crises arise. The traditional role of *citizen* has been supplemented with the *client* role, in which people are dependent on services from public organizations. The role of *user* of services provided by public organizations and the role of *customer* to public organizations is more analogous with the relationship between private producers and the market. The client role may be likened to a system of rights, the user role to a privatized democracy and the customer role to market steering of public services.

The British organization theorist Christopher Pollitt draws some useful distinctions regarding the intensity of interaction or collaboration between public organizations and citizens. This can either be one-way information from public organizations to the public at large or two-way interaction in which the public are consulted and directly involved in decision-making processes. A second relevant set of distinctions concerns the identity of different groups, for example there may be distinctions between actual users, all citizens in an area and those living in the area. The relations between these groups are elucidated in Table 6.1. By going from right to left in the table, one moves from a forum model or deliberative model towards a

Table 6.1 Identities and intensity of interaction

	Intensity of interaction		
	Information	Consultation	Participation
The public's identity			
Community	Public relations	Community planning	Community leadership
Citizens	Information for citizens	Citizen surveys Focus groups	Citizen-centred governance
Users/customers	Consumer relations	User panels User surveys	User-led services

Source: Pollitt (2003)

market model; by going from bottom to top, one moves from an individualistic identity to a more collective identity.

Motives for increased citizen participation are that this will improve the quality of services, strengthen support for policy decisions and increase the legitimacy of public organizations. Many of the arguments for increased participation arise from acknowledging that the classic form of representative democracy, with a vote in general elections held several years apart, is insufficient to ensure attentiveness by politicians towards citizens and good responsibility relations. Yet despite this, public participation is a difficult subject because many political leaders have an ambivalent attitude to it. In principle, everyone is for increased participation, yet, at the same time, a certain disquiet arises over the idea that democratically elected representatives – important links in representative democracies – should delegate some of their power to non-elected, possibly unpredictable and non-representative groups. Furthermore, inasmuch as administrative leaders are often involved in organizing the participation, this creates further challenges for the political leadership, because administrators may potentially undermine political control. The development of modern information and communications technology has increased the potential for further tensions between political and administrative leaders, because technology is a potential weapon in an administrative leader's arsenal. The possibilities for fruitful results from comprehensive reforms that aim to increase citizen participation are greatest when mutual understanding and trust obtain between political and administrative leaders. In political-administrative systems with a low degree of trust, increased participation by citizens can easily create greater problems than it solves.

LEADERSHIP TRAITS AND STYLES

Of the perspectives we have outlined, an instrumental perspective is only minimally open to the possibility that *leader traits* or qualities can be significant for how leaders exercise their roles. It is based on the assumption that the structures surrounding a leader form these traits, or that leaders can use them deliberately as tools, almost irrespective of their own personal traits. Leaders come and go, but the structures and the means of power endure. In principle it is irrelevant which qualities leaders have because formal norms steer behaviour, that is, what is decisive is the organizational framework: which type of organization one is in, which type of position one has and which types of task one carries out. According to this perspective, what counts is not what personal characteristics Bill Clinton, George W. Bush, John Major or Tony Blair have, but which organizational structure they are surrounded by and which tools they have at their disposal.

If one views leaders from a Selznick-inspired cultural perspective, leadership traits become much more relevant, even though this point is not particularly explicit in the theory. For Selznick statesmanship means not only to promote historical norms and values, but also to be able to show, by personal example or in some other way, what the cultural norms and values are and to use them to garner support and aid social integration. Which leadership traits this involves is nevertheless unclear, apart of course from more general traits such as being well versed in administrative history, inspiring trust and exuding credibility, being able to act according to norms, setting a good example and being able to assuage tensions and sort out differences.

A myth perspective would say that leadership traits are not very important, since symbols and myths are often imposed on an organization from the outside and hence are factors one must accept based on a logic of necessity or determinism. But if one gives this theory a more instrumental interpretation, one could say that deliberate manipulation of symbols and myths demands certain qualities, such as *charisma*. In order to gain support for symbols, one must come across as trustworthy and convincing. This is not all that different from the cultural perspective's view of leadership traits.

A large share of the literature on leadership is concerned with *leadership traits* or *qualities*. Such literature has limited relevance for studies of public organizations and is often marked by rather long, somewhat unprioritized lists of sundry traits typical for leaders in private organizations, which are therefore claimed to be good qualities for public leaders too. Many are primarily socio-psychological traits. These publications typically portray leaders as power-seeking individuals, a quality expressed in a person's seeking a leadership position in the first place and the active use of the effectual means such positions provide. Another quality identified is enormous self-confidence. Furthermore, leaders are frequently motivated by achievement and competition – both typically instrumental traits. Leaders are also said to have great cognitive capacity, that is they are highly intelligent and have good professional knowledge, and the ability to deal with complex information. Further traits include good social skills and the ability to be easygoing and self-assured in social settings. Leaders are typically extrovert and good at presenting their thoughts verbally. Most leaders will, of course, rarely embody all of the qualities described. Neither is it clear whether these qualities are compatible – indeed, some of them seem to be contradictory. Finally, the rather heroic terms in which such features are presented is a reason for a certain amount of scepticism.

Just as difficult a question is whether the qualities outlined have any connection with results or success in organizations and, if so, what kind. Many studies demonstrate that it can be difficult to come to any clear conclusion, and for several reasons. One reason may be that there is no sharp distinction between leadership qualities and behaviour. Second, it is much easier to measure success than to agree on what it is. A good result or success for some actors can be a failure for others. Success can be the object of competition between different definitions and symbols. As stated above, it can also be difficult to establish any connection between leadership qualities and results. There may be many factors other than leadership qualities – both internal and in the environment – which can account for good results or specific effects.

The language used to talk about leaders of public organizations is often exceedingly general and vague. It is said, for example, that former UK prime minister Tony Blair or German Chancellor Angela Merkel are successful at elections, or that top-level political leaders are good at pressuring the cabinet on specific issues. Or that particular cabinet ministers have been successful in promoting their government's or party's policies, and this is due in part to these politicians' own qualities. We can find the same argumentation in local politics, where a mayor or leader of a political party is claimed to be successful owing to certain exemplary qualities. Nevertheless, in such situations it is seldom clear how these personal qualities relate to the complexity of certain policy areas or decision-making situations, let alone to all the other conditions and circumstances involved. Often such success is predicated on deftness at handling the media. It is more seldom to see success attributed to administrative leaders in the public sphere, even though this may occasionally occur for top leaders in central government or in municipalities. The lack of attention to success may be explained in cultural terms, namely that these positions are seen as part of a system or collective and are not differentiated to any great degree. The situation is, however, changing, since top positions in public administration are increasingly subject to media attention, public scrutiny and performance indicators, tied either to institutional or individual performance contracts, which heightens the focus on administrative leaders. This serves to highlight which features they have or should have.

A country's general cultural context can also help explain why particular emphasis is placed on leadership traits or qualities related to success. This is particularly typical of a country such as the United States, where individualism is stressed. A series of academic studies of public leaders, both political and administrative, have been done which assume that a leader's success is due to certain personal qualities, and these are often presented in heroic or dramatic terms. Examples are John F. Kennedy, US president in the early 1960s, and J. Edgar Hoover, director of the FBI for thirty-nine years. In more collectivist political systems there is much less focus on individual or heroic features.

The literature on *leadership styles* is less comprehensive than the literature on leadership traits or qualities, but it deals with some of the same types of issues. A basic question is what leadership style actually is. It is often claimed that leadership style has something to do with the *appearance or presentation of leadership*, how leaders appear when carrying out various tasks. The question, then, must be: is our perception conditioned by the expectations we have of leadership roles, or do we see the leaders as they really are? Or is it perhaps a cross between the two? There is no clear answer to this question, but the latter seems most probable. Many studies of leadership styles concentrate on the distinction between instrumental and cultural style. Recently, the instrumental style has come to be regarded as less 'appropriate'. The *instrumental* and *authoritarian leadership style* is said to be more case-oriented and objective, perhaps also more analytically focused, with vertical one-way communication from leaders to followers. The *democratic* and *institutionally oriented leader*, on the other hand, is seen as being more directed towards improving cooperation and social integration, and towards care and support of employees' tasks and functions. Such leadership involves reciprocal and horizontal communication as well as participation by those being led. We find this classic distinction repeated in newer studies on the difference between *instrumental transactional leadership* and *transformational leadership,* where, in the latter, the leader helps to create and administer a social community inside an organization. The literature on leadership styles has, to a lesser degree than the literature on leadership traits and qualities, been concerned with how relevant these styles are for success or results. One reason may be that leadership styles and the actions of leaders are partly overlapping constructs. It has been claimed in some studies that, for example, an authoritarian style is most conducive to effectiveness, and it is often pointed out that different leadership styles are appropriate in different contexts and thus vary according to the conditions for action.

Our somewhat sceptical view of the literature on leadership traits and leadership styles can be summarized using a metaphor of leadership as a light bulb, borrowed from Professor James G. March at Stanford University. According to March, leadership is important in the sense of being the light cast by a bulb, but the individual leader is not all that important, in the same way that an individual light bulb in a room with many light bulbs is not very important. Replacing one bulb with another does not make a big difference but turning the light off does. Leaders are socialized into an organization in relation to the formal framework that surrounds them and are 'coloured' by the organization's culture. Hence leaders faced with similar obligations and constraints are likely to think and act in similar ways.

LEADERSHIP AND CONTEXT

It is often said that leadership is *situationally contingent*. Different situations demand different leadership types or styles. This is a relatively general claim, the interpretations of which are numerous. One interpretation is that leadership is exercised in *different contexts*, and thus will vary in thinking and behaviour. The contexts can also change over time. If we now use our three perspectives as the point of departure, leadership will be exercised within a set of structural, cultural and symbolic givens or constraints, and these will function in different combinations and to different degrees. The conditions for a leader's actions will therefore vary. Some leaders will have a tighter formal framework of clear goals, organizational structures and position-instructions or leader contracts, but be given few cultural or symbolic guidelines. Other leaders will act according to historical traditions, with few formal directives for their behaviour, while others again will exercise symbolically oriented leadership because their tasks and traditions are unclear and the pressure from the environment is great. Perhaps it is most realistic to point out that leaders operate in exceedingly complex contexts and conditions for action, which we described earlier in relation to cabinet ministers. The latter interpretation can also be qualified further by pointing out that the balance between internal and external factors will vary over time and thus render different conditional frameworks for leaders. To make things more complex still, there are also different combinations of leadership traits, characteristics of work situations and tasks both for those in subordinate positions and for leaders, all of which result in variations in how leadership is exercised.

A second interpretation of situation-determined leadership is that it is *temporal* and changes rapidly. This view is derived from the so-called 'garbage-can' model of James G. March and Johan P. Olsen. Attention is a limited resource among leaders. They must often cope with unpredictable fluctuations in decision-making processes and situations. Participants come and go, problems are defined and redefined in rapid succession, and solutions can come before the problems. Hence the possibilities for decision-making are in a state of flux. This is often referred to as *organized anarchy*. In such unpredictable situations, leaders are not primarily trying to steer organizations and processes, but rather trying to adapt themselves to continually mutable situations that demand a large degree of flexibility. According to this model, great ambiguity and rapid change result in leaders often taking recourse in symbols.

Many interpretations focusing on 'garbage-can' processes are barely concerned with leadership styles. To the extent that one can speak of a leadership style, it must be symbolically oriented, flexible and able to grasp the dynamics of fluid decision-making processes. An interpretation of turbulence and crisis often found in the academic literature describes a type of heroic leader who musters special personal qualities in times of need. This phenomenon is found in the biographies of well-known politicians and military leaders. In fact, though, it is quite difficult to systematically categorize these special abilities or traits, and so they tend to be ad hoc explanations.

A third possible interpretation of situation-determined leadership, which borrows elements from the first two, is to link it to *a stability and turbulence continuum*. Some leaders set the agenda while others are mostly reactive. Some leaders' workdays are characterized by great stability, even though they may vary along structural, cultural and symbolic lines. Other leaders will regularly experience turbulence or variability in their conditions for action, be they of an internal or external character. This may cause a leader to adjust his or her profile according to the situation at hand.

From an institutional perspective, there are, for example, analyses of how leaders experience long stable periods – periods of great significance for cultural and historical traditions – suddenly being interrupted by external shocks and crises, after which stability is restored on a new institutional track. The American political scientist John Kingdon develops this reasoning in his book on 'windows of opportunity', where, using the 'garbage-can' model, he points out that a stable institutional development may be disrupted by sudden changes because new solutions sew new problems, external pressure is great and some actors will assert the will to change. This opens a window of opportunity in which change occurs rapidly before the window abruptly closes again. The significance of this reasoning is accentuated in studies of the radical public reforms in New Zealand at the beginning of the 1980s. New Zealand used to be a social democratic welfare state with a relatively large public sector, but a combination of factors – including leadership with a long-standing aversion to change, deep economic crisis and ready-made economic reform programmes offered by prominent economists – made it possible for the finance minister, Roger Douglas, to rapidly push through radical public reforms, in spite of cultural resistance.

LEADERSHIP AND STEERING IN PUBLIC ORGANIZATIONS

Leadership in public organizations is marked by a large degree of complexity and change. Public leaders must cope with many diverse issues while working within a multi-structured and complex apparatus. They must take into consideration well-established cultural traditions that are nevertheless in a state of flux as well as constant yet changing pressures from the environment. The challenges in new administrative policies are therefore legion. In order to illustrate public leaders' roles and conditions for action in a modern government, we shall examine more closely some key results from studies of government cabinets in such countries as Australia, Norway, Sweden and the United Kingdom, and also comparative studies covering several countries.

Let us take cabinet ministers as our point of departure. Their work is constrained by a constitutional or structural framework, which includes relations with parliament, important laws and rules, case-treatment procedures for compiling and presenting governmental records, and guidelines for how to conduct negotiations formally and correctly, etc. The office of the executive political leader – the president or prime minister – often plays an important role in coordinating the formal aspects of decision-making processes and assures the quality of juridical aspects. Yet the cabinet's work is also guided by long cultural traditions, which also allow for the possibility of change, for where formal aspects allow latitude for action, cultural aspects will be brought to bear. Moreover, a cabinet is a social community where specific social norms and values develop, although these need not be consistent. The work of the cabinet also needs a social framework, which nowadays takes the form of diverse social gatherings surrounding newly formed cabinets which are important for the mode of operation. Symbolic aspects are also manifest in cabinet ministers' work. Cabinet members are in a unique position to play upon symbols of national unity in situations of crisis, to use them in garnering support for government policies, for supporting national groups or for enlisting solidarity with countries and suffering groups throughout the world. Furthermore, it is important for a cabinet to create a common image, for instance regarding its attitude to reform. Margaret Thatcher used the term 'Next Steps' as the catchphrase for comprehensive agency reforms, while Tony Blair talked more about 'joined-up government' and the 'third way'.

Moreover, pressure from the environment upon a cabinet is great. In minority governments, pressure from the parliament is intense and often unpredictable, while majority governments can avoid it to some extent. It is also crucial to cultivate relations with special interest organizations and lobbies. In light of the mass media's increased role, cabinet members have to spend more time communicating with the media and planning their strategy towards it, but their agendas and attention are also continually disrupted and changed. Further, cabinet ministers have to deal with many unexpected situations and crises, large and small. This requires the power to act, clear-mindedness and attention. Not least, they have to cope with the international environment – for example dealing with the tensions involved in being a member of NATO, international involvement in Afghanistan or Iraq, the situation in the Middle East or facilitating political negotiations in international hotspots such as Sudan, Guatemala or Sri Lanka. Through membership of the European Union, many governments have had to adapt themselves to new European laws and rules. Or, in a more international context, governments throughout the world face reform pressures from the OECD, the World Bank, the IMF and the WTO. This, combined with pressure for concrete adaptation and change, makes political leadership particularly fraught.

What form does leadership take in cabinets facing such complex conditions? On the one hand, there are clear similarities between the exercise of leadership in different governments, largely due to common and, to some extent, stable structures and cultural frameworks. On the other hand, there are clear variations between governments regarding modes of operation. One central factor in accounting for this is the design of the prime minister's role. Although this role is formally weak, in practice it is highly significant. The prime minister influences a government not only through specific personal qualities, but also because successive prime ministers organize work in different ways. They use both the formal framework and historical traditions each in their own way. Other factors affecting how leadership is exercised is whether there is a one-party or coalition government, a majority or a minority government, and which types of party are represented.

Another possibly significant factor for the exercise of leadership is the aggregate of politicians with little or a lot of experience, various parliamentary backgrounds and differing levels of education. A cabinet minister with long parliamentary experience but without higher education will act differently from an academic who has no parliamentary experience. There are also cabinet ministers who have little political experience but a lot of experience with administrative leadership, which will be reflected in a different profile of contacts and experiences and therefore a different leadership style.

Leading a ministry involves a different framework and set of demands than does participation in the cabinet. While the latter context requires comprehensive and collective thinking, the former needs specialized attention and interest in a limited area. There are features that are particularly characteristic of how cabinet ministers perform the leadership function. First, the cabinet minister must help to organize and run the daily decision-making process with a view to achieving particularly political objectives. This requires him or her to have good contact with the ministry's civil servants but also with subordinate agencies and the leaders of state-owned companies. In addition, a minister is expected to make wise use of the human resources in his or her ministry, whether this concerns career plans, development dialogues and recruiting, or developing the social community. One could call this the cultural side of leadership. It is also worth mentioning that in exercising these two leadership functions, the cabinet minister will, to varying degrees, take recourse in myths and symbols depending on the extent of instrumental change.

The desire for instrumental implementation of reforms often encounters cultural resistance and cognitive problems, and this results in more widespread use of symbols and increased cynicism. For example, the Bologna process and higher education reforms in many countries have been marked by the use of many political symbols by political leaders emphasizing the qualitative gains for education these will bring, while academics and students are often more sceptical. Another example is the increased competition surrounding public services, including competitive tendering and private providers, which is often portrayed by political leaders as increasing efficiency and quality. In fact such reforms meet with resistance from professional groups, unions and user organizations.

In spite of the stable structural and cultural framework that surrounds the roles of cabinet ministers, their exercise of leadership varies. Some are more bureaucratic, in- and out-box ministers; they expedite the cases put before them by administrators, thus displaying a rather stiffly defined instrumental form of leadership. Others select certain policy areas, focus most of their attention on these and let other areas run on their own. This may reflect the traditional prioritization of political parties, but also the minister's background. A third way of describing the minister's role is to say it is largely steered by mass media coverage and attempts to influence that coverage and is hence a more situational and symbolically oriented role. A fourth category encompasses those ministers who spend much of their time outside the ministry, often for cultural or symbolic reasons – for instance because they want to be closer to voters or in contact with people in the public organizations they lead.

A second group of public leaders in focus are top administrative leaders in ministries. They go by many names: permanent secretaries, chief executives, secretary-generals or director-generals. Their role is characterized by cross-pressure between three main elements. First, they must have tight relations with the leaders of the political executive, which involves helping to prepare cases for parliament, handling special interest organizations and the mass media, and engaging in international and local contacts. This support function, often called the 'secretariat of the political leadership function', has gained importance over time and is rather unpredictable. Second, there are often occasions when an administrative leader must set aside all present activities in order to help out a political leader, and it is difficult to set up clear structures and routines for these eventualities. Particularly important for this role is to give the cabinet minister the potential to realize his or her goals without creating unnecessary problems. Civil servants have a clear interest in the political leadership appearing to be dynamic and successful vis-à-vis the parliament and the mass media. Third, conflicts in the relationship between top political and administrative leaders concern how closely political leaders try to involve administrative leaders in political or party-political debates.

Administrative leadership in a ministry also involves organizing internal activities, namely, preparing cases related to planning, budgeting, accounting and controlling, as well as issues of law or personnel policy. Problems of attention and capacity may arise here as well. In this mode of exercising leadership the structural and instrumental aspects are key, but it is also crucial to nurture historical traditions and to provide colleagues with new challenges and competence to allow them to develop. These are for the most part culturally oriented processes. An additional function is to steer subordinate agencies and state-owned companies or other units. Again, much of this leadership activity has an instrumental character related to the dialogue of formal steering, letter of allocation (activities demanded and resources provided), formal meetings and performance reports, but it is also critical to maintain informal dialogue between levels, and this will be influenced by historical traditions.

The role of a top administrative leader in a ministry can be exercised in a number of ways and can reveal different ways of balancing the three main aspects of the role. It may also, however, reflect different ways of dividing up labour, the unique personnel history of the organization, wide-ranging educational backgrounds and the diverse historical traditions of different ministries. Governments will vary in how much contact top administrative leaders have with each other and in the extent to which their role-enactment is eventually standardized.

A third group of important governmental leaders are the directors of agencies and state-owned companies, who, often through NPM, have received increased autonomy in relation to political leaders. They experience cross-pressure between ongoing political obligations to political leaders and the necessity to exercise their increased autonomy. Some use their increased freedom to be more directly active vis-à-vis the parliament, almost assuming the role of lobbyists, while others increase their contact with stakeholders and users of services. Relations between agency directors and the political leadership are more distant than some years ago, because reforms have weakened the political levers of control and increased the distance to subordinate units. Although this may potentially undermine political control, informal contacts and mutual trust may compensate for this.

From all this one might conclude that public leadership has changed over time. The old visionary and educative type of political leader – while still distinguishing himself or herself in highly significant as well as more mundane cases – is under threat. The new political leader, however, is under greater pressure from external actors, has capacity problems and must act in an ad hoc manner; but he or she is also more decoupled from administrative leaders, commercial leaders of state-owned companies and the daily activity of administration, where the doctrine is one of remaining passive and 'steering once a year'. Political leadership is now more marked by a conception of leadership borrowed from what Johan P. Olsen calls a 'supermarket state model', and although ideals from the centralized, integrated, sovereign and rationality-bounded state model have receded, they may be reappearing in post-NPM reforms in some countries. Administrative leadership is also undergoing change. Leaders are now more frequently called 'managers' or 'chief executives' than 'top civil servants', and recruitment from the private sector is on the increase, especially for agencies and state-owned companies.

CHAPTER SUMMARY

- Leadership and steering in public organizations comprise a complex combination of formal steering instruments (instrumental elements), interaction and integration (cultural elements), and symbolic (myth) elements.
- Central political and administrative roles in public organizations have a wide variety of contextual components, which are both internally and externally defined.
- The connections between leadership styles/traits and organizational performance are often elusive and ambiguous in public organizations.

DISCUSSION QUESTIONS

Take as your point of departure a public organization you know of.

1   Try to identify some of the major ways leadership and steering are conducted in this organization, based on the instrumental, cultural and myth perspectives.
2   Discuss some of the main contextual constraints to which leaders in this organization are subjected, both internal and external.
3   Discuss whether you find elements of what Selznick defines as 'statesmanship' in this organization.

REFERENCES AND FURTHER READING

Aberbach, J.D. and Christensen, T. (2001) 'Radical Reform in New Zealand: Crisis, Windows of Opportunities and Rational Actors', *Public Administration*, 79 (2): 404–22.

Barnard, C. (1938; 30th anniversary edn 1968) *The Functions of the Executive,* Cambridge: Harvard University Press.

Brunsson, N. (1989; 2nd edn 2002) *The Organization of Hypocrisy: Talk, Decisions and Actions in Organizations,* New York: John Wiley; 2nd edn Oslo: Abstract 2002.

Byrkjeflot, H. (1997) *Fra styring til ledelse (From Steering to Leadership),* Bergen: Fagbokforlaget.

Christensen, T. (2001) 'Administrative Reform: Transforming the Relationship between Political and Administrative Leaders?', *Governance,* 14 (4): 457–80.

Christensen, T. and Lægreid (2002) *Reformer og Lederskap (Reforms and Leadership),* Oslo: Universitetsforlaget.

Christensen, T. and Lægreid, P. (2003) 'Complex Interaction and Influence among Political and Administrative Leaders', *International Review of Administrative Science,* 69 (3): 385–400.

—— (2005) 'Autonomization and Policy Capacity: The Dilemmas and Challenges Facing Political Executives' in M. Painter and J. Pierre (eds) *Challenges to State Policy Capacity,* London: Palgrave.

Cohen, M.D. and March, J.G. (1967; 2nd edn 1986) *Leadership and Ambiguity,* Boston: Harvard Business School Press.

Dunn, D.D. (1997) *Politics and Administration at the Top: Lessons from Down Under,* Pittsburgh: University of Pittsburgh Press.

Gulick, L. (1937, reprinted 1987) 'Notes on the Theory of Organization', in L. Gulick and L.F. Urwick (eds) *Papers on the Science of Administration,* New York: Institute of Public Administration; reprinted New York: Garland.

Kingdon, J. (1984; 2nd edn 1995) *Agendas, Alternatives, and Public Policies,* Boston: Little, Brown; 2nd edn New York: HarperCollins.Lundquist, L. (1993) *Ämbetsman eller director: Förvaltningschefens roll i demokratin* (*Top Civil Servant or Manager: The Role of Administrative Executives in Democracy*), Stockholm: Norstedts.

March, J.G. (1984) 'How We Talk and How We Act: Administrative Theory and Administrative Life', in I.T. Sergiovanni and J.E. Carbally (eds) *Leadership and Organizational Culture,* Urbana: University of Illinois Press.

March, J.G. and Olsen, J.P. (1976) *Ambiguity and Choice in Organizations,* Bergen: Universitetsforlaget.

Olsen, J.P. (1981) 'Regjeringen som samordningsorgan: muligheter og begrensninger' ('The Cabinet as a Coordinating Body: Possibilities and Constraints'), *Nordisk Administrativt Tidsskrift* 62 (4): 363–89.

—— (1988) 'Administrative Reform and Theories of Organization', in C. Campbell and B.G. Peters (eds) *Organizing Governance, Governing Organizations,* Pittsburgh: University of Pittsburgh Press.

Pollitt, C. (2003) *The Essential Public Manager,* Maidenhead: Open University Press.

Rhodes, R.A.W. and Weller, P. (2001) *The Changing World of Top Officials: Mandarin or Valets?,* Maidenhead: Open University Press.

Selznick, P. (1957, reissued 1984) *Leadership in Administration,* New York: Harper & Row; reissued Berkeley: University of California Press.

Thompson, J.D. (1967; new edn 2003) *Organizations in Action,* New York: McGraw-Hill; new edn Somerset: Transaction.

Chapter 7

Reform and change

LEARNING OBJECTIVES

By the end of this chapter you should have a clear understanding of how the institutional, cultural and myth perspectives can be used to:

- analyse general and specific reform programmes and reform initiatives;
- analyse the course and outcome of general and specific processes of change;
- analyse the relationships between reform programmes and the course, and the outcome of specific processes of reform and change.

REFORM AND CHANGE IN PUBLIC ORGANIZATIONS

Reform and change are not new phenomena for public organizations, since many of them have been experiencing attempts to bring about change and reorganization for a long time. For example, the question of delegation of central authority for public services from a ministry to an autonomous agency has been a central controversy in many countries such as Sweden or Australia for a century. What is new is that since the early 1980s administrative policy has grown into a separate policy area with its own discourse and administrative units, and reforms are now often launched under the auspices of more comprehensive reform programmes.

It is important to distinguish between reform and change in public organizations. By *reform*, we mean active and deliberate attempts by political and administrative leaders to change structural or cultural features of organizations; *change* is what actually happens to such features. Change is often a gradual process in organizations, taking place in the course of routine activities and in small increments, but sometimes it can take the form of abrupt and powerful upheavals, the potential for which has built up over a longer period of time. Indeed, many gradual changes have no background in reforms. Hence, it is a myth that public organizations do not change even while remaining robust and stable. Examples of continuous change can be the adoption of information and communications technology, such as the Internet and e-mail, or the gradual adaptation to external pressure through increased integration in the European Union, which influences organizational forms in public administration.

A hierarchically based instrumental perspective would expect there to be a close connection between reform and change. The point of departure here is organizational reform in the sense of a planned attempt by leaders to bring about change. Nevertheless, it is possible to think of situations where reform does not lead to change, for example where it fails to be implemented and remains a reform on paper. Reform and change in public organizations can occur simultaneously, yet be partially decoupled from one another, in the sense that reforms may be based on initiatives from the top, while change can occur continuously at lower levels of the organization.

Viewed from a negotiation-based instrumental perspective, deficiencies in carrying out reforms may stem from resistance to leaders' plans for change from actors inside or outside the organization. A cultural perspective usually uses as its point of departure the actual organizational changes or the element of stability over time, where the degree of change and stability is measured against the existing cultural characteristics of an organization. A myth perspective focuses on the symbolic aspects of reform and change.

What precisely are leaders attempting to change when they decide to carry out organizational reforms, and what happens to structural or cultural features when organizational change occurs? Chapter Four mentioned six categories of reform recipes for different aspects of public organizations: leadership, the design of formal organizational structure, human resource management, organizational culture and work environment, the organization of work processes, and financial control. The three perspectives outlined in the first part of the book emphasize different types of reform and change. An instrumental perspective, for example, will usually focus on reforms connected to structural features, while a cultural perspective will more often focus on stability and change in cultural features. Just as important is that these perspectives offer different conceptions of the course and outcome of processes of reform and change and of whether these processes can be controlled, and, if so, how. The three perspectives also offer different views of the connections between how reform processes and changes are organized and their actual content, that is, the organizational solutions employed.

One aspect of organizations as instruments is expressed in the notion that hierarchically responsible leaders implement reforms in an instrumentally rational way; another instrumental aspect is that leaders organize reform processes on the basis of means–ends considerations. There will also be a connection between how a reform process is organized and what course it takes and what the outcome is, because organizing creates capacity for analysis and action. In addition to this, conceptions of the existing organizational structure may help to determine how problems and solutions are defined. From a negotiation-based instrumental perspective, existing organizational structures and ways of organizing the reform process may be the result of previous bargaining and compromise. Just as important will be that existing organizational structures and ways of organizing the reform process provide directives for the course and outcome of reform processes, because there are vested interests in these structural features. Reform processes may therefore create conflicts because they revive old conflict patterns and may lead to changes in these.

From a cultural perspective, it will be important to clarify how the course and outcome of processes of change will be influenced by an organization's established cultural features. Informal norms and values will be relatively stable over time and may determine the reform method (i.e. ways of organizing the process of change, such as which actors should be involved) and, to some extent, the organizational solutions (i.e. the content of change) regarded as appropriate in the light of tradition. Similarly, from a myth perspective, there may at all times be recipes for organizing reform processes and for reform content, but these institutional standards may fluctuate over time. Public organizations attain legitimacy by deploying organizational reform methods and solutions regarded as modern and acceptable by the environment at a given period in time.

From the three general perspectives, moreover, there will be different ways of understanding the connection between reform initiatives directed towards a wide range of organizations and what happens in specific organizations, as well as different ways of understanding the varying content of reforms and changes over time. From the standpoint of hierarchically based analytical problem-solving, these connections and variations are closely tied to how leaders formulate their goals and define their problems. If these are consistently the same for all organizations, the outcome of reforms will be the same in different organizations regardless of the time period, whereas differences in goals and problem definitions over time will produce variations in what kinds of organizational solutions are used. Here negotiation features may entail modifying how reform initiatives are implemented, based on the existing distribution of interests and resources in individual organizations at various points in time. From a cultural perspective, reforms may vary immensely across organizations. There may be loose coupling between general reform initiatives and what happens in specific organizations, but within each organization there may be a great degree of stability over time. From a myth perspective, however, a similarity or isomorphy between organizations will occur, expressed either in general similar features based on widespread myths, or similar features within families of recipes, and if prevailing doctrines change there will be corresponding changes in the institutional standards.

124

In this chapter we will first outline central aspects of how reform processes in public organizations are organized. Thereafter, we will take as our point of departure reform programmes and initiatives directed towards a wide set of public organizations and will discuss their origins and fates. We will also discuss how the course and outcome of processes of reform and change in specific public organizations can be analysed in the light of the three perspectives. Here the most pertinent example will be the history of how the central authority for the Norwegian police force is organized.

ORGANIZING THE REFORM PROCESS

In Chapter Two we saw that the design of a formal organizational structure depends on the degree and form of specialization and coordination and that bureaucratic organizational forms involve hierarchy, routines and divisions of labour. Such structural features may also apply to ways of organizing the reform process within and between public organizations. As for *specialization*, organizational questions may be allocated to positions and units specifically designed for organizational tasks, for example units for organizational development, or positions and units whose tasks concern selected parts of society, for example units that organize contact with specific user groups. How specialized this work is depends on how many such positions and units there are and how many organizations they serve. *Coordination* means linking organizational reforms to other types of tasks and decisions within an organization or with organizational reforms in other organizations.

The reform process also entails *vertical coordination* – that is, elements of hierarchy within and between public organizations involving superior and subordinate ordering. In central government, for example, the political and administrative leadership of a ministry will take charge of organizational design for all levels of that ministry and may influence the organizational design of its subordinate agencies as well. In many countries, it is more common for organizational questions to be dealt with via vertical coordination of this kind than for these to be assigned to, say, a ministry or government administration that is hierarchically superior to ministries focused on specific fields of expertise. What is more, a hierarchy also implies vertical specialization because different types of tasks are placed at different levels. For example, there may be organizations at a subordinate level routinely focused on reform issues, such as *special units for organizational questions* in a ministry or a separate agency giving advice to other public organizations. Setting up individual units for dealing with organizational questions or issues is more characteristic of horizontal specialization, and the relationship between these and other units on the same level may be regulated through various forms of horizontal coordination.

There may also be other organizational forms for designing the reform process that are alternatives or supplements to a hierarchy. Experts on organizational questions – be they from private consulting firms or from public consulting agencies – can be directly involved in reforms, by participating in public commissions or by producing tailor-made organizational reports commissioned by an organization's leaders. If reforms are to be wide-ranging, if patterns of interest and conflict are particularly complex, or if the reforms necessitate changing laws, the practice in many countries is for the proposed reform to be reviewed by a public commission, consisting of representatives from a wide range of stakeholders, which formulates recommendations for the political and administrative leadership. Participation by actors other than leaders involves negotiatory features that are expressed in *participatory arrangements for employees.* For example, in the Scandinavian countries such participation often happens through union spokespersons, who have extended rights to take part in negotiations and discussions. In addition, they have the right to information about plans and resolutions that are important for government employees. In particular internal organizational changes of a more or less permanent character, which involve a reshuffling of manpower and equipment, are often the subject of negotiation within the guidelines drawn up through political prioritization.

While from an instrumental perspective structural features of organizations and reform processes are critical, from a cultural perspective it is the cultural features tied to these issues that are most central. Special units dealing with organizational questions will, in the same way as other public organizations, be characterized by their own informal norms and values. Some methods of implementing reforms will be considered appropriate, while others will not be as relevant because they break with the existing culture. In Scandinavia, for example, it has been traditional for government employees' unions to be involved when a ministry or agency undergoes reorganization, even beyond the bounds of their formal rights of participation in such cases.

Likewise, from a myth perspective, the special units dealing with organizational questions will be relevant interpreters of popular recipes for what organizations should look like and how they should function. Such units will usually be among the foremost interpreters of key international trends, and they can indicate how the trends should be translated to national and organizational contexts, as well as the possible outcomes. This interpretation often has clear symbolic overtones: the promising aspects of relevant reforms are over-emphasized while counter-arguments are devalued and labelled as old-fashioned and regressive.

How and to what degree is it possible to *design reform processes?* From an instrumental perspective it is important to organize systematic attention around organizational reforms. From the leadership's vantage point, this can be done by setting up separate units for organizational questions, building a knowledge base in these and influencing their horizontal and vertical placement within public administration. Civil servants and their unions can be drawn into a reform process if they are perceived as having important knowledge or insight into the consequences of actual reform initiatives, or if their participation is perceived as facilitating the implementation of reform initiatives leaders deem desirable. A consequence of setting up commissions for organizational reforms is that their composition determines who has the right to participate, and its mandate specifies which goals, organizational solutions and consequences are relevant. In this phase of the reform process actors whose points of view support the leadership can be included, while dissenters can be excluded. Alternatively, in order to increase the legitimacy of the reform processes, the process of determining alternatives for reforming an organization can be made to include many different interests. As a rule this will facilitate implementing reforms and increase the legitimacy of the leadership, but it will also make them less radical. Participatory agreements with employees and diversely composed commissions will necessitate modifying hierarchical control. Such negotiatory features allow actors with goals and interests that do not necessarily harmonize with those of leaders to voice their views.

From a cultural perspective, reform happens slowly and in increments. It is evolution rather than revolution, a process where traditional norms and values are balanced against new ones, through a process of adaptation to internal and external pressure. From a myth perspective, it will be seen as necessary to develop and spread recipes for ways of organizing reform processes and to gain legitimacy from the environment by using generally accepted methods. Imitation, in the sense of using models from other countries or advice from international organizations, may be such a method. Another method, already mentioned, might be public commissions whose composition cuts across ministries. These may have a symbolic role because they are tightly controlled by political and administrative leaders.

How then will the course and outcome of reform processes be influenced by how they are organized? From an instrumental perspective, the way capacity for analysis and action is built into units responsible for reform-related tasks is important because this capacity can be used by the hierarchical leadership. A negotiation-based instrumental perspective is concerned with how interests and resources are built into individual organizations and how organizing the reform process constrains and enables the articulation of interests and the use of resources. Such negotiatory features can be deliberately exploited by political leaders in order to control the reform process. Moreover, reforms can often be easier to carry out if the affected parties in an organization, such as employees and their unions, participate in the process prior to actual reform implementation. Nevertheless, other actors can exploit negotiations too, for, by engendering conflicts, they can influence the outcome of reform processes, even to the extent where the reforms turn out differently to how the leaders desired.

From a cultural perspective, the links between formal aspects of preliminary reform work and actual outcomes will not be entirely clear. The way reform processes are organized will provide the basis for coming up with good solutions and determining appropriate action. Nevertheless, it is the informal norms linked with organizational forms and organizational methods for change that are the most important. A myth perspective allows formal structural features to be decoupled from concrete action linked to reforms to an even greater degree. The goal of reform processes may very well be to achieve political gains without having to make substantial changes, but by organizing the reform process in a particular way, this goal can be presented so as to give the impression of a modern political leadership open to change.

REFORM PROGRAMMES AND REFORM INITIATIVES

Many organizational reforms in the public sector in the last two decades can be related to NPM. As outlined in Chapter One, NPM plays down differences between the public and private sectors and instead emphasizes the great benefits of adopting the organizational models and forms of control used by private organizations for public organizations. The theoretical underpinnings of NPM are rather mixed, combining elements of both *new institutional economics* and *managerialism*. The main tenets of organizational economics, such as *Public Choice Theory, Principal Agent Theory* and *Transaction Cost Theory,* presuppose actors trying to maximize self-interest. As in the older theories mentioned in Chapter Two, here, too, the emphasis is on controlling public organizations. Structural features within and between organizations (e.g. specialized structures based on Public Choice Theory, contracts and delegated authority based on Principal Agent Theory, and the market as an alternative to hierarchy based on Transaction Cost Theory) can be used as tools by top-level leaders for influencing the work of subordinates via a system of rewards and sanctions. As we saw in Chapter Six, new management theories contain structural as well as cultural aspects. Here revised versions of Taylorism are supplemented with ideas and initiatives such as Service Management and Value-based Management. Compared with economically based organization theories, service- and value-based management theories place stronger emphasis on giving organizations more autonomy and flexibility. While concern for commercial freedom and the efficient use of resources points in the direction of increased autonomy for public organizations, concern for control points in the opposite direction. NPM is, in other words, not a consistent and integrated theory for modernizing the public sector, but is better characterized as a wave of reforms composed of some principal reform ideas together with a loose cluster of reform initiatives pointing in various directions. Thus, NPM constitutes a set of organizational recipes that can be translated and spread to numerous public organizations, as described in Chapter Four.

According to recent comparative studies of public-sector reforms, there have been some similarities as well as differences in reform types over time and across countries. For example, in comparing Norway, Sweden, Australia and New Zealand, the political scientist John Halligan distinguishes between four main types. The first type is the *reluctant reformer* (e.g. Norway), who implements some reform principles but is essentially old-style (or in slow transition) and carries out reform on a sectoral basis relying on adaptation and incrementalism. The second type is the *specialist reformer*, where the focus is on one or more distinctive types of reform (this has applied to all four countries at some point). The third type is the *ambivalent reformer*, where there is a commitment to general change, but cross-cutting pressures (or inertia) mean that implementation varies (Sweden, Australia up to 1986). The fourth type is the *comprehensive reformer*, who makes a major commitment to reform and employs a range of reform measures (Australia and New Zealand).

Compared with Anglo-Saxon countries such as Australia, New Zealand and the United Kingdom, the Scandinavian countries have clearly pursued less radical reform strategies, yet, even in these countries, many organizational reforms carried out since the mid-1980s have been marked by NPM. In contrast to reforms in earlier years, the initiatives have been launched through more comprehensive *reform programmes*. All the same, they have remained a loose collection of ongoing reform initiatives and new reform ideas, rather than a coordinated and unified plan (by a series of governments) to change public administration. The similarities between the programmes are more striking than their differences. They have been marked by pragmatism and consensus rather than ideology, and they have focused more on increasing efficiency in public administration through restructuring than on dismantling the public sector.

Why, then, have reform programmes such as those in the Scandinavian countries developed with the specific form and content we have witnessed in recent years? From an instrumental perspective, such programmes can be understood as tools for solving current problems. The cabinet and the political-administrative leadership in the ministry with chief responsibility for national administrative policy have certain goals for developing the public sector. For them, organizational reforms are a possible means towards this end, and bringing a set of reforms together in a reform programme is critical for solving problems. If this is the case, one would expect the programmes to contain clear goals and means–ends relations and a unified plan for changing the public administration. From a negotiating perspective one would, however, have compromises about both goals and means and greater ambiguity in the reform process. From a cultural perspective, reform will entail acting in a way that corresponds with the national culture, for the form and content of reform programmes will be influenced by such cultural features. The impression we have of most reform programmes thus far is that they are less well-integrated than a hierarchically based instrumental perspective would indicate. Their rather non-cohesive content suggests also, however, that many organizations with differing interests and cultures have been involved in the planning, a phenomenon accounted for by a negotiation-based instrumental perspective and a cultural perspective. Seen from a myth perspective, such reform programmes will be part of an international trend, and initiating reforms will be an expression of the desire to gain legitimacy in the international environment (e.g. in other countries and in the OECD). This would seem to apply to many reform programmes in Western countries.

One central element (or recipe) used in NPM reform programmes in recent decades is performance management or MBOR and structural (vertical) devolution. But there has also been a focus on market orientation, openness to competition and increased horizontal specialization expressed in an emphasis on non-overlapping functions and roles and on single-purpose organizations.

MBOR can be seen as a structural-instrumental tool for political and administrative leadership. It involves a significant amount of delegation through liberalizing the general regulations on financial management and human resource management in central government. The increased flexibility is, however, counteracted by increased performance reporting and monitoring of results. As mentioned in Chapter Five, control techniques consist of three main components. First, clear, consistent, stable and concrete goals must be formulated. The content of these goals may vary, but it is up to leaders to determine it. The critical issue is that goals should be operational, that is, that they function as adequate 'measuring sticks' of whatever results are achieved. Second, control entails measuring results based on specified performance indicators and reporting back on these results to superior levels. Performance measurement systems make this possible, because they systematically test outcomes in relation to resources used. Third, results must be followed up, based on the principle that success and good performance should be rewarded while bad performance should be punished. In other words, results should also have consequences for behaviour and allocation of resources and personnel. In Chapter Eight we shall discuss how these last two components function in practice.

As noted in Chapter Five, MBOR is often associated with activity planning. In the Scandinavian countries it was launched as a concept with overarching relevance in central government, but it has changed over time. Thus, the focus has shifted from formulating goals to reporting results, and qualitative aspects have supplemented more quantitative indicators. Furthermore, activity planning has become more integrated into budget preparation, and there is a greater willingness to adapt the concept to the particular conditions and circumstances of individual organizations.

Structural devolution concerns a subordinate public organization's *form of affiliation* to top political and administrative authorities, that is, its relations with ministries, the cabinet and the parliament. Although the OECD has recently tried to develop common denominators for agencies, authorities and other governmental bodies outside ministerial departments, organizational forms still vary greatly from country to country. However, in many countries, three main organizational forms related to central government often exist alongside ministries. *Civil service organizations* and central agencies are normally part of the state as a legal entity, subordinate to a ministry and its responsible cabinet minister and controlled through many general regulations, such as those pertaining to financial management and human resource management. *State-owned companies* share certain core features.

They are separate and independent legal entities, have their own board of directors and are responsible for their own economic resources. The central state authorities primarily control the companies through their position of ownership. *Governmental foundations* are independent legal entities and are self-owned. Control is exercised by the central state authorities primarily via regulations and funnelling by providing the basic capital when a foundation is first established.

Structural devolution involves decentralization and increased vertical specialization among public organizations. This may mean changing the organizational form of existing organizations in the direction of greater autonomy as well as creating new organizations with greater autonomy than was previously the case for organizations with similar tasks.

Recently, academic discussions of public organizations that address structural devolution have focused on the development of *agencies*. For example, in a comparative study on semi-autonomous state agencies in four sectors in Finland, the Netherlands, Sweden and the United Kingdom, Christopher Pollitt and colleagues used a working definition of an agency as an organization which has its status defined principally or exclusively in public law. It is functionally disaggregated from the core of its ministry, enjoys some degree of autonomy not enjoyed by the core ministry, but is nevertheless linked to the ministry in ways that are close enough to permit ministers to alter the budgets and main operational goals of the organization. An agency is not statutorily fully independent of its ministry, nor is it a commercial corporation. As Australian political scientist Roger Wettenhall notes, however, this definition may be regarded as too hard (or narrow), for it fails to take into account softer (or broader) versions and sub-types of 'non-departmental public bodies' (NDPBs) that have existed for a long time. For example, what in Australia used to be called statutory authorities and corporations go back more than a century, and in Sweden and other Scandinavian countries semi-autonomous agencies go back even farther.

A comparative study of New Zealand, Australia, Sweden and Norway shows that in all four countries reform initiatives for structural devolution have been launched during the last two decades. In general, the prevailing international doctrines and the national administrative doctrines in these countries from the late 1980s onwards prescribed increased structural devolution. In the 2000s, however, doctrines in New Zealand and Australia have tended to reverse the trend and they now prescribe less structural devolution. In New Zealand, Australia and Norway, comprehensive reviews have resulted in clarifying the possible organizational forms and assessing the conditions under which each of them is relevant. For example, in Norway, where control by politically elected leaders is particularly important, it was decided that the organizations carrying out tasks directly linked with exercising public authority or politically defined revenue-redistribution between groups in society should be civil service organizations. At the same time, the importance of efficiency and managerial discretion made it desirable for the production of goods and services by the government on a commercial basis to be put under the auspices of state-owned companies. Such reform initiatives are also spawned by a structural-instrumental mindset, but rather than prescribing one universal solution, it was emphasized how the organizational form of concrete organizations would vary according to their goals and tasks. The use of different organizational forms has also been discussed in Sweden, but here the set of alternatives has remained stable and more limited.

A common characteristic of MBOR and structural devolution is that they focus on vertical control and coordination within each individual sector. Yet, even so, these recipes contribute little to strengthening horizontal coordination in public administration, which probably is at least as big a problem.

How then have such reform programmes and key reform initiatives been followed up in practice? The point of departure from an instrumental perspective is the government and the particular ministry responsible for national administrative policy. In addition to clear goals and a clear understanding of means and ends, successful implementation, seen from the vantage point of these actors, will depend on them having political control over what happens to the programmes and initiatives. A main characteristic of the proposed Scandinavian reforms, particularly in the initial programmes, was that they were advisory rather than mandatory for subordinate organizations. Thus, the follow-up has been built more on persuasion rather than coercion.

From a cultural perspective, one would expect the fate of reform initiatives to depend on the degree to which there is normative correspondence between them and the organization as it already exists. Reform initiatives that are incompatible with established norms and values in organizations will be rejected, while parts that are compatible will be implemented; controversial parts will be adapted so as to be made acceptable. From a myth perspective, reform initiatives that correspond with current doctrines about 'good organization' will gain acceptance more readily than initiatives that diverge from what is thought to be modern. The greater the correspondence between, on the one hand, problem definitions and suggested solutions in reform programmes, and, on the other hand, the circumstances of organizations perceived as well-run models for other organizations, the easier it will be to gain legitimacy and endorsement.

In sum, an instrumental perspective that looks solely at the capacity for analysis and action of the cabinet and the ministry with overarching responsibility for national administrative policy cannot capture all aspects of how reform programmes and key reform initiatives are carried out. National and organization-specific interests and cultures, as well as national and international trends in administrative doctrine, are also highly significant.

COURSE AND OUTCOME OF REFORM AND CHANGE PROCESSES

When analysing what happens in processes of reform and change in specific public organizations from a *hierarchically based instrumental perspective* it can be relevant to start the inquiry by examining the organizational leadership and superior authorities who may use the organization as a tool. For example, attempts to bring about change in an agency may come from the agency's leaders, from political and administrative executives in the parent ministry, or from the cabinet. Similarly, plans to organize and control a public university in new ways may come from university leaders, from a ministry for education and research, or from the cabinet. Even though the key agent of reform varies, it will, from such a perspective, be important nevertheless to clarify and understand that agent's capacity for analysis and action.

Similarly, from a *negotiation-based instrumental perspective* it will be important to map the interests and resources of different actors within the organization and of other actors who may be affected by the reforms. Relevant actors will therefore include the organization's leaders and superior authorities, and all actors will be expected to act in an instrumentally rational way, based on self-interest. From a *cultural perspective*, the culture in specific organizations will be more relevant to the process of change than the national culture cited when the reform programmes are presented. From a *myth perspective*, the focus will be more on how recipes are adopted in specific organizations than on how they are developed and mediated. For a public organization, the degree to which reform symbols are adopted in other organizations as well will nevertheless be very significant, since adopting the solutions found in other organizations it wants to compare itself with will be a good way for an organization to acquire external legitimacy.

As for the course and outcome of processes of reform and change in public organizations, we will here particularly emphasize the significance of the existing organizational structure and how reform processes are organized. From a *hierarchically based instrumental perspective*, organizational changes are desired and planned by an organization's leaders or by superior authorities. The question of reform and change will, in the first instance, be influenced by these people's goals and perceptions of the situation at hand. Reforms are likely to be put on the agenda if new leaders or new people in superior authorities arrive with new goals, or if those already occupying these positions change their goals. Another reason for reform to be put on the agenda is if new knowledge is gained about the consequences that new organizational forms will have and about how they might be implemented. The reforms will be characterized by clear goals, clear means–ends relations and control over implementation. This will include an overview of who may be involved and an assurance that the favoured alternatives are possible to implement.

From a *hierarchically based instrumental perspective*, the organization's leaders or superior authorities will calculate the costs and benefits of the organization's existing form and other relevant forms and will recommend reforms in cases where alternatives are deemed to be better for achieving the organization's goals. Here bounded rationality means that there may be costs tied to acquiring information about the consequences of different solutions, and there can also be costs for implementing these solutions. If one takes into consideration information and implementation costs, then the present organizational form will have a certain advantage. Information about other organizational forms and relevant reform proposals will not be readily accessible, and leaders or superior authorities must therefore expend efforts to acquire it. The costs of acquiring insight into means–ends relations will then be added to the utility calculations of various reform proposals.

From a *negotiation-based instrumental perspective*, negotiations will serve to make reform plans concrete, and their outcome will be determined by conditions several actors have a certain amount of control over. The organization's leaders must therefore enter into coalitions with other actors in order to further their own goals and interests. The existing organizational structure and design of reform work will be significant in that these conditions provide the foundation for the actors' interests and resources. Even if some actors perceive the existing organizational structure and design of reform processes as unsuitable for realizing their interests, it is unlikely they will be able to change them on their own. Current organizational structures and ways of handling reforms will therefore have a different status to possible alternatives.

As the American organization theorist Jeffrey Pfeffer points out, reform initiatives will most likely come from those actors who believe they can gain something through reorganization, that is, from those who foresee increased influence and control once reforms are implemented. Actors will want reorganization provided their position improves and the likelihood of success is great enough to compensate for uncertainties and the possibility that they may end up worse off than before. The existing organizational structure, in itself, will be a part of the power base of the dominant coalition. Demands for change will therefore come particularly from outside the coalition. Supporters of reforms will be those who believe they have some bases of influence not currently recognized.

From a *cultural perspective*, reform and change are linked with actions that correspond with established norms and values. The question of reform and change will therefore chiefly be influenced by the informal norms and values found in an organization at a given point in time. Reforms will be launched because perceptions change about the situation the organization faces, about the organization's identity or what it stands for, or about what are appropriate rules for action. Hence it is a question of the relationship between situation and identity. Existing organizational features will be significant to the extent they provide a basis for understanding what good solutions are and what action is appropriate. Prevailing norms develop slowly and cannot simply be changed by any one actor. As we mentioned in Chapter Three, the development of organizational forms will be path-dependent. Changes are characterized as gradual adaptations centring around a state of equilibrium, punctuated by abrupt and powerful upheavals, and then followed by a new phase of small changes centred around a new state of equilibrium.

Such radical changes are most likely to happen at what are called *critical junctures*. It is therefore important to clarify what precipitates these junctures. Public organizations usually have specific cultures, which may involve variations in structural arrangements between the different ministerial areas or between different parts of municipal administration. Internal traditions and norms will vary from sector to sector and provide the basis for path dependency. Internal forces contributing to the organization's robustness and stability will be more important than shifting political signals, and the links between general doctrines of reform and any actual changes will be rather loose. Reforms that are incompatible with the established organizational culture will not be followed through.

Seen from a *myth perspective*, and in light of the significance of institutionalized environments, the course and outcome of reform in public organizations will be linked with organizations deploying reform initiatives that are widespread. Organizations gain legitimacy by communicating that their structures and procedures correspond with perceptions about what is rational, reasonable and modern. If these impressions do not correspond with what is needed to carry out tasks and ensure goal achievement, then there will be a discrepancy between the formal organizational structure and the way actual behaviour is coordinated. Alternatively, reforms that correspond with prevailing ideas in the environment have a greater likelihood of being implemented. Here, too, it is a matter of compatibility, but in this case, compatibility with what is widespread and accepted in the environment.

REFORM AND CHANGE IN THE CENTRAL AUTHORITY OF THE NORWEGIAN POLICE FORCE

We can illustrate some of the aspects presented above by discussing specific reforms and changes in how the central authority of the Norwegian police force has been organized. This central authority was part of the Ministry of Justice from the early nineteenth century onwards, and the police force became a state service in the 1930s. Since 1960, at least nine comprehensive reports on this theme have been made, and three major changes have been implemented. In 1976, the police division in the Ministry of Justice was divided in two, but, by 1983, these two divisions had merged again. In 2001, the central authority was placed in a new, autonomous agency (the Directorate of the Police) subordinate to the Ministry of Justice. The police division in the ministry was maintained, but it became much smaller than before and acquired the more precise character of being a secretariat for the political leadership.

As for comprehensive *reports*, the Directorate of Public Management issued one report in 1964 and a public commission issued another in 1970, both proposing that the central authority should be placed in an autonomous agency. This suggestion was followed up in a bill presented to the parliament by the Korvald (Centre) government in 1973, but it was not discussed there before the parliament dissolved. After the new Labour government took over, an internal task force in the Ministry of Justice proposed that the central authority should remain in the ministry, and the 1976 changes were based on these recommendations. In a similar way, the merger of police divisions in 1983 was based on what came out of a report from a new internal task force. Between 1987 and 1997, the Ministry of Justice produced four reports on how the central authority of the police should be organized. In three of the reports it was assumed that the police's central authority would still be part of the ministry, while the creation of an autonomous agency was recommended in the report from 1991. Nevertheless, it wasn't until almost ten years later, on the basis of a recommendation made in 1999 by a public commission composed of a cross-section of people from different ministries, that the Directorate of the Police was established in 2001.

How can the course and outcome of reforms and changes in the central authority of the Norwegian police be explained? Important considerations from a *hierarchically based instrumental perspective* are whether new political leaders with new goals have entered the scene and whether leaders have changed their perception of the goals and problems at hand. Moreover, recommendations for organizational change will be based on a leader's clear means–ends mindset. The Korvald (Centre) government's proposal defined the problem as being that issues pertaining to the professional field of police work were not being properly addressed by the current arrangements. Concern about political control was also emphasized, but with the proviso that new rules regarding the right of the ministry to command and instruct the agency would make this possible. After the 1973 change in government, the new (Labour) political leadership in the Ministry of Justice opposed the proposal, mainly because it believed that the creation of an autonomous agency could lead to a weakening of political control of the police. It also thought it would be difficult to distinguish between 'administrative issues' and 'political issues', and that it would be possible to strengthen the professional field of police work by keeping the central authority within the ministry. The internal task force drew up two suggestions for how the central authority could be strengthened within the ministry:

- establishing a police division with two sections for different types of tasks;
- the creation of a new section for planning and inspection activities, in addition to the existing section for administrative issues.

The split in 1976 corresponded largely with the second alternative.

The internal task force that some years later proposed remerging the two divisions assumed that the central authority of the police would remain within the ministry. This stricture was self-imposed by the task force after assessing prevailing political attitudes. The task force decided the best solution was to consolidate the central authority to make it one division of the ministry. The follow-up commissioned report was addressed in a meeting with political leaders in the Ministry of Justice shortly after the Willoch (Conservative) government took over in 1981. Even though the Conservative party had earlier supported the proposal to create an autonomous agency, this solution was not considered at the time. This may have been to do with the fact that a new minister and a new cabinet – in the phase just after a change in government – had to prioritize issues on the political agenda, and organizing the central authority of the police was perhaps not perceived as one of the most important tasks for the new political leadership.

The 1991 commissioned report took as its point of departure the tasks assigned to the central police authority and the relative importance of different types of goals and values for the fulfilment of these tasks. Two structural options were drawn up: an autonomous agency at the national level or several regional units. This indirectly implied that the current arrangement, whereby the central authority was inside the ministry, was not deemed relevant. The task force itself favoured the first alternative. These plans were nevertheless not pursued, owing to expected resistance from the parliament.

The proposal put forward by a diversely composed commission in 1999 also advocated an autonomous police agency subordinate to the Ministry of Justice. As in several previous reports, this one also highlighted the problems associated with having the professional and operative management of the police under the cabinet minister's constitutional and parliamentary responsibility. In view of the increased tasks being carried out by the police, the commission believed a ministry was no longer suitable for leading such a large public service. Moreover, it thought it would be possible to maintain democratic control through an autonomous agency. The proposal for an autonomous police agency received support from the political leadership in the Ministry of Justice as well as in the cabinet, which saw the re-organization as a response to the increase in organized international crime and the need to strengthen international police cooperation.

Using a *negotiation-based instrumental perspective*, we will limit our discussion to a few instances of *articulation of interests* by the police force unions. Since 1960, these special interest organizations have participated in many of the public commissions on reforming the central authority of the police, and they have also submitted recommendations on several other occasions. This happened, for example, in the follow-up to the proposal from the internal task force set up after the 1973 government change. The bodies entitled to comment on the proposal were asked to comment on the two relevant alternatives. Several police force unions noted that their preference for an autonomous agency remained unchanged. Of the two alternatives, they supported the option involving two police divisions, and they particularly emphasized that, through such an arrangement, professional policing tasks would be greatly facilitated. That the outcome largely corresponded with this alternative may be seen as a compromise.

The new arrangement in 1976, moreover, meant that there was now a division manned by people with police force experience and police academy education. Previously the organizational structure of the ministry had been conducive to tension between civil servants with a legal education and those with police academy backgrounds. Within a few years the Ministry of Justice became aware of a number of problems in cooperation between the two divisions, which necessitated addressing the issue anew.

Unions for police force and ministry employees were also involved in subsequent commissioned reports on reforms in the central police authority. This took the form of participation in reference groups or hearings and of participatory arrangements for employees. Important aspects of the organizational structure, such as questions about whether the central authority should be inside or outside the ministry, were interpreted as having a political character, and therefore fell outside the purview of negotiations. Several police force unions were also represented in the 1999 public commission, and in the subsequent round of hearings all the unions supported the proposal to establish an autonomous agency. Conversely, most unions for ministry employees expressed scepticism over the proposal to establish a police directorate.

A *cultural perspective* will, on certain points, coincide with a negotiation-based instrumental perspective, since, for the police force and the Ministry of Justice, which are institutions rich in tradition, it is difficult to determine whether actions are marked by an articulation of interests or based on norms. Moreover, there has over time been a great correspondence between positions/units, professions and unions. Until the 1970s, people with law degrees dominated the Ministry of Justice. Until quite recently they also monopolized Chief of Police posts and other higher positions within the police force, and they still have their own professional unions. By contrast, few people with police academy backgrounds worked in the Ministry of Justice before the mid-1970s, and on the local level they were organized in separate groups according to positions and belonged to their own unions. This could be the basis for the two subcultures within the police. These subcultures may also have been spawned over time on the local level and gained strength through the 1976 partition of the police division within the Ministry of Justice. Variations in the attitudes of different groups to questions of central police authority can most certainly be traced back to such circumstances, regardless of their being based in different interests or norms and values.

The Ministry of Justice is one of the oldest ministries in Norway, and structural and cultural features of the organization changed little and only gradually up until the mid-1970s. Since then, many of its areas of responsibility, not merely the police, have undergone evaluation and reorganization. This may have to do with the ministry's tasks increasing and becoming more turbulent, but it may also be because more social scientists have been employed by the ministry. Given their educational background, many social scientists are less likely than employees educated in law to be primarily inclined in undertaking casework based on a given set of rules and regulations. In the

Ministry of Justice, therefore, a quite homogeneous organizational culture dominated by the legal profession has gradually developed into a more heterogeneous culture, or perhaps, as the above history suggests, it has diversified into different subcultures.

From a *myth perspective*, what is important is how reforms in the central police authority have been linked with more general lines of development in central government. From the mid-1950s onwards, setting up autonomous agencies became the prevailing doctrine for how to organize central public service authorities in Norway, and several concrete reforms were proposed for the police in the early 1960s. The fact that the new Labour government did not follow up the Centre government's 1973 proposal for an autonomous agency may be linked with the perception that it would hamper decentralization to the local level, a doctrine more prevalent at the time.

In 1986 the Ministry of Justice started constructing its own reform programme. This programme was launched as the ministry's follow-up to the government's programmes of modernization and renewal. The general aim was to improve professional and administrative work in the ministry. Organizational analyses were seen as an important part of this. One of the first organizational projects was to evaluate the merger of the two police divisions. This report from 1987 was followed up by a new project and, in a subsequent report from 1990, the police division's three main types of tasks were singled out:

- functioning as the secretariat for the political leadership in the ministry;
- having administrative responsibility for all subordinate police units throughout the country; and
- being the executive authority for a number of laws and regulations.

It was decided that the order of priority for these tasks should be determined through annual activity planning. National administrative policy was also expressed in the argument that the leadership of the division should be performed largely according to MBO. In 1994, a reorganization of the police division was carried out, with the intention of achieving comprehensive control over the police force in accordance with the principles of performance management.

PERSPECTIVES AND CONNECTIONS

In this chapter we have mostly examined the three main perspectives individually. We have discussed how to interpret from each perspective reform programmes and initiatives and the process of reform for a wide set of organizations, as well as the course and outcome of specific processes of reform and change. We have also emphasized how one can, through these perspectives, comprehend connections between the design of reform processes and the course and outcome of these processes, between general and specific reforms, and between specific reforms and changes. We have shown that there are many clear differences between the perspectives but also some instances where the same observations may be made from different perspectives. This is particularly the case for established organizations (such as the Ministry of Justice and the Norwegian police force) where it is difficult to distinguish between the significance of the organizations' interests and identities when attempts are made to change them.

We also interpreted the Ministry of Justice's use of organizational forms that corresponded with prevailing doctrines as an indication of the ministry's wish to gain legitimacy in the environment. Seen from the position of superior authorities, this can also be interpreted instrumentally, because the reform measures they prioritize are implemented in the ministries. Given that leaders in the Ministry of Justice share goals and problem definitions with the government and the ministry responsible for national administrative policy, *this* too can be interpreted instrumentally by ministerial leaders. An instrumental perspective and a myth perspective will nevertheless be divided over the issue of how implemented reforms are connected to a ministry's mode of operation. We shall return to this issue in the next chapter.

Instead of addressing the perspectives individually, we can also examine the relationship between them and how they interact. In Chapter Nine we shall find that we can truly increase our understanding of reform and change in public organizations by discussing the interplay of elements from several perspectives.

CHAPTER SUMMARY

- There is a distinction between reform and change in public organizations, and the form and extent of connection between reform and change varies from one theoretical perspective to another.
- The design of reform processes also involves different degrees and forms of specialization and coordination and affects the course and outcome of these processes.
- Reform and change in public organizations involve structural and cultural features of organizations as well as reform processes, and reform myths may be related to all aspects.

DISCUSSION QUESTIONS

Choose a public-sector organization with which you are familiar.

1 Identify some recent reforms and changes in structural and cultural features of the organization.

2   Discuss one or more of these reforms and changes from the instrumental, cultural and myth perspectives.

3   Discuss the relationship between one or more of these reforms and the national administrative policy in your country.

REFERENCES AND FURTHER READING

Boston, J., Martin, J., Pallot, J. and Walsh, P. (1996) *Public Management: The New Zealand Model,* Auckland: Oxford University Press.

Brunsson, N. and Olsen, J.P. (eds) (1993) *The Reforming Organization,* London: Routledge.

Christensen, T. and Lægreid, P. (2005) 'Autonomization and Policy Capacity: The Dilemmas and Challenges Facing Political Executives', in M. Painter and J. Pierre (eds) *Challenges to State Policy Capacity: Global Trends and Comparative Perspectives,* Basingstoke: Palgrave Macmillan.

——— (2007) 'Globalization of Administrative Reforms: The Dilemmas of Combining Political Control and Increased Institutional Autonomy', in A. Farazmand (ed.) *Handbook of Globalization, Governance and Public Administration,* Boca Raton: Taylor & Francis.

Halligan, John (2001) 'The Process of Reform in the Era of Public Sector Transformation', in T. Christensen and P. Lægreid (eds) *New Public Management: The Transformation of Ideas and Practice,* Aldershot: Ashgate.

Lægreid, P. and Roness, P.G. (1999) 'Administrative Reform as Organized Attention', in M. Egeberg and P. Lægreid (eds) *Organizing Political Institutions: Essays for Johan P. Olsen,* Oslo: Scandinavian University Press.

——— (2003) 'Administrative Reform Programmes and Institutional Response in Norwegian Central Government', in J.J. Hesse, C. Hood and B.G. Peters (eds) *Paradoxes in Public Sector Reform: An International Comparison,* Berlin: Duncker & Humblot.

Mosher, F.C. (ed.) (1967) *Governmental Reorganization: Cases and Commentary,* Indianapolis: Bobbs-Merrill.

OECD (2002) *Distributed Public Governance: Agencies, Authorities and other Government Bodies,* Paris: OECD.

Osborne, S. and Brown, K. (2005) *Managing Change and Innovation in Public Service Organizations,* London: Routledge.

Pfeffer, J. (1978) *Organizational Design,* Arlington Heights: AHM.

Pollitt, C. and Bouckaert, G. (2000; 2nd edn 2004) *Public Management Reform: A Comparative Analysis,* Oxford: Oxford University Press.

Pollitt, C., Caulfield, J., Smullen, A. and Talbot, C. (2004) *Agencies: How Governments do things through Semi-autonomous Organizations,* Basingstoke: Palgrave Macmillan.

Roness, P.G. (2007) 'Types of State Organizations: Arguments, Doctrines and Changes Beyond New Public Management', in T. Christensen and P. Lægreid (eds) *Transcending New Public Management: The Transformation of Public Sector Reforms*, Aldershot: Ashgate.

Wettenhall, R. (2005) 'Agencies and Non-departmental Public Bodies: The Hard and the Soft Lenses of Agencification Theory', *Public Management Review*, 7 (4): 615–35.

Chapter 8

Effects and implications

LEARNING OBJECTIVES

By the end of this chapter you should:

- have a clear understanding of the challenges involved in measuring the effects and results of public-sector reforms;
- be able to identify different dimensions of the concept of *effects*;
- have some basic ideas about the effects of New Public Management (NPM) reforms.

DESIGN OF PUBLIC ORGANIZATIONS MATTERS BUT THE EFFECTS ARE AMBIGUOUS

Is the design of public organizations significant? What are the effects of organizational change? Answering these questions requires knowledge about public organizations' ability for rational calculation, that is, an ability to analyse plans and to foresee the consequences of alternative actions and organizational forms. The answers also require focusing on organizations' ability to *look backwards*, to learn from experience and recognize what has actually been achieved via various organizational forms and initiatives. In this chapter, attention is directed towards the latter process. In particular, we will focus on the effects and implications of reforms associated with NPM, the 'guiding light' for organizational reforms in the public sectors of many countries in the last two decades, with its emphasis on performance management, structural devolution, market-orientation, efficiency and management models borrowed from private firms.

Looking comparatively at studies of public organizations in many countries, we find relatively little systematic information about the effects of using different organizational forms. The crux of the problem is formulated by the American political scientist B. Guy Peters, who claims that organizational structure is that aspect of public organizations most manipulated but least understood. Often insufficient resources are allocated to acquire information about various possible organizational forms, their effects on society and the degree to which they have enabled goals to be achieved. A general impression is that effects are often assumed, expected or promised, but seldom well documented through systematic studies. Reform practice is often at odds with rhetoric. Hence we are faced with a paradox, in that those who prescribe NPM reforms and who argue for their legitimacy by promising results seldom examine the effects of their own reforms. Over time, however, people become increasingly eager to know what the reforms have achieved, thus *evaluation* has become the mantra of our times, just as *planning* was a buzzword during the 1960s and 1970s. Yet evaluation processes can be instrumentally directed as well as symbolic.

In studying *performance measurements* and *effect analyses*, it is important to be aware that different user-groups may be doing the evaluations. We must therefore ask for whom the results are measured. An evaluation may be conducted for administrative leaders and those overseeing an initiative, including government and cabinet ministers, who decide whether large organizational changes should be undertaken or whether an initiative should continue. But it may also be done for parliament and its control apparatus, the national auditor's office, in order to help elected politicians evaluate how well their government policies are functioning. Finally, evaluation may be undertaken for the sake of public opinion, for users and clients. It may address such questions as: how much does a particular administrative reform or initiative benefit them? Different target groups often require different forms of evaluation and performance measurement, because what may be an adequate or a good evaluation for one target group may be inadequate for another.

PERSPECTIVES AND EFFECTS

From a hierarchically based instrumental perspective, one expects behaviour and results to be influenced by changing organizational forms or structures as well as processes and personnel. An instrumental perspective presupposes a tight connection between visions, goals, programmes, initiatives, organizational forms, implementation and effects. Effect measurement and evaluation should show whether organizational forms and initiatives are functioning according to plan and point out eventual weaknesses that need to be corrected. A key hypothesis is that *formal structures influence and channel attitudes and actions*. Moreover, it is assumed that organizations have adequate information about the effects of different organizational forms and initiatives. The challenge is thus to demonstrate how much and in what way these expectations and hypotheses are obtained.

Instrumental perspectives hardly see effects and results as problematic, but, in practice, public servants are limited in their ability to learn through experience. When it is claimed that organizational structure influences participation, patterns of collaboration, attention, conflict-relations, balance of power and the ability to innovate, it is simultaneously emphasized that results can be uncertain and imprecise. Two factors make it particularly difficult to achieve full information and insight into results and their implications. To begin with, public organizations are clearly limited in their capacity and ability to receive, deal with, store and make practical use of information. Second, in many cases, special interests are vested in the information, allowing it to be used strategically.

From a negotiation-based instrumental perspective, one would expect evaluation and effect measurement to be used as political ammunition in a power struggle between different actors and groups. Information is seldom neutral. Interests, values and trust relations influence interpretations of what is considered important and reliable knowledge. There will therefore be antagonisms and conflicts over a public organization's knowledge-base, particularly if it is heterogeneous or finds itself in a heterogeneous environment.

Institutional approaches will place more emphasis on using evaluation and result measurement for the sake of legitimacy but also in order to shape and change people's attitudes and impressions. The longer the tradition of an organizational form, or the longer it has enjoyed hegemony and been accepted as the best and most effective form, the less need there will be to examine its effects. From a cultural perspective, decisions to introduce new structures or initiatives may encounter rejection, resistance or sluggish implementation because they are on a collision course with informal norms – understandings and traditions that have long dominated an organization. Effects will therefore not be obtained, and decisions will loosely couple with implementation and results.

From a myth perspective, one expects that decisions and concrete action are frequently decoupled. If there is broad consensus in the environment on the best form of organization, it will be unnecessary to examine the effects of alternative organizational forms. Although the reforms have apparently been carried out, in reality decisions and their implementation are decoupled from practice and action. In such situations evaluations will often have a symbolic function; ritual aspects will be central, and controlling the evaluation will be important for strengthening legitimacy.

MEANING OF EFFECTS

By *effects*, we mean the consequences of organizational forms, organizational changes and public initiatives. A distinction is often made between a narrow and an expanded concept of effects. A *narrow concept of effects* directs attention to intended or desired effects, such as effectiveness and efficiency, and is a key component in an instrumental perspective. Effects are measured according to the model's own preconditions. Does the organization live up to the intentions of the reforms? Organizational reforms are thus evaluated according to whether they effectively translate given goals into decisions, output and outcomes. Such a narrow concept of effects implies *single-loop learning* because instrumental approaches usually operate according to a one-way process: from a decision via implementation to effects and implications. In practice, however, we are often faced with processes that have reciprocal influences. The revealed effects and implications can boomerang and change structures and initiatives, and hence also the conditions for future action.

An *expanded concept of effects* will also concern itself with side effects and societal and political effects, such as those that come from political-democratic steering. For example, one might ask whether the underlying model is reliable. The question is thus more about whether the NPM model, in itself, is good. Viewed through this extended effects concept, organizational reforms lead to so-called *double-loop learning* because the way things are organized also affects how goals are structured, as well as norms, beliefs and opinions – all key factors in an institutional perspective. It will therefore also be important to map the relationship between how things are organized and the development of meaning, conditions of trust, legitimacy, levels of conflict and types of conflict in the public sector. Yet in spite of these important gains from an expanded effects concept, the difficulty increases of evaluating goals in relation to each other and of having certain knowledge about means–ends relations. In situations where the extended effects concept is deployed, uncertainty and ambiguity over effects grow, and interpreting how different organizational forms and public-sector reforms function becomes all the more important. In situations where changes occur at an increasing pace and the level of complexity and uncertainty rises, the instrumental perspective's supposition about 'reality' being simple and straightforward becomes problematic.

Analyses of the effects of different organizational forms must take into account variations in tasks as well as conditions for action. Today's reform programmes are primarily concerned with efficiency and productivity, with emphasis on performance management and little emphasis on management by rules. Nevertheless, public organizations operating on the basis of clear rules for action can be very effective under certain conditions. Management by rules will function well if the tasks and environment are relatively stable, or if they change relatively slowly and predictably. Effectiveness lies in not needing to constantly evaluate methods for achieving various objectives. That said, rules and standard procedures for action become problematic if tasks and environments change rapidly and in unforeseeable ways.

It is important to distinguish between the effects on main goals and the side effects on other goals that the reform initiatives were not meant to target. It is also important to distinguish whether the effects correspond with intentions, whether they are counterproductive, or whether the results are neutral, in the sense of having neither a positive nor a negative effect. Table 8.1 reflects these distinctions.

The best of all situations is when positive effects are achieved for the main goal and there are also positive side effects for other goals (2). This can be the case when organizational reforms intended to increase efficiency obtain and also have positive effects on other goals such as political control. A more common situation is when reforms have positive effects for the main goal, efficiency, but negative side effects for quality of service (3). A further example of side effects is that the introduction of performance measurements and quantitative performance indicators can lead to over-measurement of easy cases and those relations that can be numerically determined, at the expense of non-quantifiable relations and difficult cases. With hospitals, for example, it is easier to focus on internal pricing between sections or to determine how long a patient has been in hospital, than to measure care, human compassion or whether the patient gets well.

The main hypothesis of NPM reforms is that they will have *positive effects on the main goal, efficiency, yet avoid negative side effects for other goals* such as quality, political control and rule-of-law values (1 and 2). Even so, it is difficult to show clear effects for the main goal, and one gravitates towards boxes four to six, or in the worst cases, boxes seven to nine. In a multifunctional public sector, we would expect that positive results for the main goals without side effects (1) would be the exception rather than the rule. There is often an element of ambiguity in identifying the side effects of organizational change and reform initiatives, because the goals are often formulated imprecisely. One person's or group's side effects can be another's main goal, and compromises and ambiguous goals are often key elements in the process of establishing reform coalitions. This will particularly be the case for a negotiation-based instrumental perspective.

A distinction can be drawn between *internal administrative effects* on the one hand, and *external, political* and *societal effects* of modern reform initiatives on the other. *Internal effects* concern productivity, increased efficiency or changes in administrative

Table 8.1 Effects of public sector reforms

Side-effects	Effects on main goal		
	Positive	None	Negative
None	1 Expected result	4 No result	7 Negative results
Positive	2 Expected result plus bonus	5 No expected results, but bonus	8 Negative results plus bonus
Negative	3 Expected result plus risk	6 No expected results plus risk	9 Negative results plus risk

Source: Hesse, Hood and Peters (2003), modified

culture, steering and control. This entails *administrative learning,* facilitating the achievement of politically mandated goals, that is, learning to find good ways of achieving goals and following those goals through. *Political learning,* connected to the latter distinction, focuses more on how citizens and political leaders learn to hold public organizations accountable for their activities. Do organizational reforms strengthen or weaken the opportunities for political-democratic steering and control? Is there more steering in large issues and less steering in smaller issues, or is this even desirable from a democratic point of view? Do the conditions of power and trust change between leaders and followers?

Societal effects involve the transmission of organizational change – that is, to what extent do implemented organizational decisions go on to affect people's lives and situations? This phenomenon is often referred to as effectiveness. From this there arises a second core distinction, between *effects of process* and *effects of content*. Processual effects concern whether one has carried out tasks in an acceptable way and followed the relevant and appropriate procedures and methods for casework. The decisions are acceptable because one has made them in the correct way, not because one has achieved the expected results. This is often not efficient in a narrow sense of the term, for instance casework for building applications or asylum applications, according to the rule of law and legal protection. Reform initiatives for cutting the amount of time it takes to handle cases, encouraging a more service-oriented mentality, or introducing 'one-stop shops' are all examples of instrumental or cultural initiatives that will influence processes. The course of a reform process is often easier to observe and describe than its outcome and effects. Examples of this difficulty are performance management and performance audits. Although the ambition is to measure outcome, societal results and effects – that is, what consequences initiatives have for citizens, users and clients – in practice, one often measures output, activities, the use of resources and whether or not relevant rules and regulations are being followed. One measures, for instance, the length of time it took to handle a case at the welfare office, the number of days a patient was in hospital, or readmissions to hospital per patient, rather than whether the decisional content is correct or the patient got well.

A second and related distinction is that between *content-related effects* and *symbolic effects*, which we can understand from an instrumental perspective as well as from a myth perspective. While the first type concerns the content of decisions (who gets what benefits and burdens), the second type concerns effects on opinions, beliefs, attitudes and interpretations. Organizational reforms belong to the practical world as well as the world of ideas. As well as affecting practice, reforms can affect ideas and influence people's and civil servants' understanding of public organizations. The effects are 'bricks' in building opinions and conceptions of what are thought to be relevant problems and good solutions; they are not merely tools for changing public organizations' actions. For example, performance management can help change organizational culture in the direction of a more performance-oriented, less procedure-oriented culture.

Finally, there is the matter of learning from the effects of reforms. A distinction is usually made between two forms of experience-based learning: *learning as a result* and *learning as a process*. In the former, learning is understood as the ability to reveal and correct mistakes in order to improve an organization's mode of operation. Organizational learning involves identifying, remembering and using structures and procedures that improve an organization's problem-solving ability. Learning, understood as positive results or improvements, is largely associated with an instrumental perspective. Parallels are drawn with scientific experiments, where rational adaptations are made, based on simple, complete learning curves founded on explicit experiences.

Although instrumental perspectives presuppose a complete learning cycle, the real world often deviates from this. Since organizations struggle with problems of capacity and motivation and must function in institutional environments and networks, public organizations involved in political processes often face ambiguity, uncertainty, conflicts and powerlessness. Notwithstanding, organizations try to distinguish between success and fiasco, to repeat successful reforms and initiatives, and to avoid those that are failures. As such, learning is a process where one acts on the basis of experiences that must be interpreted. Learning happens, therefore, when observations and experience-based actions create lasting changes in an organization's structures and procedures. Yet these changes are not necessarily improvements. The learning cycle may fracture and result in *superstitious learning*. Such learning is often biased and selective. One sees what one wants or expects to see, or one sees the things seen by trusted individuals, such as would be expected from a cultural perspective. When many public organizations and strong professional groups claim that their actions are based on facts, this may be interpreted in two ways: it may reflect increased emphasis on so-called 'objective knowledge', or facts and learning based upon this. However, from a symbolic perspective, one could say that a particular person or group's mode of defining connections and learning has won, regardless of how solid the facts are.

DIFFICULTY OF MEASURING EFFECTS

There are many reasons why it is difficult to measure the effects and results of organizational change and public initiatives. First, we are faced with *problems of motivation*. It is not in everyone's interest to examine the results of reforms and public initiatives. Asking questions of a politically or administratively sensitive nature can often engender opposition from certain actors or groups. Independent evaluations can be interpreted as threatening to political and administrative leaders. Politicians are often more concerned with boosting their own image by launching new programmes and initiatives than with evaluating earlier reforms, because the political gains from such evaluations are limited. Also, reforms usually look more attractive

149

and elegant beforehand than after they have been allowed to work for a while. Moreover, administrative leaders can limit access to information or direct attention to positive aspects of the reforms and thus hamper political leaders' evaluations.

Second, we are faced with a *problem of independence*. In order to achieve reliable performance measurements, it is imperative that those doing the evaluation are independent from those being evaluated. At the same time, a certain closeness is needed in order to understand the values and perspectives of different actors. The result can easily be a sort of compromise, where all points of view come to expression but no independent conclusion is drawn. Disputes therefore arise when public units evaluate themselves and often conclude that their own actions were positive. A second example is when a public organization 'commissions' an evaluation of its outsourced activities and the evaluation turns out to be positive. When national auditor's offices expend time and energy on performance audits, this indicates a re-evaluation of current political processes. This easily creates tensions, regardless of whether the auditor's office functions as an independent unit or 'teams up' with opposition parties in the parliament.

Third, there are often *manifold criteria* for evaluating results, all of which are *conflicting, unclear and unstable*. In order to speak about a better-organized public sector and about improvements, one must clarify which criteria are being used to evaluate whether public organizations function well or poorly. No evaluation can be done without some form of criteria. In a pluralistic society, different groups and actors often have different ideas about what good or bad modes of operation are, not to mention positive or negative developmental features. There will be different opinions about the normative and political foundation for the public sector and about which criteria should be used to evaluate public organizations' modes of operation. There may be conflicts over the public sector's size, financing and structure between political parties, organizations and groups in society, leadership levels, sectors and professions. One individual group may even want public organizations to be responsible for issues that are not necessarily compatible, for example economy, efficiency, being representative, responsiveness to voters, professional quality, performance, service quality, safety and security, due process, control, neutrality, equal treatment, impartiality, public transparency and openness, predictability and rights of participation. In other words, organizational reforms confront us with a great many partially conflicting concerns. Claiming that 'it is the results that count' obfuscates the norms and values tied to processes, means and modes of operation, for there is much more at stake than substantial results.

In a political-administrative system with a style of decision-making traditionally characterized by political collaboration and a culture oriented towards consensus, divergent normative and political criteria often cause actors to seek compromises, which in turn contributes to goals being ambiguous and partly conflicting. This situation is heightened in the case of a coalition or minority government. In a culture of partnership with a high level of mutual trust, combined solutions are often sought

150

so that everyone will be able to support them. Agreements and compromises are usually based on elastic formulations – long unprioritized wish-lists or 'catalogues' of good intentions that are open to interpretation. This is not necessarily a sign of weakness, but can be interpreted as characteristic of a democratic mode of steering in a pluralistic society. Often, unclear goals are intended to be unclear, even though they are symbolically presented as being clear. This is apt to be politically necessary for garnering sufficient support for a reorganization process or for new initiatives and programmes, yet unclear and partly conflicting goals obviously make it more difficult to measure effects and results.

In addition to problems of precision and consistency, we are confronted with the problem of *unstable goals and criteria*. Unstable goals obstruct performance measurement and tend to be a product of changes of government when there is a concurrent change in goal-formulation and priorities. At lower levels we are often faced with situations where there are unstable measurement methods and performance indicators. The general tendency is for performance indicators to change frequently. Altogether, this creates problems for measuring results and effects over time. In situations where expectations about clear goals and certain knowledge of means–ends relations cannot be fulfilled – as an instrumental perspective would want them to be – the evaluations will be more social tests than efficiency tests, and the measurement devices will be relative. A main strategy of social tests is *benchmarking*: either a public organization tests its own performance in relation to its previous performance record, or it compares itself with other similar organizations whether public or private. An important precondition for such benchmarking is to be well acquainted with the starting point as well as with the modes of operation in similar organizations. Finding models to emulate from the world of private organizations has triggered a debate over this method of comparing results in public organizations.

Fourth, there is the *problem of timing*. When should effect studies be carried out? If effects are measured shortly after an initiative has been launched, the measurements will pertain mainly to the adaptation process. Although initial phases usually entail a fair amount of uncertainty, resistance and confusion, these eventually decrease as reforms become established in an organization. One advantage of early evaluation, however, is that it makes it easier to intervene and change the course of reform. If one waits until it is possible to reveal all the consequences, it may be too late to influence political decisions about the initiatives and the programme's future.

If one waits until the adjustment phase is over to perform an evaluation and then measures effects, it is more likely that the lasting effects and implications of a more normal operational phase will be revealed, hence it may be easier to demonstrate efficiency. Yet the more time that passes, the greater the difficulty of isolating the effects of a specific organizational reform initiative from other reforms and changes that have occurred concurrently or in the intervening time. This leads us to a serious methodological problem of effect measurement, namely, *the problem of attribution*.

The attribution problem arises when one tries to identify and isolate the effects of one single reform initiative or reorganization. Evaluating a formal organization's mode of operation is not like a traditional controlled experiment, such as we might find in hard science, where it is easier to hold all relevant factors constant and then read off the effects of only the manipulated or changed conditions. Social systems will normally be unstable; they experience uncontrolled change in internal and external conditions beyond those attributed to reforms or organizational changes under observation. It is therefore difficult to grasp the *contra-factual*, that is, what would have happened without the ongoing reform. A particularly difficult task is to isolate the effects of a single reform measure in a period when many other reforms and comprehensive changes are underway. When a public organization becomes formally more independent, the effects will be difficult to isolate if at the same time that its tasks are changed it also moves to a new location and experiences a major employee turnover.

Organizational reform and change often happen when there is a gap between performance and expectations or demands. When results fail to correspond with goals this usually initiates a demand for change, reform and renewal. Yet the dynamics of reform often lead to the problem of *over-selling*, accounted for by a myth perspective. Since scepticism and opposition to reform and change often arise in organizations, in order to enlist support and arouse enthusiasm, the agents of reform may promise more than they can in fact deliver. Expectations of what can be achieved become unrealistically high, with consequent frustration among organizational members when results do not obtain. In other words, reforms can increase expectations more than they increase performance, and the gap between expectations and performance can even be larger after the reforms have been initiated, even though performance may have improved. This scenario may be found in recent Norwegian hospital and university reforms. It also suggests two ways to close the gap between performance and expectations: either one improves the performance level or one reduces expectations (the latter being difficult if one hopes to gain support for carrying out reforms). Public organizations probably experience just as great problems with excessive demands and expectations being placed on them relative to available resources as with unsatisfactory performance.

CHALLENGES IN PERFORMANCE MEASUREMENT AND EFFECT STUDIES

In light of the difficulties mentioned above, we are faced with a series of challenges and dilemmas in measuring the effects and implications of reform in public organizations. There are no easy answers, but it is important to pay attention to these issues. Aided by the research of Christopher Pollitt and others, we will now give an account of these problems and particularly focus on how they come to expression in NPM reforms.

The problem of politics and control

A fundamental problem with performance measurement, from an instrumental perspective, is that it presupposes two independent processes: one superior political goal-formulation process and one subordinate technical-neutral implementation process followed by a performance report. Politicians' goals are limited to formulating primary goals and to evaluating results, while the rest can be delegated to managers and experts. The problem is, however, that practice diverges from this ideal.

A great challenge for performance management lies at the threshold between politics and administration. That tension arises between a political and an administrative logic is not surprising, given that one of the hallmarks of the political world is conflict of interest. *Administrative logic* is proactive, concerned with administrative control, consistency and long-term planning. *Political logic*, by contrast, pulls in the direction of being reactive, of responding to current and unexpected events, where small issues can be used to signal a political stance to voters. *If* politicians adhere to an instrumental perspective, *then* this will not be sufficient to compel them to behave in the way that reforms require, for they will be more concerned about setting up new initiatives than about evaluating existing organizations and initiatives. Consequently two steering systems develop that are relatively loosely coupled to each other: a political steering-system and a performance-management system, largely delegated to administrators, professionals and experts. Many politicians experience the demand for result control as burdensome when the parliament, the national auditor's office and the mass media are continually asking for results. Yet just as burdensome is the task of trying to hold politicians accountable after the fact, when they no longer hold their previous positions of responsibility.

The problem of responsibility

Performance measurement and effect analyses prompt some key questions: who should be held responsible for poor results and who should be rewarded for good results? Is it the case that politicians want to take the credit for good results, but pass responsibility for bad results onto the organizations that actually carried out the work? In the traditional bureaucratic organizational form – with hierarchy, routines and little room for discretion – a civil servant's responsibility is primarily to follow correct procedures, rules for casework and set practices, while the content of decisions and their effects is the responsibility of politicians.

The *principle of ministerial rule* is central in many representative parliamentary democracies. This means that the individual cabinet minister is responsible for everything that happens in his or her subordinate organizations. At the same time, performance management, contractual steering models and the structural devolution of public organizations that has come about through the establishment of state-owned companies and changing forms of affiliation all allow greater autonomy for administrative executives and structurally devolved organizations.

153

The tension between control and autonomy is a persistent and fundamental dilemma in administrative reforms. On the one hand, organizations attain greater autonomy through structural devolution and an increased capacity for exercising discretionary judgment in everyday tasks. On the other hand, in order for superiors to control whether or not organizations have achieved targeted goals, the latter are held accountable by being subjected to more rigid performance management systems. One can either have greater control or more autonomy, but it is difficult to have both at the same time, or to find a stable balance between the two. There is much to suggest that the increased freedom to manage allocated resources is accompanied by more intensive reporting and surveillance systems, which results in the paradoxical development of increased autonomy and structural devolution leading to an explosion in auditing and control.

One problem is that managers are only held responsible for what is stated in their contract, whether it is an individual contract, such as we find in pay-for-performance systems, or organizational contracts such as letters of allocation from parent ministries to subordinate agencies, or arrangements about paying for non-commercial, societal or sector-related policy tasks in state-owned companies. Since contracts can engender a 'check-list approach' to questions of responsibility, this pulls in the direction of short-sighted aspects, individualized accountability and a weakening of broader, long-term and collective notions of responsibility. Market systems and contracts may therefore strengthen *administrative accountability* – for agencies must now account for themselves by submitting regular performance reports – but weaken political responsibility. One example of this is responsibility for supplying energy, where long-term responsibility for infrastructure and stable delivery of affordable energy to all users can suffer in a deregulated and marked-oriented system. Such problems are difficult to solve through more specified contracts or detailed performance indicators, but could be helped by clarifying political responsibility.

The critical question is to what extent politicians can waive responsibility for the consequences of how means are used in structurally devolved or market-exposed public organizations with limited transparency. At the end of the day, politicians are held responsible, often for results over which they have diminishing control. This gap between responsibility and power is an important source of the legitimacy problems that public organizations increasingly face in relation to the general public.

The problem of performance measurement

A key question for performance measurement is which results are being measured. One main intention of the new administrative reforms is to turn attention from procedures, that is, processes and allocating resources (input), to activities, products, services (output) and societal results (outcomes). Thus, one of the main objectives has been to redirect the focus – from factors related to *ex ante* control to *ex post* result control. Yet devices for measuring performance are often difficult to construe for public programmes and one ends up measuring activities and processes as *surrogates* for results and effects in society. One reason for this is that the results of many initiatives are not apparent until many years later, nor will results necessarily follow the budget year – one need only think of initiatives for crime- and disease-prevention.

Another reason for using surrogates, which we have already touched upon, is that the reported results will only partially be determined by the specific initiatives or already-accomplished organizational changes. Furthermore, there is no guarantee that poor results will necessarily lead to initiatives being discontinued, such as is predicted for reforms based on performance management, where successful results are rewarded and deficient results are punished. An increase in the percentage of resolved police cases is not necessarily a good indicator of a reduction in crime, for it may just as well indicate an excessive focus on small and easy cases at the expense of big and difficult cases. Political goals for creating jobs and reducing crime will be just as important even if results are not obtained, and there may also be good reasons for supplying unsuccessful initiatives with more funds in the hope of achieving better results. Automatically coupling performance measurements with resource distribution is, therefore, often neither technically nor politically acceptable. The consequence of poor results cannot always be to reduce budgets.

In practice, less knowledge is gleaned about results – whether or not public organizations have become more efficient or effective – than one would have expected from the intentions behind NPM reforms. There are problems in creating a logical chain of goals and objectives, where an overarching main goal is broken down into sub-goals and result indicators. It is difficult, in practice, to account for the furthest links in the result chain. The easiest task is still to check that the administration is following approved resolutions and that the right systems are in place. Instead of studying the effects on society, one often resorts to scrutinizing whether there have been changes in the way public organizations plan and collect information, the content of the plan, and managerial routines and behaviour. This is a paradox, since the main goal of performance management is to reduce the focus on procedures, processes and activities and concentrate attention on results. Initiatives are often planned with a goal in sight, while the follow-up is based not on objectively measuring concrete results but on a discussion forum where there is room to interpret what has happened.

Deficient performance measurement may also have to do with such measurements tending to be trivial, uncontroversial, apolitical and vague. Politically explosive performance indicators have a tendency to be removed, leaving one with neutral indicators of little political relevance. In a political world, it is difficult to commit oneself to performance indicators that are disputable. This means that the less politicized an organization's sphere of activity is, and the farther it is from the political centre, the easier it will be to develop performance indicators. Performance management becomes increasingly difficult the more politically controversial an organization's activities are and the more it is marked by inherently conflicting values and concerns that are difficult to quantify.

Surrogates for performance indicators are *structural indicators* that focus attention on an organization's capacity to carry out expected activities. Structural indicators concern the number of personnel, their skills, expertise and competence. In light of these indicators, a distinction can be made between an organization's *capacity for analysis* and its *capacity for action*. As mentioned earlier, analytic capacity involves the ability for calculation, evaluation and planning, whereas the capacity for action involves the ability to carry out tasks. Often, therefore, an organization's operations are more driven by what it has the capacity to do than by what is said and thought.

The problem of reporting

How reliable are the results and information reported back to leaders? Since NPM-related reforms are based on an incentive mindset that presupposes organizations and employees pursuing self-interest, good results should be rewarded while bad results should be sanctioned. Yet if one takes into account that reported information is seldom neutral but can be used strategically in order to promote self-interest, one is faced with a situation that encourages information passed upwards in an organization to be biased. Thus, there is a risk of gaming, of strategically over-reporting successes and under-reporting failures in order to strengthen one's own organization. Examples of this are unemployment offices cheating on their reports, medical personnel manipulating their reported diagnoses, or activity-based resource-allocation, which may lead to hospitals 'courting' the most lucrative patients. Experts and professionals in subordinate agencies who have superior information can act strategically, while ministries often have a limited capacity to specify performance measurements and evaluate results. Acknowledging such problems has prompted national auditor's offices to conduct quality-control reports through validity audits, in order to find out whether reports are reliable and valid.

Yet performance reports also raise other ethical problems. Public organizations have, over a long period, developed measures to ensure that employees are honest, honourable, truthful, reliable, non-corruptible and non-partisan. These measures include fixed salaries, tenure, management by rules and clear casework procedures, limited opportunities for exercising discretion and clear divisions of labour between the public and private sectors. Such means are now under pressure from NPM reforms that are based on incentive, mistrust and the assumption that organizations and employees act according to self-interest. It can become more a question of what is economically feasible than what is ethically proper. The degree to which ethical erosion has occurred remains to be seen, however, for the problem has not yet been studied systematically.

In connection with this, the problems of reporting also include mismeasurement and goal displacement. *Mismeasurement* happens when less important but quantifiable aspects of organizational activities are reported, whereas more crucial but non-quantifiable aspects remain unreported. One measures something other than what was originally intended by only accounting for quantifiable and calculable circumstances. *Goal-displacement* arises when primary and legitimate political goals are displaced with organization-specific or individual employee-related goals, not publicly known or not in accord with primary goals. Such developments result in goals being transformed into means, and means into goals.

Finally, reporting involves the *problem of isolating the results* of a single organization's activities from all the other activities of public organizations. In an organizational landscape where many challenges lie at the interface between organizations, and where organizational boundaries break down or become blurred, it is difficult to operate with a closed organizational perspective that would allow one to specify a single organization's goals and read off its results. In practice, public organizations are often intertwined with other organizations in society, not to mention those beyond national borders. There are, for instance, demands for service offices in which numerous organizations may collaborate; they may cooperate, form partnerships, share team leadership and be involved in national as well as transnational networks. This may also include public–private partnerships. Service offices can render better results, but will also make it more difficult to measure the results of each individual organization's activities.

The problem of follow-up

As mentioned, one of the central elements in performance management is that, whatever results are achieved, they should have resource-related, personnel-related or organizational consequences. Such follow-up practices are, however, difficult for many public organizations. One example is the pay-for-performance systems for administrative executives, whereby they receive salary supplements for good performance and lose supplements for poor performance. These have had only limited success as performance incentives. Likewise, government resources are seldom allocated on the basis of performance or results, partly because budgeting processes are seldom consistent in providing good, reliable information about results. Furthermore, using information about results in order to allocate resources works better at lower public-sector levels than at higher levels. When, for example, a minister of education has to divide resources between primary schools, secondary schools and universities, it is difficult to argue that the minister should allocate on the basis of results. If primary education shows poor results, should the minister take resources away from primary education and give them to other levels that show better results? Or should primary education receive more resources so it can rise to an acceptable standard? Good primary education will be a fundamental political goal regardless of how bad performance is, and problems in lower grades tend to continue into higher grades.

Another example of how difficult it is to operate with a narrow focus on results limited to one public organization or unit is the relationship between the police, the courts and the prison authorities. An effective police force can create problems and queues for courts, and effective courts can create prison queues. One organization's success becomes the next organization's problem. A further problem of follow-up is that subordinate agencies can never be completely sure how information about their performance will be used by those in superior posts. Do superiors, for reasons of capacity or motivation, immediately file the report without reading it? Do they habitually respond by rewarding good results or by sending more resources to areas with poor results? This creates opportunities for manipulation by superiors, and uncertainty for subordinate organizations.

Evaluating what should be done with good and bad results must also be seen in relation to the tasks different organizations have. Many public organizations must cope with problems of wickedness that will never be completely resolved, such as crime, drug abuse, alcohol abuse, unemployment and environmental protection issues. For such tasks, poor results will often entail more resources, not fewer.

KNOWLEDGE ABOUT EFFECTS

The main hypothesis of NPM reforms is that *increased market orientation and management leads to increased efficiency, without causing negative side effects for other goals and concerns.* Our argument is that it is still necessary to treat this as a hypothesis to be studied empirically, not as an established fact or evidence-based knowledge. We have not come so far as to say that this has been studied and confirmed. Hard evidence is often lacking, and we also lack systematic and reliable studies of the effects of reforms and organizational forms. Often strategies, plans and selective success stories are the focus of attention, rather than systematic analysis of results. Research has generally focused more on answering questions about why reform and reorganization happen than on trying to reveal the effects of initiatives.

Our argument is that the NPM hypothesis is not valid as a general characteristic for all public organizations. It is necessary to specify and examine under which conditions it will be valid. An extended effects concept must not simply focus on economy or efficiency but must also take into account the effects on democracy and on governance and coordination in a more fragmented, complex public sector. For example, the transition from an integrated organizational model – in which divergent demands and considerations were moulded or adapted to one another within one organization – to a single-purpose organizational model – in which a separate organization is set up for each individual goal – will not merely affect efficiency. Such a change will also have consequences for the balance of power, coordination, the level of conflict, conflict resolution and for prioritizing between diverse concerns such as impartiality, security, service quality and political control.

We know less about external political learning and societal effects than about internal administrative effects on efficiency, such as those that have resulted from internal audits in ministries and their subordinate organizations. It is nevertheless unclear whether performance reporting to politically elected officials has become better as a result of reforms. The further an organization is to one end of the effects chain, the more difficult it is to put goals into operation and to identify results, and the more uncertain are the learning curves.

What seems to have been learned is that there is no one-to-one correspondence between organizational structure and effects. Even so, we can say something about likely directions of correspondence and suggest their strength. Organizational forms seem, in many cases, to be rough and robust categories that allow great variation in actual behaviour and patterns of action, contingent on their context and which situational factors they face. If we take, for example, organizations working with issues that have a low political profile or tasks demanding technological knowledge and professional expertise, or whose finances are independent of state budgets, these may have greater freedom and latitude in their daily running of affairs than other public organizations.

There may be an interaction between market adaptation and political choice, for example in the education sector free choice of schools within an expanding privatized school system can lead to self-reinforcing developments that weaken existing public school systems. The majority of citizens may become victims of their own small decisions, for there is no guarantee that privatizing education will produce better results for the majority.

Our present knowledge of NPM reforms is that in some cases there can be positive effects on efficiency, but that the efficiency gains also vary according to tasks. The Australian organization researcher Graeme A. Hodge has found a significant association between cost savings and contracting out corresponding to a level around 6–12 per cent. Comparative studies often claim that competition brings economic benefits: savings on costs, more efficient production and more flexible and user-friendly services. Yet these studies often have a narrow economic orientation and do not take into account negative side effects in the form of increased social problems, for example unemployment, lower pay, short-term contracts or problems in the work environment when public monopolies are dissolved. There are, at the same time, many negative reports of the effects of opening up the public sector to competition, for example railway privatization in the United Kingdom, private companies offering collective transportation in Stockholm and the deregulation of energy markets in Norway and California.

The effects on efficiency are usually less than reform advocates predict. This is partly a product of over-selling, as has been mentioned, but also because transaction costs, as well as administration and operational costs of the new arrangements, may not have been taken into consideration or were under-evaluated. Studies from the United Kingdom, by George A. Boyne and colleagues, show that through reforms in health care and social housing from the 1980s onwards, structural devolution and increased competition have led to increased efficiency, at least in the short term, but the situation is more uncertain in education. Responsiveness to users has improved within the housing and education sectors, but it is more uncertain in the health-care sector. How much in fact is achieved in efficiency is difficult to determine accurately because of the problem of identification and the lack of comparable data from before reforms were introduced.

In the three sectors studied by Boyne and colleagues, there are clear indications of a reduction in equality. It appears that improved efficiency and responsiveness have been achieved at the expense of equal treatment. This is also confirmed in a Swedish study of schools and hospitals by Paula Blomquist and Bo Rothstein, where, in particular, the free choice of schools has led to social segregation and increased gaps between resourceful users who were able to make use of the new possibilities and other users. On the other hand, there has been a positive effect for democracy in the form of increased freedom of choice of services, which has been expressed in the free choice of schools and hospitals, for instance. Danish studies on increased competition, conducted by Jørgen Grønnegaard Christensen and Simon Calmar Andersen, show that being able to freely choose a school has created greater social differences between schools, increased segregation, no cost savings and no learning improvement. Freely choosing one's hospital, on the other hand, did not create greater differences in the health-care sector, but neither did it produce more efficient solutions.

One conclusion to be drawn from these studies is that the design of various market-models may vary considerably between countries, tasks, sectors and administrative levels and will have consequences for effect studies. The implication is that discussions of the effects of reform must strive for exceedingly precise terminology and must not be conducted at a general level.

A fundamental dilemma for many organizational reforms is the tension between autonomy and control. Organizations should have enough freedom to run in an efficient way, yet not be so free that superior levels of leadership lose power and control. Organizations should have greater freedom in how they use allocated resources so that they can function efficiently, but the price of increased autonomy is subjection to a more rigid performance management system. One wants to achieve more freedom and greater control simultaneously. More rigid, formalized and comprehensive systems – with performance indicators, reporting and evaluation – strengthen the top echelon's control, but simultaneously public organizations become structurally devolved through changes in forms of affiliation and by giving managers more discretion in using allocated resources. Whether or not this strengthens political control and leads to better political steering is an open question. Some will claim that the reforms promote increased autonomy for non-ministerial organizations and a transfer of power and influence to state-owned companies and autonomous agencies.

Others will claim that steering is and will remain steering, regardless of the concept used – that the performance-indicator trend is first and foremost a tool for improving top-level administrative control.

The likelihood, in any case, is that the new organizational forms will lead to changes in how public organizations are controlled. The traditional, informal, internal, collegial and trust-based forms of control are waning, and the more formal, external, professional and distrust-based forms of control are waxing. Using performance indicators means that a hierarchically based inspection of whether or not regulations are being followed will change from being a monitoring of procedures and compliance to being a control of performance and results. Moreover, elements of control through increased competition and market-oriented organizational forms are growing at the same time that internal, informal and collegial controls abate. One presupposed system effect of NPM reforms has been that they would reverse citizens' depleted trust of public authorities. This connection is, however, difficult to prove, and most likely is related to reforms not being based on assumptions of a large degree of trust between public organizations at different levels.

In sum, one can only confirm the impossibility of saying unequivocally what the effects are of alternative organizational forms. The knowledge-base for correspondence between organizational forms and effects is ambiguous and deficient. Organizational forms are often rough and robust categories that allow great variations in actual behaviour. Instead of fine-tuning organizational forms in order to achieve the desired effects, one should focus on more robust and rough categories that are able to say something about the likely connections and directions of development. One implication of this is that radical reforms will not necessarily lead to greater effectiveness and better control than moderate reforms.

THERE IS NO BEST SOLUTION – LEARNING AND EFFECTS

There are no simple recipes or one optimal organizational solution for achieving a better-organized public sector. One important reason for this is that the *context is significant for the results*. Public organizations are not merely of one kind; they represent a wide spectrum of functions, tasks and target groups and exist in different administrative cultures and under different conditions and circumstances. They demand different approaches and different mixes of goals and values. It is, therefore, very unlikely that one single set of organizational forms, steering models or performance management systems will work everywhere, in all times and for all situations. One reason for this is that the contexts and environments many public organizations operate within are fundamentally different from that of private organizations. Politics is frequently absent from many of the general recipes and accompanying analyses presently on offer.

161

If the context of public organizations is so important for their mode of operation and achievement of results, what can we say about the significance of context? The three perspectives we have followed emphasize different aspects of this. An instrumental perspective underscores the significance of political signals for steering and the professional base of knowledge. A cultural perspective directs attention to internal contexts embedded in traditions and organizational cultures, while a myth perspective underscores the significance of the external institutionalized environment in relation to which organizations function. The problem with all these contextual factors is that they often operate at a high level of generalization, which gives few directional lines for concrete action in specific cases. In the next chapter we will specify some of these contextual factors in more concrete terms.

We will also warn against excessive optimism as regards learning. Unambiguous cause–effect relations are certainly seldom occurrences in social science. There are no controllable experiments where one can straightforwardly read off objective results, as is sometimes the case in hard science. Rather than assuming that political and administrative leaders act in accord with a planning ideal, we should ask questions about how one leadership functions in situations marked by a lack of time and attention, where goals are unclear and there is doubt over the best means for achieving them as well as over which results will actually be produced. Politicians do not always need clear goals, but rather models of steering that can be deployed when goals are unclear. This raises the question of whether there is a need for *goal-free evaluation*, where performance evaluation is not limited to one pre-determined goal but also takes into consideration consequences for other areas and other goals. Often one learns how the world looks from the standpoint of a given policy model, but if the underlying model is wrong the learning will be futile. We must learn not only whether the organizational form functions in accord with the underlying model, but also whether the model itself is founded on faulty or sound assumptions.

If we, from an instrumental vantage point, define effects narrowly – for instance scientifically tested effects of the final results of an organizational change – the last decade's public-sector reform programmes would not have needed results in order to energize continuing reform efforts. This is no surprise from a myth perspective, for it emphasizes the symbolic and rhetorical aspects of reform. Perhaps the most important effects of reform work have been the changes in the way we speak about public organizations, which indicates a cultural shift in our understanding of what public organizations are and how we expect them to function.

In this chapter we have focused on problems of performance measurement and effect studies. Evaluation is an important but difficult activity that indicates a desired direction for development. Used with wisdom, and keeping in mind the limitations and conditions, performance measurement and effect studies could be important contributions for increasing the knowledge-base of how public organizations function. Although a difficult and challenging activity, this does not mean one should discontinue studying effects and results. First, if evaluations were not carried out, how would it be possible to control whether public organizations and initiatives are functioning? Second, it is naive to suppose evaluations render final answers that are immediately implemented by eager politicians and administrative leaders. Many other factors besides performance measurement will also influence how public organizations and initiatives are evaluated, interpreted and changed. Third, evaluation and performance measurement can be difficult, but this does not mean they are not worth trying.

CHAPTER SUMMARY

- It is important to apply an extended concept of effects.
- The effects of public-sector reforms are uncertain and contested.
- Because of the significance of context, there is no best solution for administrative reforms.

DISCUSSION QUESTIONS

Choose a public-sector reform with which you are familiar.

1 Identify the main goals behind the reform.
2 Discuss the effects of the reform by referring to a narrow and extended concept of effects, the difficulties of measuring effects, the effects on the main goal and possible side effects.
3 Identify how the context might be significant for the results of the reform.

REFERENCES AND FURTHER READING

Andersen, S.C. and Serritzlew, S. (2007) 'The Unintended Effects of Private School Competition', *Journal of Public Administration Research and Theory*, 17 (2): 335–56.

Blomqvist, P. and Rothstein, B. (2000) *Välfärdsstatens nya ansikte (The Many Faces of the Welfare State)*, Stockholm: Agora.

Boyne, G.A., Farrell, C., Law, J., Powell, M. and Walker, R.M. (2003) *Evaluating Public Sector Reforms*, Buckingham: Open University Press.

Brunsson, N. (2006) *Mechanisms of Hope: Maintaining the Dream of the Rational Organization*, Malmø: Liber.

Brunsson, N. and Olsen, J.P. (eds) (1993) *The Reforming Organization*, London: Routledge.

Christensen, J.G. (2003) *Velfærdsstatens Institutioner* (*The Institutions of the Welfare State*), Aarhus: Aarhus Universitetsforlag.

Christensen, T. and Lægreid, P. (eds) (2001) *New Public Management: The Transformation of Ideas and Practice*, Aldershot: Ashgate.

Hesse, J.J., Hood, C. and Peters, B.G. (eds) (2003) *Paradoxes in Public Sector Reform*, Berlin: Duncker & Humblot.

Hodge, G.A. (2000) *Privatization: An International Review of Performance*, Boulder: Westview.

Hood, C., Scott, C., James, O., Jones, G. and Travers, T. (1999) *Regulation Inside Government*, Oxford: Oxford University Press.

Lægreid, P. (2001) 'Mål- og resultatstyring i offentleg sektor- erfaringar og utfordringar' ('Management by Objectives and Results in the Public-sector – Experiences and Challenges'), in A.L. Fimreite *et al.* (eds) *Lekmannstyre under press*, Oslo: Kommuneforlaget.

March, J.G. and Olsen, J.P. (1975) 'The Uncertainty of the Past: Organizational Learning under Ambiguity', *European Journal of Political Research*, 3(2): 147–71.

Olsen, J.P. (1997) 'Institutional Design in Democratic Context', *Journal of Political Philosophy*, 5 (3): 203–29.

Olsen, J.P. and Peters, B.G. (eds) (1996) *Lessons from Experience: Experiential Learning in Administrative Reforms in Eight Democracies,* Oslo: Scandinavian University Press.

Peters, B.G. (1988) *Comparing Public Bureaucracies: Problems of Theory and Methods,* Tuscaloosa: University of Alabama Press.

Pollitt, C. (1995) 'Justification by Works or by Faith? Evaluating the New Public Management', *Evaluation*, 1 (2): 133–54.

—— (2003) *The Essential Public Manager*, Maidenhead: Open University Press.

Pollitt, C. and Bouckaert, G. (2000; 2nd edn 2004) *Public Management Reform: A Comparative Analysis,* Oxford: Oxford University Press.

—— (2003) 'Evaluating Public Management Reforms: An International Perspective', in H. Wollmann (ed.) *Evaluation in Public-Sector Reform,* Cheltenham: Edward Elgar.

Radin, B.A. (2006) *Challenging the Performance Movement: Accountability, Complexity and Democratic Values,* Washington: Georgetown University Press.

Chapter 9

Understanding and design

 LEARNING OBJECTIVES

By the end of this chapter you should:

- have a clear understanding of how the different perspectives relate to and mutually influence one another;
- be able to identify what is meant by a 'prescriptive organization theory' and by a 'transformative approach';
- have some ideas about possible scenarios for future developments in public-sector organizations.

PERSPECTIVES, DESIGN AND STRATEGIES

In the previous chapters we have presented an instrumental perspective, a cultural perspective and a myth perspective and related these to various core aspects of public organizations, such as goals and values, leadership and steering, reform and change, and effects and implications. In this chapter we will first discuss the relationship between the perspectives and show how one might arrive at a *transformative approach*, which argues that a complex public sector must engage with elements from all three perspectives. It also emphasizes processual aspects and the dynamic interplay that takes place through various forms of translation, editing and adaptation that occur in the process of renewal and modernization in the public sector.

In this chapter we shall discuss the possibilities for developing a *prescriptive direction* in organization theory for the public sector. This emphasizes a normative foundation for what public organizations should do, by balancing a diverse set of values in multifunctional political-administrative systems. The chapter culminates in a discussion of which strategies *can* be used in reforming the public sector, given the existing knowledge of how public organizations function, and concludes by discussing *possible lines of development* for public organizations.

The three perspectives represent different interpretative 'lenses' through which we can view the activities of public organizations. Seldom are actors in public organizations one-dimensional. Rather, they have normally multiple identities and their actions are usually based on a complex logic because many different concerns must be attended to. It is therefore necessary to discuss the complex and dynamic interplay between processes and effects marked by instrumentality, culture and myths.

Studies of how political and administrative leaders have adapted to modern reforms show how these actors exist in complex contexts and how their actions are based on many different *logics of action*, which represent a multifaceted mix of formal frameworks, cultural concerns and symbolic conditions. The world surrounding a government is exceedingly complex and continually undergoing change. These factors make manifold demands on how the roles of the government and its members are designed. In addition, the reforms may be of different kinds – performance management, leader contracts, contracting-out or structural devolution – which further complicates the logics of action.

COMPLEX AND DYNAMIC LOGICS OF ACTION

Of the various ways of viewing the relationship between the different logics of action, one approach is to analyse how they work together and influence one another. There are also variations on this analytic method. First, it is possible to start from one perspective and then include elements from other perspectives to modify it. For instance, the European Union's effects at the national level can be analysed by looking at how influence from the European environment is constrained by national cultures and is thus coupled with the instrumental actions of domestic political and administrative actors. An analysis of how a national health authority is faring can be carried out on the basis of hierarchical steering, but this can be constrained or enhanced by negotiation-based elements and cultural features. A second method of analysing the relationship between logics of action is to emphasize that a transformation happens when the various logics confront each other and qualitatively new structures and cultural forms arise. This transformation can happen in different ways: new reforms may be implemented partially or completely, but they are adapted, combined, whittled down or translated via their confrontation with existing structures and cultures.

Instrumentality and culture

Chapter Three underscored that the dominant theories about organizational culture see cultural development as taking place through natural and gradual adaptation processes. The theories state that it is difficult to intervene in such processes and that instrumental features will be constrained by cultural traditions and path dependency. Here, however, we will first discuss the antithesis of this view, namely, that *instrumental actions can largely influence informal norms and values*. A general precondition for this possibility might be that a public organization's culture is minimally influenced by its members' social backgrounds, and what they bring with them into the organization, but operates largely on the basis of internal cooperation, with the formal structure as the most important frame of reference.

Political and administrative leaders can deliberately attempt to design their organizational culture. Such designs can have a more general objective, for example to establish and develop certain informal institutional norms in order to help show outwardly what the organization stands for. Internally, the cultural design might facilitate socializing new members and give established members clear guidelines for action, but the objective could also be to deliberately build support for hierarchical steering. An example of this could be steering related to organizational reforms. Leaders may be aware of the great potential for cultural opposition to proposed reforms and changes and know that a key condition for introducing the reforms is to change the culture and structure simultaneously. This can be done in different ways, either through an *incremental strategy*, where, over time, leaders try to alter the organizational culture in a desired direction, or through a *confrontational strategy* that involves a rapid break with certain traditional norms in order to begin a new cultural path.

A design strategy presupposes that leaders have enough insight into the cultural changes needed, and also have at their disposal the means or devices as well as the power to carry them out. All these preconditions can be problematic to achieve in practice. Gaining adequate insight can be difficult because structural changes are much easier to grasp and understand than culture, which is harder to articulate and relate to a structure. Structural means of change are also easier to use, while cultural means are often more controversial and can easily provoke resistance to change.

Cultural design strategies have been more common in private organizations than public organizations, yet with the NPM movement, they have become central. The ideology behind NPM points not only to public organizations needing to be reorganized for greater efficiency, but also to the need for their culture to change so that structural change can happen. Put differently, an organization must be imbued with a *corporate culture*. Civil servants must think less about job security and personal interests, be less rigid and rule-oriented and be more oriented towards the users of public services. How this can come about is not always easy to say, however.

167

One way is to focus on human resource management, that is, how to develop the skills of personnel and change their attitudes and ways of thinking.

Cultural design has not generally been a central issue in public organizations. There are, however, examples of large projects to bring about cultural change in government ministries, which critically focus on employees' informal norms and values and whether these are well-adapted to their roles and tasks. Cultural change has become more relevant in NPM-based reforms because it is recognized that cultural resistance is problematic for implementing reforms. Yet although private consulting firms have often pointed out that existing culture must change in order to achieve greater efficiency, it has nevertheless been shown that such reform strategies have often not been all that clear or well-founded, and neither have they been easy to implement.

In Australia and New Zealand, post-NPM reforms have focused on nurturing a strong and unified sense of values, building teams, encouraging the involvement of participating organizations, promoting trust, value-based management and collaboration, and improving the training and self-development of public servants. What these governments seek is a cultural shift in the state sector, the argument being that much can be achieved by trying to build a common culture, collegiality and a shared understanding of norms and values that bind all ministries and agencies together through a single, distinctive public service ethos. Under the slogan 'Working Together', the Australian government has emphasized the need to build a supportive public-sector culture by formulating value guidelines and codes of conduct, so as to re-establish a *common ethic* and a *cohesive culture* in the public sector.

Personnel policies under the regime of NPM are also concerned with cultural aspects, for they have modified a number of laws and regulations in the area of human resource management. For example, in reform programmes under slogans such as 'An inclusive and stimulating personnel policy', cultural aspects are unmistakeably present. Reform programmes state that it is important to encourage cultural diversity among staff and to adapt to change through active personnel policies. Primary emphasis is placed on positive aspects of policies, for example increased postgraduate education and freedom in the work place, yet there is little focus on declining job security and increasing employee differentiation in the new system. In the most recent strategic plans for individual ministries and agencies, cultural change is usually mentioned in much the same way, namely, that changing the internal culture will not only be more important for individual employees but will enable the organization to do a better job for its users.

We have previously described how a *logic of appropriateness* is a core aspect of cultural perspectives. What is seen as appropriate in public organizations may vary, because their cultural paths are divergent and they are partly influenced by their cultural roots. If we link this insight to an instrumental perspective, it may be the case that *what is appropriate in a public organization is to act according to an instrumental logic of action*. When, during the 1980s, five different Swedish authorities were pressured by the superior political-administrative leadership to introduce 'three-year budgeting', their initial reaction reflected their institutional or cultural traditions. One public organization in particular – the Central Agency for Statistics – was relatively positive. One reason for this was that the organization's cultural traditions were based on an economic-instrumental mindset, well suited to the new reform's cultural norms and values. This made it easier to introduce the reform. A contrary example is the introduction of performance-management-based *activity planning* at the largest public university in Norway in about 1990. The humanities and social sciences faculties found this reform controversial because their cultural traditions did not embrace an 'efficiency mindset' and therefore the reform was seen as culturally incompatible. By contrast, the reform was welcomed by the medical faculty and the faculty of sciences, which claimed to be already using such planning methods.

A further way of viewing the dynamic relationship between instrumentality and culture is to emphasize that *cultural traditions influence the instrumental logic of action*. More generally, it may be that traditional informal norms and values are built into instrumental norms and therefore acquire high status. Examples of this are when constitutional habits, customs or practices almost acquire the status of formal laws and rules, or when leaders of reform processes impose restrictions on themselves, that is, although they could exercise stricter instrumental control, they refrain from doing so because they feel compelled to maintain certain cultural norms. This has been typical for a number of reform processes in higher education and research organizations. Informal norms can over time become so dominant that they influence formal structures and lead to changes in them.

The dynamic relationship can also be interpreted by considering *the degree of compatibility* between formal norms and informal norms and values as a crucial factor for understanding decision-making processes in public organizations. Many studies of reforms demonstrate this. That NPM as a reform wave has been received differently in different countries can be understood as reflecting varying degrees of compatibility. If a political-administrative leadership tries to introduce NPM in a country marked by strong rule-of-law values or egalitarian norms, such as Norway, France or Germany, cultural compatibility is relatively low. This can lead to variations in the course of reform processes. One option is for political-administrative leaders to give up reforms because they recognize that the internal, cultural resistance is too strong. Another course of action is for leaders to try to overcome the resistance, often incurring problems of legitimacy as a result. Alternatively, leaders can introduce those aspects of reforms that are most compatible with traditional norms and then modify those elements that are most culturally controversial. By contrast, the experience of a number of Anglo-American countries, where clear compatibility between cultural traditions and the content of reforms has been quite different, is that reforms have been easier to implement.

Instrumentality and myths

In Chapter Four we emphasized that myth perspectives, like cultural perspectives, are marked by ideas and supporting arguments about natural developmental processes. Myths grow on a macro-level and spread quickly between and within different types of organizations, but it is unclear which role intentionality plays in the process. One could say that, based on this reasoning, myths have an advantage over instrumentally driven decision-making processes, because myths can thwart such processes, as can be seen in reform processes where myths highlight and exaggerate the negative effects of planned changes and thus undermine the reform process. Yet myths can also aid reform processes. An example of this is when NPM is associated with modernity and efficiency, while traditional systems are claimed to be rigid and old-fashioned. It is common for divergent myths to confront each other through reform processes. We have seen this in a number of reform processes in Europe, such as partial privatization, hospital reforms, quality reforms in higher education and competitive outsourcing in municipalities. One of the most recent examples of *myths in confrontation* is a discussion over what status public universities should have if they change their form of affiliation to the state. Advocates of one reform use the symbolic slogan 'Universities need greater freedom' and argue that this can be achieved by giving universities the status of state-owned enterprises – separate and independent legal entities that have their own board of directors and are responsible for their own economic resources. Those opposing reform, by contrast, emphasize symbols connected to commercializing research, higher revenues for universities and shrinking professional freedom. In Norway this opposition has manifested itself, among other ways, in an official appeal against becoming state-owned enterprises signed by several thousand university employees.

In examining the effects of myths, an oft-heard claim is that *myths do not have instrumental effects*, they merely act as varnish on organizational structures. Myths receive exposure in order to promote a leadership's legitimacy but have few implications for action. This position can, however, be challenged. On a general level, myths can be seen as guidelines for action or change in that they may function as a sort of theory about decision-making behaviour. Otherwise, it is possible to implement some aspects of myths while other aspects remain abstract, and some myth-related concepts can be translated or adapted to existing practices. Generally speaking, however, the myth concept has a slightly negative connotation and it is not always easy to differentiate between non-scientifically justified general ideas and recipes that function well in practical situations and those that do not.

If, however, one claims that *instrumentality takes precedence over myths in decision-making processes*, this permits the possibility of other courses of action. First, the leadership can deliberately create specific myths in the environment that can be instrumentally justified, so that reforms thought to be absolutely necessary and impossible to avoid are, in reality, discretions the organization has itself created.

There may, for example, be groups of countries, such as the Anglo-American countries, that contribute to the spread of reform myths, either via the international organizations they dominate or directly between countries. Alternatively, there may be reform entrepreneurs within a country who certify reforms by pointing to their general acceptance throughout the world.

Second, certain actors can consciously cull reform concepts from the environment and manipulate them in order to increase their legitimacy and the possibility of carrying them out. In the event that myths are implemented, either completely or partially, they would not merely be varnish on a meta-level. Such a course of action may apply to deliberately imported organizational recipes. A deliberate use of myths may also be instrumental for adapting other myths to concepts or practices, by, for example, completely or partially whittling down or translating the concepts and practices.

In examining how NPM has been implemented in many countries, one could say that the process is based on key political actors winning an instrumentally based battle over symbols and that several myths are usually deliberately linked together. Many NPM reforms have been initiated by defining a crisis, for example that the economic situation is terrible, the public administration is inefficient or people are dissatisfied with public services. The assumption of a crisis is frequently taken for granted and acquires a myth-like character, without complete clarity over what that assumption is founded upon. Crisis definitions can sometimes start to take on lives of their own, even when exposed as empirically unfounded. Attempts by various political and administrative actors to contradict such myths are often viewed as 'trying to save a sinking ship', and as evidence that the situation, defined as a crisis, indeed corresponds to reality. When a crisis definition is established radical reforms are often proposed, yet without complete clarity over why certain reforms should be deployed or what the possible effects will be. Once again, it is possible to identify a *form of ideological dominance* that helps reform entrepreneurs dominate the reform process. When reforms are introduced and their effects evaluated, it is often the same actors who control the evaluation and the symbols surrounding them. They commonly come to the conclusion that the reforms have been successful, yet without explicit reference to what criteria their conclusion is based on. Hence one discovers that reforms may be characterized by a chain of myths manipulated and controlled by reform entrepreneurs.

Culture and myths

Cultural and myth-marked processes share in common that they are often thought to be natural developmental processes based on commonly held definitions of social reality. Nevertheless, cultural processes may be distinguished from myth processes because they lead to distinctness or uniqueness, while myth processes lead to isomorphy or similarity between organizations, at least superficially. The reason for this is that cultural institutionalization processes entail adaptation to a unique combination of internal pressure and pressure from the environment, while myth-related processes exert pressure in one direction. An in-between position is that public organizations seldom import similar super-standards through natural processes but rather deliberately introduce elements from diverse organizational fields and use them as 'building-blocks' to construct different multi-standard organizations. The 'buildings' may be different, but still belong to the same family of reform concepts; thus there would be a combination of dissimilarity and similarity.

If one holds that *culture has priority over myths*, cultural traditions can be the wellspring of myths. This can happen by exaggerating institutional features and presenting them in the form of myths. The culture in a particular organization is idealized by its members and its good aspects emphasized, while other cultures are defined as negative. This can take on the character of superstitious learning, where one's own organization stands for everything good, while others represent all that is bad. Positive actions in a decision-making process are linked to organizational members' own attitudes and culture, while negative actions are linked to actors from other organizations with a different culture. The same can be experienced in reform processes. The example already mentioned, about the introduction of performance-based *activity planning* at universities, reveals a battle between reformers and opponents. The reformers claimed that introducing the recipe would produce mainly good results, while opponents anticipated the worst case scenario.

A third example of the confrontation between the 'best' and the 'worst imaginable' is the battle over the fate of the Norwegian Health Authority in the early 1990s. Leaders in the Ministry of Health were convinced that dismantling the agency would lead to the greatest good, since it was an organization dominated by a coalition of doctors and lawyers who 'feathered their own nest', while the agency and its allies defended their own culture and existence through various symbolic means, including citing doctors' professional knowledge and lawyers' due process orientation as being the best guarantees for patients. If we look at a higher political level, the US Secretary of State's distinction between the 'old' and the 'new' Europe during the Iraq War, begun in 2003, is also an example of a myth-influenced cultural distinction between 'us' and 'them' – the nations that supported the US president in attacking Iraq were the 'good' powers from the 'New Europe', while the other countries were regarded as not entirely trustworthy.

If one turns this assumption on its head and asserts that *myths have priority over culture*, myths can be wellsprings for cultural features. For example, strong external pressure may influence informal norms and values in organizations. For example, if the *zeitgeist* has a great influence on reform processes, this may help weaken cultural resistance to reforms and engender new norms in the cultures of public organizations. This is what happened in New Zealand from the mid-1980s onwards, when extreme reforms and concurrent myths led, in the course of a few years, to more emphasis on dissimilarity, individualism, competition and market-orientation at the expense of a public organizational culture quite similar to that in Scandinavia. A second example is the adaptation to the European Union of the Norwegian state monopoly agency for wholesale and distribution of pharmaceutical and health-care products. Within the agency an internal preference emerged for a set of myths claiming that the tight affiliation with government hampered the organization's ability to respond to increasing competition. This led to a change in the internal culture, which in turn resulted in a rapid, almost over-eager adaptation and subsequent privatization of the organization. Also, more generally, these myths have come to reflect themselves in leaders' attitudes in other state-owned companies.

Transformation and translation

In this book we have underscored that if one wants to understand how public organizations are established, maintained and changed, it is insufficient to resort to a one-factor explanation or one single perspective. Only in exceptional cases can a public organization's mode of operation be understood solely as a result of instrumental processes and strategies by leaders, solely as a product of historical legacy or informal norms, or solely as an adaptation to environmentally determined myths. Instead, the life of an organization must be viewed as a complex interplay between planned strategies, cultural features and external pressure. In some situations, strategies, historical legacies and myths work together and lead to comprehensive change, while, in other situations, different circumstances can work against each other and thus help maintain an equilibrium. We argue that *at the nexus of these diverse factors of influence, a transformation will often occur.* Reforms and attempts at reorganization will be reformulated, adapted, modified and reinterpreted. Translation, revision or editing arise from the contextual conditions an organization is confronted with. Automatically copying reforms – from one country to another, from the private to the public sector, or from one public organization to another – is seldom successful and occurs only in exceptional cases.

Transformation is often a two-way or reciprocally influential process. Reformers regularly play active roles in interpreting reforms or the space for action the reforms represent; at the same time, adaptation is controlled by divergent rules of interpretation, which imply that adaptation processes may take place mainly on the formal level rather than in daily practical work. All things considered, patterns of reform and change will be marked by divergence and variation more than convergence and parallel directions.

In addition to examining the three paired relations between instrumentality, culture and myths, it is also important to look at the dynamics between all three perspectives. When different logics of action confront one another in a public decision-making process, new hybrid formal organizational structures emerge along with new informal norms and 'creole' cultures arising at a cultural crossroads. These are all different types of transformation.

A transformative approach and its arguments are used in studies of how NPM has been implemented in Norway, Sweden, New Zealand and Australia. In these studies, variations in the effects of reforms are seen as complex interplays, where political and administrative leaders' latitude for action in promoting reforms is contingent on several factors. First, there are the factors of polity or the formal frameworks reformers work within: general constitutional features, features of parliamentary systems and their constellations and structures in public administration. Second, there are the historical–cultural traditions and the degree to which reforms or attempts at change are compatible with cultural contexts. Third, there is the factor of how strongly environments exert pressure for reform and change. This includes whether or not crises are defined, particularly economic ones.

When examining developments in administrative reform in relation to these factors, one can say that the radical reforms in New Zealand can be explained by the combination of an economic crisis, the existence of a strong Westminster-type majority government and a confrontational policy style. In contrast, the reluctant Norwegian reforms can be seen as the result of an absence of economic crisis, a cultural collision between reform ideas, and the strongly collectivistic and egalitarian welfare-state culture, weak consensual minority governments and a cooperative policy style.

These factors are also in the process of changing in many countries as traditional structural and cultural forms blend with rapidly growing new forms resulting from the neo-liberal reforms of structural devolution and market orientation. Taken all together this comprises a transformation. Similar explanatory factors are used to understand how central governments in the Nordic countries have adapted themselves to the EU and increased European integration. Here environmental pressure plays a significant role, expressed in different forms of affiliation with the EU, and also length of membership. Furthermore, national strategies – how the various countries organize national EU coordination, and historical traditions represented by different administrative models – are significant for a central government's adaptation to the EU.

In addition to recognizing the mutual influence and interplay of instrumental elements, cultural features and myths, one does well to recognize how these influence outcomes and organizational modes of operation. Elements from other perspectives can help strengthen or weaken the core features of the perspective used as a point of departure. Equally possible is that core features of one perspective may determine the framework for how elements from the other perspectives play an active role. From an instrumental perspective, for example, trying to steer reforms through a hierarchy can be constrained by articulation of interests and negotiations, established organizational cultures and dominant myths in the environment. Political decisions, articulation of interests and external events can be interpreted and filtered through informal norms. It is therefore important to be open to a synthesis of elements tied to deliberate choice, established cultures and myths. Rather than cultivating a 'pure' instrumental perspective, one can also consider how planned proposals for organizational reforms are modified by deficient knowledge, conflicts of interest, informal norms and dominant doctrines in the environment. Institutional theories stress that at a certain point, existing structural and cultural features will determine the framework for the results of change processes. Steering proposals, articulation of interests and external events will be interpreted and filtered through ingrained rules and norms.

It is therefore important to allow for mutually influential processes or reciprocal action between elements from different perspectives. Yet it is also worth noting that there can be a two-way influence between structural framework and action. New organizational forms will influence how organizational members act, and such new patterns of action will, in the next instance, influence future reforms. A reform programme built on the assumption that public organizations and employees are out to maximize their own interests, can, if implemented, lead to organizations and employees gradually changing their informal norms and values in the direction of becoming more self-interested. This is one way normative foundations change and thereby influence the possibilities for future reform.

Such co-evolutions break down the clear borders between dependent and independent variables and allow for a dynamic process of reciprocal influence between factors. It is, therefore, necessary to take into account how behaviour and outcomes of reform and change processes will, at a certain point in time, exert an influence on which changes are relevant at a later point in time. The result of the processes together with actors' interpretations of what happened will influence the framework for future action.

TOWARDS A PRESCRIPTIVE ORGANIZATION THEORY FOR THE PUBLIC SECTOR

A distinction can be forged between, on the one hand, models for achieving an adequate understanding of an organization's mode of operation, and hence one that includes many relevant explanatory factors, and, on the other hand, design-oriented instrumental models more concerned with prescribing variables that can be used as means. A design model involves variables that can be manipulated for, by deliberately manipulating means, one can affect desired changes in an organization's decision-making behaviour. One programmatic declaration along these lines was formulated by Johan P. Olsen: 'Reorganization as a political means and political science as an architectural discipline'. Over time, the supply of, as well as the demand for, knowledge about public organizations' modes of operation and their effects have increased. Practitioners have increasingly emphasized design problems and voiced the belief that one must understand an organization's mode of operation in order to successfully introduce reforms. Academics, for their part, have increasingly acknowledged that

175

an organization theory for the public sector must have a practical objective, and contributions by professionals have been most relevant when they have successfully combined an interest in current problems and courses of development with an interest in general problems.

A key contributor to this *prescriptive tradition* in the study of public organizations is the Norwegian political scientist Morten Egeberg, who has developed a design model in which the criteria for selecting explanatory factors is that they, in addition to being relevant for understanding variations in decision-making behaviour, must also be manipulable and operational. Egeberg emphasizes three main groups of explanatory factors: formal organizational structure, organizational locus and organizational demography. These can all be changed, to a certain degree, through deliberate manipulation. Meanwhile, empirical studies have shown that various formal structures, physical structures and compositions of personnel will also have consequences for decision-making behaviour in organizations. An example of this type of design thinking can be a government's proposal to reorganize its subordinate regulatory agencies. By making the agencies more autonomous, through changes in rules for casework and the channels for lodging a complaint (formal structure), agency relocation (organizational locus) and employee turnover (organizational demography), the government should expect changes in the agencies' decision-making behaviour.

In order to carry out a prescriptive analysis of what can be done to affect decision-making, we need to have insight into connections between *organizational forms* and their *effects,* based on empirical research. Quite clear connections between formal structures and decision-making behaviour have been shown, for example that organizational mergers increase the potential for conflict, while splitting organizations helps transfer conflicts to higher organizational levels. Moreover, changes in forms of affiliation, from civil service organizations to state-owned companies, although weakening the possibilities for political control, will strengthen commercial considerations. Clear effects have also been shown for personnel composition. An organization's profession-based composition will influence which problems will receive attention, which cases will be prioritized and which solutions will be proposed. An organization dominated by lawyers will have different perceptions of values, situations and social identities to an organization dominated by economists. Organizational locus has also been shown to influence decision-making behaviour. For example, it is significant whether a ministry of defence and the military's top echelon of commanders are located in the same building or placed in different locations within the capital city.

That said, it is as well to remember that evidence-based knowledge about many of the connections between organizational forms and their effects is still uncertain and incomplete. Research in this field has not yet come far enough for us to be able to say, from an empirical base, that connections have been researched and tested to the extent that we know what works best. There are no clear, unambiguous empirical answers. Although a design model can help strengthen applied organizational research, the provable connections indicate a *direction for development* more than a precise statement about the strength or extent of changes in decisional content when formal structures, physical structures and personnel compositions change.

NORMATIVE FOUNDATION FOR PUBLIC ORGANIZATIONS

In addition to an empirical knowledge-base, a further condition must be taken into consideration in order to make a design model of public organizations work. We have to ask the normative question: what should public organizations do? A prescriptive analysis that proposes how public organizations should be designed must use measuring devices grounded in values and considerations rooted in the public sector generally and in the concrete values of specific organizations. Put differently, one must have some *normative standards* or criteria in order to determine whether changes in decision-making behaviour are positive or negative. Changes in an organization's mode of operation must be evaluated by comparing them with the baseline of values in a multifunctional state. For example, to what degree do the changes strengthen or weaken values related to majority rule, professional rule, attending to affected parties or to values concerning rule of law, such as equal treatment, impartiality, predictability and public transparency? One must also ask whether the criteria take into consideration past and future generations.

Measuring according to these criteria is seldom an unambiguous or stable process. It is usually marked by compromises and flexible wording that can generate different content and interpretations, according to which group is doing the measuring. A common, clear and stable standard for evaluating reforms, such as an instrumental perspective provides, is difficult to live up to. How different values, norms and considerations are emphasized will vary according to individuals, groups, organizations and cultures. A good, positive development by one organization or group may be experienced as less desirable or as negative by others. Some will focus on equity more than on efficiency, while others will do the opposite. In increasingly pluralistic societies, there are fewer commonly held assumptions about what good reforms are. The need therefore arises for a normative analysis of which values and concerns should provide the foundation for planned changes and how organizational reforms can be justified.

In public organizations one must learn to live with partially conflicting goals and values. Actual reforms and changes are permeated with permanent tensions, dilemmas and unintended effects. In evaluating them, one can therefore not afford to be one-dimensional and focus on only *one* value such as efficiency, without also taking into consideration how the reforms affect other important values and concerns included in a public organization's mandate. Despite the precedence accorded to efficiency, the NPM movement acknowledges that there are other values but views them as more or less unproblematic concerns that will not be influenced negatively by increasing the focus on efficiency. The assumption that one can increase efficiency without incurring negative consequences for other considerations is, however, often a problematic one.

It is important to recognize the complexities modern organizations face. Standardization based on a single ideal of steering, or on one value, is clearly limited. Twenty years of public-sector reforms have taught us that public organizations and the public sector are exceedingly nuanced and heterogeneous. Economic concerns must be weighed against *democratic values*: public organizations and their leaders should be loyal to the prevailing government at all times, while also being politically neutral and serving each successive government in equal measure. They should be effective entrepreneurs of policy but politically responsible at the same time. They should ensure due process and defensible casework without succumbing to excessive formalism. They should emphasize rapid casework, but also precision and quality. They should be good stewards of professional knowledge and contribute professional expertise, yet avoid becoming an insensitive technocracy. They should ensure central steering, standardization and control, but also decentralization, flexibility and autonomy. They should contribute to innovation and renewal but also ensure predictability and stability. Deregulation occurs simultaneously with reregulation in many policy areas. Public organizations and their leaders should be efficient, but not at the expense of equal treatment, quality, openness and security. They should be sensitive to signals from users and clients, yet also exercise justice and impartiality and avoid favouring strong groups.

There is no panacea for how to balance these diverse concerns. Attempts to solve one problem, or to take one concern into account, will easily create new problems and challenges along other dimensions. The implication is, therefore, that reforms engender further reforms. It is difficult to create a stable and enduring balance for all the different values and concerns.

SIGNIFICANCE OF CONTEXT

Multifarious values and uncertain knowledge about the connections between organizational forms and effects point to the impossibility of forming universal principles. The wisdom is that one must take into consideration the contexts organizations act within, such as they are presented in the three perspectives and in discussions about steering, leadership, effects and implications. Reasonable deliberation and balance in one situation, for one organization or at one point in time, can be unreasonable in other contexts. Different organizations must cope with different economic, technological, demographic, political, social and cultural conditions. They have different tasks and face different task environments as well as general environments, target groups, clients, users and customers. Each has its own set of problems, all somewhat different from each other; at the same time, the organizations share partly overlapping frameworks for action.

Particularly important for public organizations is to acknowledge two crucial contextual factors that make them fundamentally different from private organizations. First, they are *subordinated to a politically elected leadership* and fall under a parliamentary chain of governance. Second, they are *multifunctional* – in other words, one consideration alone cannot normally be singled out as a superior value from which all other values can be derived. These two fundamental distinctions between private organizations and public organizations mean that there are clear limits to how far public organizations can go in imitating private-sector models of organization and leadership.

In addition to these two systemic features, other more specific contextual conditions of organizational form can be taken into consideration when evaluating alternative organizational forms in the public sector, as Christopher Pollitt and others have stressed. Values and considerations are emphasized differently in different contexts, and the balance between values varies according to the organization's historical legacy. First, appropriate organizational form can vary according to how politically salient or controversial an organization's tasks are. Giving great autonomy to public organizations that deal with politically sensitive policy areas with the potential for conflict can lead to significant problems. This will particularly be the case for policy areas where it is difficult to determine in advance what the political and administrative issues are. For policy areas where every single issue can be politicized, keeping the organization at arm's length from political influence and control by establishing state-owned companies and autonomous agencies will be a costly process. Examples of this might be the policy areas of immigration and health care. A lot of political attention demands public transparency and openness, but this can be difficult to achieve in state-owned companies exempt from the Freedom of Information Act. Organizations such as an immigration agency or health enterprises that deal with politically sensitive issues require greater openness, transparency and accountability than organizations dealing with non-politically salient issues such as metrology.

Second, the appropriateness of organizational forms will vary according to the degree to which tasks are standardized, how observable an organization's activities are and the degree to which it redistributes goods and services. Performance management systems and contractual steering models are difficult to introduce for non-standardized tasks or in situations where activities or results are difficult to observe. This is why there is an essential difference between, on the one hand, a passport office or a department of motor vehicles, and, on the other hand, a primary school or a social welfare office. Non-standardized activities presuppose a more discursive approach with an emphasis on dialogue, and reporting therefore takes longer and requires a less quantifiable format. In such situations mutual trust and professional standards are at a premium.

The lack of observable activities and results make contract steering difficult. Pinpointing responsibility becomes more complicated and, as mentioned, the value of trust increases. Difficult activities to observe include such things as counselling and providing moral support. Results in society can be difficult to observe because they take effect over long periods of time or because they have manifold causes. Examples are pollution or new teaching programmes for primary schools. For tasks with low observability, there is a particular need for organizational forms that maximize good professional ethics. The latter is also the case for organizations with high-technological tasks operating on a high level of scientific knowledge and involving monopolized expertise. In such situations it is difficult for the top executives to formulate clear operational goals for subordinate organizations. If an organization redistributes goods that cannot be divided – in the sense that if one party receives the goods, the next party will not – the organization will be particularly exposed to criticism. Examples of this are when agencies are relocated, hospital wings shut down or schools and municipalities merge. These questions easily lead to political conflicts and tugs-of-war and therefore must be resolved largely by democratically elected political entities, rather than delegated to more or less independent groups of experts or commercial organizations.

Third, for organizations that lay claim to large financial resources but do not have their own revenue-generating activity, tight political steering and control will be an appropriate organizational form. This is particularly the case if intense political attention is focused on the policy area. The lack of such tight steering is well illustrated by the problems of hospital reform, with autonomous health enterprises held at arm's length from politics.

A fourth important contextual condition is risk. Organizations that work with issues involving great risk, or where the consequences of actions are great, will have a particular need for reliability, effectiveness and an ability to react quickly. Examples of this are police, fire and ambulance services, yet also regulatory agencies in such policy areas as health care, and food and drug administration. In times of crisis and disaster these organizations face completely different challenges than when carrying out routine activities.

Finally, an organization's history and culture will help determine the form that is appropriate for it, for over time organizations develop institutional rules and identities that establish what are considered reasonable behaviours, relevant problems and appropriate solutions. The institutional features determine the latitude for reform and change. Introducing, say, a performance-salary system in a Norwegian civil-servant culture marked by strong egalitarian and collectivistic norms will be done quite differently than in a more elitist and individualistic civil-servant culture, such as is found in New Zealand. Also important to take into account is that effects and implications are not only matters of technique; they also require room for interpretation and political processes. This will particularly be the case when goals are unclear or conflicting, or when means are uncertain. Results are often accepted because procedures for casework have been followed correctly, not because one necessarily agrees with the results. Most people can accept that an internal revenue service makes mistakes, as long as their procedures allow them to receive complaints and correct mistakes.

These examples of different contextual conditions demonstrate that it is impossible to operate with one universal solution. NPM reforms will therefore appear as special cases that function best in situations where an organization's activities and results are observable, where the organization works with minimally controversial political issues and where its tasks involve relatively low-level technology.

HOW REFORMS SHOULD BE CARRIED OUT

On the basis of the knowledge we have gained about redesigning and changing public organizations and about their mode of operation and effects, is it possible to outline how one should go about introducing reforms in the public sector? The first lesson to be learned is that one must be careful not to adopt the latest fad from consulting firms, no matter how popular it may be with the firms themselves, with international organizations or among organizational gurus. One must refrain from purchasing a ready-made diagnosis, an organizational form or steering techniques from such external bodies. There is no alternative to making a thorough analysis of the challenges confronting a particular organization and to identifying what its main problems are. The point of departure should be problems, not solutions. Organizational reforms must be anchored in the organization itself and motivated by demand. Such an analysis should not be carried out in a closed, narrow process, but should involve employees, stakeholders, user groups and political leaders.

Second, one should recognize that reforms require time and resources. Often it is more appropriate to function like a *gardener* rather than like an *engineer* or *architect* of reform: if one is fortunate enough to have good soil, and the garden is well tended, with good fertilizer and growth conditions, then one will harvest abundant fruit. Those who want to reform public organizations should not be too hasty but rather should exercise perseverance, patience and tolerance. Third, reformers need all the help they can get. Resistance and suspicion always coincide with reform and change. Allies are therefore needed along with leaders, and it is best if leaders come from the organization itself. As a rule, reformers will fail unless they operate in tandem with leaders who give them their wholehearted support.

Fourth, one should take care not to 'throw the baby out with the bath water'– in other words, avoid ruining the strong, positive aspects of an organization through the process of reform. Trust is easy to damage but difficult to rebuild. If a reform demoralizes key groups of competent employees so that many quit, this is a serious danger signal. Well-functioning services should not be closed down before new services have been tested in practice. Fifth, it may be advantageous to focus on robust reform measures that are perceived as reasonable, relevant and appropriate but which influence administrative practice in an ambiguous and imprecise way and therefore allow different modes of action and results. Such reforms will be easier to gain support for than controversial and contentious reforms that are tailor-made and finely tuned to solve specific problems or to reach a concrete political goal. This implies that political leaders should use more energy on planning procedures than on planning the substance of reforms.

Finally, one should be prepared to be accommodating, and to modify reforms 'en route', because we do not have strong, pre-tested models for what should be done. Since there is no best method, it is important to build good reporting mechanisms, feedback loops and evaluation procedures into the system, for these will make it possible to learn from experience. If a reform is first and foremost perceived as installing a predetermined technique, the possibility of failure increases. Instead of committing oneself too strongly to reform initiatives such as TQM, Balanced Scorecard, service declarations, purchaser–provider models, out-sourcing, public–private partnerships or structural devolution, and letting such measures dominate the agenda, one should focus more closely on the goal of a better-organized public sector and better steering or services.

PROSPECTS FOR THE FUTURE

What future developments can be expected for public organizations around the world? The last twenty-five years' experience with administrative reforms provides the basis for three different scenarios. The first is the conception of a *linear development* towards more management, efficiency and market-orientation. We may have witnessed merely the beginning of the NPM movement, so that a possible future development might be continuous, increasing dominance of the new administrative dogma. In a world of increasing globalization and internationalization there may be no alternatives to NPM reforms. They will exert pressure, appear essential and lead to increasing similarity and convergence between public and private organizations and between public sectors in different countries. Market-oriented solutions will function as mechanisms for selection, and organizational reforms not in compliance with them will be rejected or resisted. Economically oriented reforms will enjoy ideological hegemony or be perceived as the most functional solutions; hence they will be necessary instruments for counteracting telltale signs of 'sickness' in the public sector and may ensure survival in an increasingly competitive situation. The rhetoric behind NPM reforms will spread triumphantly from country to country, and a common vocabulary that underscores efficiency and modernity will develop for reform concepts anchored in NPM. As a result, the large, planning-oriented state will be displaced by a slimmer *supermarket state*. The implemented reforms will be perceived as successful and will spread across national borders with increasing strength and intensity. Important aspects of the reforms will become irreversible, as is illustrated by the way former UK Prime Minister Tony Blair perpetuated central elements in reforms introduced by his Conservative predecessors.

A second scenario is that after a period of NPM reforms and one-sided emphasis on one particular value, a *reaction* will come and public organizations will redeploy certain key aspects of good old-fashioned administrative principles. Development is seldom as deterministic as a linear perspective implies, for cultivating a pure universal model of organization and leadership in a pluralistic society and a multidimensional public sector can give rise to counter forces that focus on those values and concerns demoted or neglected during NPM-dominated reforms. The complexity of steering systems in modern representative democracies, with their mix of values and concerns that must *all* be maintained, makes it difficult, over time, to stick to reforms that cultivate only one value. Reforms, therefore have a tendency to appear as cyclical processes. A period of centralization will be followed by a period of decentralization, specialization creates new needs for coordination, and, after a period where efficiency is stressed, non-economic values and ethical concerns will again come to the fore. The ideas behind reforms can change over time, in conformity with political and ideological trends. This is also the case for the dominant coalitions underpinning specific NPM reforms. The various reforms have their day, a window of opportunity opens but later closes – for actors, problem-definitions, values and solutions. Thus relations between different values and between different actors are better understood as a movement of ebb and flow, rather than as a constantly rising water level.

Such a scenario is sceptical towards NPM reforms as a panacea. In recent years there has been a gradual reduction in enthusiasm for universal reforms. In the most eager NPM countries, such as New Zealand, this type of reform seems to have reached saturation point, and international organizations, such as the World Bank, the UN and the IMF, have been more reticent to propose NPM as a 'medicine' for developing countries. The significance of historical-institutional contexts has been rediscovered, and understanding has increased of the significance of starting from the particular and unique situation of each country. Priorities have shifted from making organizations more efficient and autonomous and of establishing state-owned companies, to finding a good balance between responsibility and autonomy. This is done by focusing on the need for coordination, building up and maintaining ethical capital, administrative capacity and competence in the public sector. 'Joined-up-government' and 'whole-of-government' initiatives have been launched in the aftermath of NPM, as a response to reduced policy capacity in central governments and increased fragmentation in the most radical NPM countries such as the United Kingdom, New Zealand and Australia.

A third possible line of development questions the notions of straight-line development or swings of the pendulum and asks whether a *dialectical development* can happen. Are the public sectors in modern welfare states at a historical watershed, where old-style public administration meets NPM and amalgamates into a new synthesis, different from both the NPM ideal and traditional organizational forms? Are public organizations changing in new, more complex and complicated ways? Instead of linear or cyclical processes, we could be facing a situation where reform ideas, administrative practice and organization theories reciprocally influence one another in a search for a new institutional balance between different forms of governance.

Such a scenario would render hybrid structural solutions that are the result of complex environments and confrontations between divergent principles for the design of public organizations. Market orientation can, for example, create new organizational forms that break down the threshold between the public and private sectors through public–private partnerships. This could make public organizations less distinct. MBO could meld with MBOR into a Rule-oriented MBO. NPM could also lead to a form of cultural 'creolization', in which new, economically oriented values meld with traditional administrative values and create qualitatively new organizational cultures. Symbols and myths may also increase in significance in the new era, as an outcome of increased complexity in the public sector and the need to develop simple guide-lines for action. Yet symbols and myths may also emerge as a result of NPM reforms having led to qualitative changes in leader roles in the public sector.

Do public sectors face a situation where their administrative practices follow in the wake of societal developments, but are simultaneously in the vanguard of theoretical development? Even if this were to be the case, it is important to stress that democracy is an open project. Values and norms in public administration can change over time, among other ways, through experience with organizational reforms. The content of neo-liberal reforms based on NPM ideas will, for instance, strengthen an aggregative and individualistic concept of democracy while weakening a more integrated and collectivistic concept. The normative challenge is, therefore, to modernize the public sector in ways that can take into account the complexities inherent in forms of leadership, steering and organization in modern democracies, and to ensure the development of a democratic political order through active training and socialization, for citizens, civil servants and political and administrative leaders.

CHAPTER SUMMARY

- To understand how public organizations are established, maintained and changed, it is insufficient to resort to a one-factor explanation or a single per-spective. A transformative approach is needed.

- To apply a design model to public-sector organizations one has to take their normative foundations into consideration.
- Context plays a significant role in understanding how public organizations work in practice, how they change and how reform processes should be organized.

DISCUSSION QUESTIONS

1   What are the main dependent and independent variables in a design perspective?
2   Discuss what is meant by a transformative approach and how useful it is to understand reforms and change in public organizations.
3   Discuss the future for public-sector reform in your country by applying a linear, a cyclical and a dialectic scenario.

REFERENCES AND FURTHER READING

Christensen, T. and Lægreid, P. (eds) (2001) *New Public Management: The Transformation of Ideas and Practice,* Aldershot: Ashgate.

—— (2003) 'Administrative Reform Policy: The Challenge of Turning Symbols into Practice', *Public Organization Review,* 3 (1): 3–27.

—— (2007) *Transcending New Public Management: The Transformation of Public Sector Reforms,* Aldershot: Ashgate.

Egeberg, M. (2003) 'How Bureaucratic Structure Matters: An Organizational Perspective', in B.G. Peters and J. Pierre, (eds) *Handbook of Public Administration,* London: Sage.

Jacobsson, B., Lægreid, P. and Pedersen, O.K. (2003) *Europeanization and Transnational States: Comparing Nordic Central Governments,* London: Routledge.

Lægreid, P. and Roness, P.G. (1999) 'Administrative Reforms as Organized Attention', in M. Egeberg and P. Lægreid (eds) *Organizing Political Institutions,* Oslo: Scandinavian University Press.

March, J.G. and Olsen, J.P. (1983) 'Organizing Political Life: What Administrative Reorganization Tells Us about Governance', *American Political Science Review,* 77 (2): 281–96.

Olsen, J.P. (1988) 'Reorganisering som politisk virkemiddel og statsvitenskapen som arkitektonisk disiplin' ('Reorganization as a Policy Means and Political Science as an Architectonic Discipline'), in J.P. Olsen (ed.) *Statsstyre og institusjonsutforming* (*State Governance and Institutional Design*), Oslo: Universitetsforlaget.

—— (1992) 'Analyzing Institutional Dynamics', *Staatswissenschaften und Staatspraxis,* 3 (2): 247–71.

—— (1997) 'Civil Service in Transition: Dilemmas and Lessons Learned', in J.J. Hesse and T.A.J. Toonen (eds) *The European Yearbook of Comparative Government and Public Administration,* vol. III, Baden-Baden: Nomos.

—— (2004) 'Citizens, Public Administration and the Search for Theoretical Foundations', *PS: Political Science & Politics,* 1: 69–79.

Pollitt, C. (2003) *The Essential Public Manager,* Maidenhead: Open University Press.

Pollitt, C., Caulfield, J., Smullen, A. and Talbot, C. (2004) *Agencies: How Governments do things through Semi-autonomous Organizations,* Basingstoke: Palgrave Macmillan.

Index